Pedal To The Metal Leadership

ACCELERATE YOURSELF
AND YOUR TEAM

❖   ❖   ❖

Dr. Arlen Burger

Published by Docento Press, 849 Almar Ave. Suite C150, Santa Cruz, CA 95060.

ISBN: 0989976211
Print ISBN: 9780989976213
Ebook ISBN: 978-0-9899762-2-0

All trademarks are trademarks of their respective owners. Rather than put a trademark symbol after every occurrence of a trademarked name, we use names in an editorial fashion only, and to the benefit of the trademark owner, with no intention of infringement of the trademark. Where such designations appear in this book, they have been printed with initial caps.

This book is available at special quantity discounts to use as premiums and sales promotions, or for use in corporate training programs. For more information contact Arlen Burger at arlen@fasterleader.com.

TERMS OF USE

Pedal To The Metal Leadership

Contents

Dedication

❖ ❖ ❖

I'd like to dedicate the book to the hundreds of leaders I have worked with over the past twenty five years. They were fundamental in my journey of becoming a leadership coach. Their openness, insight, hunger for learning, and willingness to experiment helped create the foundation for Pedal to the Metal.

Acknowledgements

❖ ❖ ❖

WRITING A BOOK IS AN exercise in community. You need advisors, editors, sounding boards, and a task master to keep you focused. Thankfully, I've had a great community in my corner as I tackled Pedal to the Metal.

First and foremost, I'd like to acknowledge my wife Mary who stuck with me during the entire project. Her feedback and encouragement made it all possible.

I'd like to thank my kids Kelsey and Tyler. They always listened to my ideas and helped make them better. They helped turn me into a leadership story teller.

I'd like to acknowledge Henry DeVries for his help in visualizing the book and working with me closely on getting a pile of notes into a draft that made sense.

Sharron Stockhausen rolled up her sleeves and provided invaluable editing advice. Her feedback helped create a product that was more readable and flowed from chapter to chapter.

Joni McPherson did an outstanding job in designing the cover of the book.

Thank you all for helping me to finally get the book across the finish line!

Part I: The Race Is On

❖ ❖ ❖

Introduction: Refuel the Leadership Mission

❖   ❖   ❖

REVOLUTIONS ARE HAPPENING AROUND US all the time. The introduction of the smart phone changed forever the way we communicate, connect and share our lives. Solar power is reshaping the grid. Medical breakthroughs like genetic engineering are improving the quality and extending the length of our lives.

The consequences of these revolutions affect the way leaders need to engage the organization. But, there is a problem. Most of our traditional leadership approaches and tools are just too slow and cumbersome to be effective in a work environment that continues to get faster and more complex. These leadership models were created and refined during a time when the pace of work was different, the pace of change moved slower, and people had different attitudes towards leaders.

What is needed now is a basic refueling of the leadership mission. Having coached hundreds of leaders over the past twenty five years, I have personally seen the need for this revolution gain momentum. Fundamentally, leadership needs to be approached differently given the pace of change. There is a whole new set of skills leaders need to master to be effective in the always on, always connected world.

The core premise of the book is that leaders need to get faster in how they exercise their leadership while at the same time helping their organizations to also get faster.

Leadership speed is simply not enough; organizations need to get faster too. If the speed gap between the leader and the organization becomes too large, performance is impacted in a negative way. The need to accelerate touches all types of leaders and organizations whether they are non-profit, academic, or commercial enterprises.

You can use the book like a leadership flight manual to map out your course and strategy for accelerating your leadership skills. It will become an important resource for you as you refine your skills. You'll find tips, resources, models, and suggestions for becoming a faster leader. Although the book outlines a leadership system, each chapter is written to stand on its own. You can jump into it at any point of interest. I include an application exercise at the end of each chapter to help you apply the concepts and principles. You can download the exercises from the website (**www.fasterleader.com**).

To simplify the narrative, I use the masculine pronoun throughout the book. No slight is intended to the excellent female leaders who hopefully will find the book useful and transformative. I have had the opportunity to work with many exceptional women leaders and they shaped many of the concepts I write about.

What is faster leadership and how is it different than more traditional forms of leadership? Let me clarify at the outset, the emphasis on faster is about being faster in the things that really matter. It is about smart speed. It is not about being frantic, reactionary, or an adrenaline junky. It is not about just moving quickly, it is about cultivating agility and the ability to change quickly. Faster leadership requires significant investment in time and resources, and it is not easy to attain. Indeed, faster leadership can be defined as the capacity to help your team or organization get ahead of and navigate change.

Don't get me wrong. Characteristics such as credibility and integrity are still important for effective leadership. But it is the leader's ability to accelerate and make their team faster that is increasingly the difference between success and failure.

Faster leadership is not just reserved for the C Suite. Successful organizations cultivate leadership throughout the organization and promote a **leadership everywhere** philosophy. Distributed leadership is critical because so many of the big problems and challenges facing organizations don't fit neatly into organizational structure and responsibility. The CEO can't be the only one focused on the big picture and the future of the organization.

The faster leader model proposed in this book emphasizes four factors that drive speed and you'll be reading about them throughout the book.

- **Navigation** is about the leader's ability to chart a course through a chaotic environment and get the team over the finish line. It incorporates concepts like vision, mission, strategy and the leadership dashboard.
- **Energy** is the motivational fuel that the leader taps into to drive performance. A key source of creating organizational energy is to build a high engagement culture.
- **Optimization** references the leader's drive for continual improvement in efficiency and effectiveness.
- **Resistance** is the fundamental force that slows everything down and the leader's goal is to minimize it at all costs.

While leaders have always been dealing with these forces to a degree, the pace of change magnifies the consequences of those forces and challenges the leader to dramatically improve their skills. To master the forces of speed, the leader needs to become an expert in the **FASTER** skill set.

F: A leader's sense of **focus** needs to be rigorous and extreme. They need to make sure the organization is focused on the critical variables that drive success. They need to be vigilant about combating the forces of distraction.

A: The leader needs to drive **alignment**. All parts of the organization need to support each other and be working for the same goal. The leader needs to be constantly on the lookout for misalignment and friction, and quickly act to bring things back into alignment.

S: The leader needs to have excellent **self-awareness** and the ability to be self-critical. Blind spots and rationalization lead to ineffective leadership behavior, and erode the credibility and trust that allows a leader to accelerate. Your personality is the engine by which you exercise your leadership, and it needs to be in tune.

T: The leader needs to place a high value on **time** and how it is used. They need to reinforce the concept that everyone's time is valuable and time management is an organizational priority. They need to be a model of efficiency and speed in setting strategy, execution, decision-making, and resolving issues.

E: Faster leadership doesn't happen unless the leader **engages** the organization. A leader can't do it alone. He needs to have an organization that is committed, involved, and invested. By building and reinforcing a culture of engagement, the leader fosters self-management and leadership.

R: Speed without **results** is just meaningless activity. The faster leader places results at the top of the priority list and holds people, including himself, accountable for achieving results that matter.

THE FASTER LEADER ROLES

In addition to the FASTER skills, leaders need to master several specialized roles that build on those skills and help drive speed and acceleration. While you don't have to excel in every one of them, you'll want to develop proficiency in as many as you can. The ten faster leader roles include:

1. **Chief Engagement Officer**: The key focus of this role is on engaging the organization at a high level. Building strong personal connections throughout the organization is a top priority. This role is covered in Chapter Four.

2. **Chief Architect**: Leaders have an important role in designing effective cultures and organizations. To build a fast culture, a leader needs to understand the principles of speed. They need to think like an architect. I cover several important design concepts and this role in Chapter Eight.

3. **Chief Assessment Officer**: As the work environment continues to speed up, the ability of the leader to quickly diagnose problems and issues becomes critical to success. The role of Chief Assessment Officer is discussed in Chapters Three, Nine, and Eleven.

4. **Chief Time Manager**: One of the most important things a leader can do is optimize how time is spent both personally and for the organization. Time is one of the most precious commodities and leaders need to place a high priority on how it is used. I cover this role in Chapters Two and Six.

5. **Chief Information Officer**: Good information is the key to good decision making and strategy. In this role, the faster leader ensures the organization has accurate information flow in areas that matter most. See my discussion in Chapter Nine.

6. **Chief Recruiting Officer**: The ability to attract and retain talent is one of the most important skills of the faster leader. Rather than leaving it to others, I suggest leaders play a primary role in recruitment. I cover this role in depth in Chapter Nine.

7. **Chief Team Builder**: Putting together a top notch team is one of the most important ways a leader can build a faster organization. Having a nose for talent, having a great reputation as a boss, and creating an environment where top performers thrive is the role of the Chief Team Builder. I address this critical leadership role in Chapter Nine.

8. **Chief Perspective Officer**: Helping the organization to understand and make sense of change and chaos is the role of the Chief Perspective Officer. By providing frameworks and context, you can help the organization to make better decisions and respond to events more effectively. Chapters Four and Nine address this role and give suggestions on improving your communications in this vital leadership area.

9. **Chief Guidance Officer**: Setting the correct course for the organization and navigating through an ever-changing environment is the job of the Chief Guidance Officer. Having

a vision, mission, charter, and strategies that are aligned allows everyone in the organization to work together on the same goals. See Chapter Seven for more ideas on how to build your Chief Guidance Officer performance.

10. **Chief Focus Officer**: It is an ongoing battle to keep the organization focused on what is most important to its success. Mission creep, distraction, and too much information all contribute to an organization losing its focus. These variables, among others, challenge the leader to keep the organization on track. I give several suggestions in Chapter Thirteen on how a leader can help the organization remain focused and stay the course.

In the coming chapters, we'll explore how masters of speed practice and refine their craft. We'll dig into environments where speed is a dominant success factor. I think much can be learned by studying individuals who push the limits of performance. In particular, I'll be highlighting drivers who push the envelope in Formula One racing and pilots who have the right stuff. A common trait these speed burners possess is they get the most from everything they touch. Leaders, start your engines.

CHAPTER 1

The Need for Speed

If everything seems under control, you're
just not going fast enough.

MARIO ANDRETTI, WORLD CHAMPION RACE CAR DRIVER

IF YOU JUST KEEP PACE, you will lose the race. In today's rapidly evolving, globally connected business world, speed gives you the competitive edge. The time has come to get your leadership life and effectiveness under control.

Faster leaders are needed now more than ever. The rapidly accelerating pace of change is not going to let up. You are undoubtedly feeling the effects. Technology advances, globalization, downsizing, the emergence of the lean organization, and economic shifts continue to put pressure on leaders to step up their game. The stakes are high and any mistake a leader makes is magnified.

You can't slow down your competitors while you catch your breath. You can't stop the world from spinning as you get organized. You can't call a time out while you figure out what you want to do next.

The pace of work is a blur and the sheer volume of work to be accomplished is overwhelming leaders everywhere. Leaders are living in an "always on, always connected" world where there is no break from work. No wonder so many leaders are struggling to keep up.

There is never enough time to get everything done and everything seems to have so much urgency attached to it. Leaders are tethered to their phones, laptops, and other communication devices. Work has become a 24/7/365 activity. The result is leaders fall into constant reacting and firefighting. Leaders easily lose touch with what is truly important to success. Leaders fall into the trap of doing what can be done easily rather than what is important.

The work environment is managing the leader rather than the leader managing the environment. The constant and unrelenting competition continues to raise expectations and demands on leaders, which challenges their ability to lead and make good choices.

Over the more than twenty five years I have been working with leaders, I have seen the impact of rapid change on leadership behaviors. One of the main consequences is that many individuals in leadership roles simply stop or reduce their leadership behavior. Too much stress can act as an antagonist to leadership. The tyranny of immediacy—too much to do with too little time—puts people into coping mode. Sad to say, leadership behavior is one of the first things to drop off the to-do list. In auto racing parlance, they hit the wall. In the vernacular of flight school, they wash out.

In this chapter, I'll cover a few of the trends the faster leader needs to deal with. I'll talk about the paradox that exists at the heart of becoming a faster leader and introduce the concept of the leadership ecosystem.

Rough Roads and Turbulence Ahead

Before plunging ahead, let's step back and take a look at the landscape leaders need to deal with. Beyond the pace of change, what are the other key factors that impact a leader's ability to be faster? Out of all the pressing concerns, problems, trends, and stressors, what are the most important issues leaders should to be aware of and have an effective strategy for managing?

No doubt you are zipping along already. Driving at over two hundred miles per hour at the Indy 500 doesn't give you a great view of the scenery. When you are flying near Mach 1 at 50,000 feet, the landscape can look pretty blurry from the jet cockpit. However, in both cases, there are still navigational features that can be recognized.

Regardless of where you are a leader—in a start up, a large organization, an academic setting, or not-for-profit entity—there are ten trends that profoundly affect your leadership and how you exercise it. You have to deal with these trends if you want to lead and lead effectively. I think of these ten trends as the rough weather pilots need to navigate through to bring their planes safely home. Figurative thunderstorms, updrafts, wind shear, and ice storms will test your mettle.

Trend # 1: Uncertainty is the New Normal

Your ability to handle and navigate ambiguity and uncertainty is paramount. Stability and security are illusions. Things will not return to how they once were. The best adaptation strategy is to get more comfortable with uncertainty, see the patterns in what seems like chaos, and get ahead of events so they can be more effectively shaped. As Ana Dutra, CEO of Korn Ferry, asserted in *Chief Learning Officer* magazine, "Where tolerance for ambiguity used to be one of the top traits of leaders it is now the 'price of admission.'"[1]

Trend # 2: Time Demands Continue to Increase

Face it. You will never have enough time to do the things you need to do. There is simply too much to do and too little time. More people want a part of you, your time, and your attention. The pace of change and increase in demands stress the leader. Exacerbating the problem, people have become less discriminating in how they consume each other's time. Rather than assessing whether or not something is critical, they simply treat all things as important and pass them along, which force you to sort through an ever increasing stockpile of demands. This type of **reactive workflow** (junk work generated by others) has a hugely negative impact on focus, morale, and productivity. In fact, many of my clients say reactive workflow is the single biggest problem they deal with in their organizations. It's one of the reasons why managing your time has become such a challenge.

The challenge extends beyond just managing your own time. Leaders increasingly need to help their organizations do a better job of time management overall. Time management needs to become an organizational priority, and leaders need to drive and shape the time management budget for the entire organization. By doing so, leaders can help their organizations become more efficient and effective.

Trend #3: The Rules Change Constantly

What made you successful in the past will not always work in the future. Applying historical experience to new and novel situations is a recipe for failure. Clinging to what is familiar will leave you unprepared to deal with new rules and challenges. Being able to quickly sort out and understand the new rules that apply to your marketplace, your business, and your team will become a more critical leadership behavior. You will need to continually re-invent yourself and your business while staying true to your core value proposition.

Trend #4: We Live in an Increasingly Complex World
The variables you must incorporate into your thinking and perspective will continue to increase both in depth and breadth. New regulations and reporting, increased management oversight, and increased public scrutiny all contribute to the complexity of the leadership landscape. The emergence of the global economy, where you may buy a product from one company, package it with another, and distribute it with a third, requires the leader think beyond traditional business models. As the world becomes more interconnected and complex, you will be challenged to continually push for simplification.

Trend #5: Information Overload
Not only is the pace of work much faster than it historically has been, leaders have to contend with massive amounts of information that vary incredibly in terms of quality and accuracy. For example, The Radicati Group, Inc. estimates that 294 billion e-mails are sent daily worldwide. They found that the average corporate e-mail user sends and receives 110 messages a day, with a good portion being spam or unwanted newsletters.[2] Monitoring software on users' PCs showed that people check their e-mail up to forty times an hour. Filters help, but leaders still spend hours each day sorting through e-mail.

The proliferation of online content and the pace at which new information is published is staggering. An infographic published by DOMO in 2014 showed that every minute:

- Facebook users share nearly 2.5 million pieces of content.
- Twitter users tweet nearly 300,000 times.
- Instagram users post nearly 220,000 new photos.
- YouTube users upload 72 hours of new video content.
- Apple users download nearly 50,000 apps.
- Email users send over 200 million messages.[3]

The State of the Workplace Survey 2014 by Cornerstone On Demand, reported that more than two-thirds of U.S. workers suffer from work overload mainly caused by too much information and too many demands on their time.[4] Figuring out how to keep up with this juggernaut of information taxes even the most organized leader. Any race car driver will tell you that too much information is as bad as not enough information.

Trend #6: The Distraction Epidemic
With so many different demands and possibilities confronting people, getting and maintaining their attention is another challenge leader's face. It seems that everyone has a need to report on everything they are doing. As our attention spans have shrunk and our need for immediate feedback has increased, leaders have to focus on making their messages more compelling and attention grabbing. The rapid rise of new syntax and slang challenges the leader to be relevant and timely. Keeping important messages fresh over time and keeping people engaged is a full-time sales job.

With the explosion of social media, people are more distracted than ever. People are constantly checking their phones, texting others, and posting pictures. The next time you attend a meeting check what others are doing and you'll see what I'm talking about. Leaders are battling a distraction epidemic.

Trend #7: Adaptation Fatigue

Not only does the pace of change affect leaders, it affects everyone else. As leaders struggle to adapt, so do their teams and organizations. As a consequence, leaders are constantly combating their own reactions while simultaneously trying to influence their teams and have to fight what I call adaptation fatigue, which is both prevalent and powerful. Rather than being proactive, adaptation fatigue sets us up for failure. It starts to happen when stress and panic begin to overwhelm us.

There are the six characteristics of adaptation fatigue. Be on the lookout for them in both yourself and others on your team.

- **Our perspective shrinks.** When we get overloaded our viewpoint becomes more restricted and narrow. We miss important data that is outside our attention window.
- **We become more distracted and interruption driven**. We have more difficulty completing things and tasks are left unfinished as we move on to the next emergency.
- **We impose filters to control information**. We set up a gauntlet of steps people have to go through to get our attention. Communication becomes more challenging.
- **We respond to anything new by saying no**. We fall into a default position of rejecting any new requests because we are already swamped.
- **We increasingly rely on our past experience**. Unfortunately, many apply past experiences inappropriately to new situations. Rather than being adaptive and agile, we get increasingly conservative in our behavior.
- **We focus on short-term achievable tasks**. Longer-term thinking and planning take a backseat to our reacting to what is on our plate.

Trend #8: Work Overload

There is simply too much work to be done and not enough time to accomplish it. Organizations have adopted reduced headcount as an operating principle which puts tremendous pressure on employees to accomplish more with less. Many projects in organizations are chronically under resourced.

The fast pace of change adds to the work load. We keep piling on initiatives to keep pace with the work demands. We consistently forget to counterbalance this trend by taking things off the plate. Team members are constantly struggling to keep their heads above water. Many of the productivity improvement tools we implement actually create more work rather than eliminating it. There is no obvious end in sight. The amount of work to be done keeps increasing for all levels of the organization.

The effects of overload can be dramatic. In researching the causes of aviation accidents, the FAA found that eighty percent of the accidents were caused by human error. A key finding—too much workload and task saturation led to a reduction in situational awareness and problem escalation.[5]

Trend #9: A Challenging Workforce

Leaders have an uphill battle on more than one front. One of the biggest challenges leaders face is trying to engage a workforce that is skeptical and distrustful of leadership. Organizations have survived layoffs, outsourcing, restructuring, bad behavior by senior executives, and other challenges during recent years. The net effect is a dramatic alteration of the work contract and employee engagement level at its lowest point in generations.

The results of a Gallup poll are particularly sobering. In a broad survey of employee attitudes, 29 percent of those surveyed rated themselves as positively engaged with their work. That's the good news. The bad news is that 55 percent of survey respondents rated themselves a passively disengaged. Think of passively disengaged as doing the minimum to get by or coasting at their jobs. The final 16 percent said they were actively disengaged in their work.[6] What does this mean? A significant percentage of the work population is using work time for their interests and has little loyalty towards their employer. While more recent data suggests employee engagement is improving, leaders still have a big problem on their hands.

While you may have been conducting yourself ethically and honestly, the behavior of other leaders who have not can influence the behavior of team members towards you. It's guilty by association. Team members see bad executive behavior in one leader and transfer that impression to other leaders. Trying to manage the actively disengaged, win back the passively disengaged, and keep the positively engaged productive means leaders need to be at their persuasive best. Recovering from a trust and credibility deficiency requires patience and tenacity, and makes the job of the leader more difficult.

One of the net results of all of these trends is that people are more reluctant to demonstrate leadership. Scrutiny, higher risk, and negative attitudes contribute to lower frequencies of leadership behavior. According to Ashford and DeRue in the *Harvard Business Review*, nearly 60 percent of companies are saying they face a leadership shortage.[7]

Trend#10: The Gap is Widening
The gap between leadership speed and organizational speed is widening. This trend is primarily due to organizations being slower to adapt to change and the proliferation of tools that help leaders adapt. As a consequence, leaders are outpacing their organizations. Faster leaders need to concentrate on closing the gap. Remember, you are only as fast as your support crew. Increasingly, leaders will need to spend more of their time focusing on issues like

efficiency, process improvement, resourcing, training, and continuous performance improvement to help their teams accelerate.

PEDAL TO THE METAL: FASTER IS BETTER

While working harder and longer is certainly part of the solution, there is a point at which we hit the wall. We simply can't throw more time or energy at the challenges we face—we don't have any of either one left to give. We have to learn to quickly get things out of our hands and into the hands of our team rather than focus on gate keeping and control. We simply must get faster as leaders.

Leaders need to understand that what made them successful in the past doesn't always work in the here and now, let alone the uncertain future they face. The accelerating world demands leaders do everything quicker, better, more effectively, and more efficiently. Leaders need to become more comfortable with things like quickly assessing risk, navigating ambiguity, creating and maintaining momentum across a global network of work sites, building high energy work cultures, and cultivating top-notch talent to name a few. Mastering these skills and the leadership landscape represent adaptations all leaders need to make to be successful.

While change has always been an aspect of organizational life, there is significant evidence all around us that the pace of change is accelerating. Let me give you a couple of real-world examples.

In days past when I was helping leaders assimilate into a new work culture or company, we would jointly develop a ninety-day plan. This onboarding plan would outline the steps leaders were going to take while still giving them time to assess the organization, issues they needed to tackle, and the people they inherited over their first ninety days on the job.

Currently, when I am working this same issue, I compress the time frame to thirty days because ninety days is simply too slow.

If it takes you three months to get up to speed, you will be too far behind the curve. I coach people to adopt the perspective that the clock starts ticking the minute they walk into the door.

Another symptom of the accelerating world is that many of the planning frameworks for organizations have become dramatically compressed. While company vision statements still have a longer term horizon, the ten-year plan, once the standard, is now considered obsolete. The prevailing view is that the business climate will be dramatically different in a much shorter time span. Many people see ten-year plans as somewhat dangerous because they convey a false sense of stability. Most leaders are looking for road maps or plans with a two-year horizon and see this type of plan as the best they can hope to do.

SPEED IS THE GAME CHANGER

So, just how important is speed? In their book *Strategic Speed*, Jocelyn Davis, Henry M. Frechette, and Edwin H. Boswell found that companies that are faster at executing their strategies soundly beat companies that are slower—to the tune of *40 percent higher sales growth and 52 percent higher growth in operating profits.* The majority of organizational leaders they interviewed believed speed was critical to success, but only four out of ten believed they were faster than their competition.[8]

This perceived gap between the current pace of organizational performance versus the desired speed represents a fundamental challenge leaders must grapple with. Leaders simply have to be faster themselves and help their organizations become faster if they want to be successful.

While management and leadership experts continue to emphasize skills such as character, emotional intelligence, or vision (all of which are important), not enough focus is placed on the speed in which these skills are exercised. Outstanding skills don't do a leader any good if the leader is too slow in exercising them.

Ignoring the need for speed comes with a heavy price. Just keeping pace will put you further and further behind. Competitors will eat your lunch while you spend hours in unproductive meetings. Leaders who know how to accelerate their behavior will continue to leave you in the dust. The pace of work demands that leaders learn how to work faster.

THE PARADOX OF THE FASTER LEADER

But wait. There is more to becoming a faster leader than just being quick. You have to master a paradox that is at the heart of becoming a faster leader. What is the paradox? You have to **invest** in the right things to build a foundation before you can become faster. It takes time to become faster. Leadership speed is not an accident. It is the result of planning, practice, patience, and investment. Just like a Formula One driver, you have to log in hours and hours of time on the practice track mastering yourself and the machine you are driving.

You can be a really fast driver, but you won't win races if your pit crew is slow or doesn't work well together. You can't win by yourself. You have to invest in people, you have to invest in systems, and you have to invest in speed-enabling techniques. It's not just about being quick. It's not about frantic activity. It's about being efficient and effective in the things that really matter, those things that are on the critical path. It's what I call **smart speed**.

If you really want to become a faster leader, you have to take further steps and create a **leadership ecosystem** around you. Faster leaders rely upon a clearly defined and reinforced work culture, a strong supporting cast, efficient and effective systems, a well-mapped-out strategy, and organizational structures that are clean and non-hierarchical. The paradox is that becoming faster takes time, energy, and patience.

You don't build a leadership ecosystem by just flipping a switch or wishing for its existence—you have to put the work in. The way I look at it, there really is no way to shortcut the process. You have to put in the investment before you can savor the rewards. If you are impatient or need instant feedback and gratification, you will be challenged. While our culture emphasizes the immediate, faster leaders understand the best investments take time to realize their gains.

An effective ecosystem may take months or years to build. It takes time to assemble the right building blocks and to put them in the right order or sequence. It takes time for your ecosystem to get up and running efficiently. It takes time to find the right people. You can't become a faster leader by yourself. Complete the acceleration tool #1 at the end of this chapter to evaluate the state of your ecosystem. You can download the tool at www.fasterleader.com.

The real challenge for leaders is to budget the time and exercise the discipline to build an ecosystem in environments where time is at a premium. The pace of work makes building an ecosystem even more challenging. Many leaders are under the gun and feel they simply don't have the time to invest. Organizations make it worse by continually asking leaders to do more and by treating everything as urgent and important. Building a leadership ecosystem has to become a personal priority or it won't happen. If you invest your time and energy wisely, you will become a faster leader. We'll talk more about building your leadership ecosystem throughout the book.

The 51 Percent Threshold

Jet aircraft are routinely pulled off line so necessary maintenance can be performed. Part of faster leadership maintenance is taking time out to invest in your environment and get your own machine in tip top shape. Sometimes you have to go *slower* in order to go faster. If you are constantly racing around, you may not have created the right infrastructure for your business and eventually you will hit the wall. Faster leaders don't allow themselves to become victims of false urgency and immediacy. Instead, they take the time to think things through. They manage the situation instead of allowing the situation to manage them.

What I found in working with faster leaders is they consistently invest a relatively high percentage of their personal time in activities that have a delayed or more long-term strategic leadership effect. How much time should you budget to build your ecosystem and faster leader resources? Quite a bit it turns out. I call this target the **51 percent threshold** because it represents the average amount of time leaders must devote to creating conditions that enable faster leadership. The other 49 percent is focused on more tactical issues and problem solving.

A perfect example relates to hiring. Rather than waiting until a team member leaves, the faster leader consistently devotes time to looking for talent and informally interviewing people. One leader I worked with went so far as to devote a set number of hours per week to networking with people to find potential candidates for his team.

Why don't all leaders just pick up the pace? Well, not so fast. There are many speed bumps and roadblocks that stand in the way of a faster leader. The next chapter addresses one of the biggest challenges a leader faces—time management.

ACCELERATION TOOL #1: ECOSYSTEM AUDIT

Take some time to evaluate the state of your current faster leader ecosystem. Here are the key ingredients you will want to review. Use the following categories to grade each ingredient: in good shape, needs improvement, and lots of work needed. Pick the top three that are in the worst shape and start budgeting some time to improve them.

- A talent pool that fits your culture
- Clear roles and minimal hierarchy
- Sufficient resources
- Tools necessary to perform the work
- Alignment across teams and organizations
- Simple communication systems that work
- Accurate performance feedback loops
- Real-time visibility into performance
- A well-defined organizational strategy
- Cultural values around time and urgency
- Continuous improvement processes
- Extreme focus and minimal distraction
- Goals that are challenging but attainable
- Organizational discipline around practice and continuous improvement

CHAPTER 2

Every Race Has a Finish Line

❖ ❖ ❖

At some point, you simply run out of runway
and need to get your wheels in the air.

WHETHER YOU ARE A FORMULA One race car driver, a jet fighter pilot or a leader in a nonprofit organization, your goal is to win the race, complete the mission or meet your goals. You are either competing against others, yourself, obstacles, or the environment, and how you spend time drives your success or failure. You are always racing against the clock.

It seems that everything you do has an implicit or explicit time line or runway attached to it and the clock keeps ticking whether or not you want to acknowledge it. This chapter focuses on the time element of the faster leader model I talked about in the preface.

While most leaders understand the importance of time, the reality is that poor time management has become the number one problem in organizations. Against the onslaught of all of the trends I talked about in Chapter One, our ability to manage time has been eroded to the point that we have lost control of it. But, losing control of our time didn't happen overnight. It was a gradual process made up of many work/life compromises and fostered by advances in technology.

Why don't more leaders focus on time management? The problem lies in our orientation to time management. People generally think of time management as **an individual problem, not an organizational one**. Additionally, a lot of bad habits have been developed in organizations around the use of time. One classic example is inefficient meetings in which people waste their time. This bias towards time management as an individual problem leads us to develop tools and approaches that focus on the individual and not attacking the issue at its foundation.

Leaders have historically not focused on organizational time management as one of their areas of responsibility. While time management doesn't seem like a high leverage impact issue, as Peter Drucker maintains, if you can't manage time you really can't manage anything else.

The crisis is real. The consequences of time management erosion are everywhere. Here are just a few of the effects I have observed in my work with organizations:

- People have become less respectful and valuing of other's time
- Multitasking has become standard work practice. Ironically, it leads to lower productivity and increased distraction.
- People are too busy to lead. Although many people want to lead, it often doesn't show up in their priorities.
- There is more focus on what can be accomplished rather than what is strategically important.
- Meetings have taken over organizational life.
- People have lost control of their calendars.

On your path to becoming a faster leader you will need to view time as your ally, not your enemy. Time forces you to focus on the things that really matter and it drives a relentless prioritization. At the heart of becoming a faster leader is helping your organization to value time more effectively and to accelerate in ways that are meaningful and impactful. I challenge leaders to think of time management as one of their top leadership priorities.

In this chapter I'll talk about a few principles of effective time management, discuss a new role a leader can play in helping their organization to get back on the time management wagon, and tackle the number one time management problem. Let's get started with five principles that can guide your time management strategy.

PRINCIPLES OF TIME MANAGEMENT

Principle #1: Value other's time as much as you value your own. Regardless of a person's status or place in the organization, treat their time as important. As the old adage states, you get what you give. If you value other's time, you increase the possibility that other people will value yours.

Principle #2: Establish a no-fly zone. Military mission commanders will often set aside an area of territory that planes are not allowed to fly over. The objective is to create an area of safety for non-combatants on the ground. Likewise, there needs to be a time in the organizational work cycle that cannot be interrupted or compromised. Set aside a block of time that is a no-fly zone and will be respected throughout the organization. You will teach the organization that time management can be done while reinforcing the idea of respecting boundaries.

Principle 3: Remember the ripple effect. Because of the interconnected nature of work, a single individual can disrupt the schedules of many people. These time ripples can spread throughout the organization and compromise performance. Make sure people understand the consequences of their behavior on others.

Principle #4: Practice time reciprocity. Your team can quickly become overloaded if things are continually added to their plate without something coming off. Time reciprocity is basically a balancing act to counteract overload. You can apply the principle to meetings, schedules, workload, or anything that has a time value attached to it. If you add a task that takes additional time to complete, be sure to eliminate another task to compensate.

Principle #5: Time management, as a discipline, begins at the top. Leaders need to model good time management behavior. The next section covers in more detail what a leader can do to improve time management within their organization.

LEADER AS CHIEF TIME MANAGER

Leaders need to understand that ultimately they are only going to be as fast and agile as their team allows them to be. Leaders have to help their organizations to get faster if they want to be successful. Leaders need to address issues and invest in areas that have not typically been part of leadership responsibility to achieve this goal.

When leaders are looking for ways to help their teams accelerate, I typically point them to time management. I suggest that they think of it as one of the most important components of the organizational engine.

Time management is your secret weapon against the challenges of an accelerating world. I challenge leaders to think of themselves as a CTM (**Chief Time Manager**).

Your human capital is your most important asset. How your people spend their time has a real impact on how your organization performs. When your team is focusing on the most important things, great performance is possible and morale can be high. When your team is distracted or focused on the non-essential, performance slips and morale suffers.

I suggest that leaders approach **time management as an organizational priority**. Strategic time management is the foundation of the faster organization. It is the chassis on which you build a high performing organization.

How your team members spend their time is the most critical variable in driving the performance of your organization. If your team is wasting time by focusing on low priority items more critical issues will be ignored. The best way a leader can help their team deal with the time management problem is to emphasize the strategic value of time and give their team the tools to better manage their time. As I mentioned previously, a principle of organizational time management is to set and respect boundaries. It is fundamentally about applying discipline and control. I suggest using four steps to put time management discipline into practice and close the speed gap.

Step 1: Establish a Strategic Time Allocation Budget (STAB)
We create budgets to help us monitor performance in many different areas but time often doesn't show up on the spreadsheet as one of the variables we track. At the executive level, I recommend leaders create a strategic time allocation budget or STAB for their

organization that clearly identifies the strategic priorities for the organization in terms of time allocation.

A STAB establishes a success formula for the organization to follow by clearly articulating concrete targets for time allocation. It answers the question of how should we be spending our time if we want to be successful as an organization. If your sales people are spending too much time on product quality issues and not on selling, you are going to have big problems. Let me be clear, this is not about micro-management but rather about aligning how time is spent in the organization with strategic priorities. This master time allocation budget can then be used throughout the organization to drive better time management.

The best place to start in developing a STAB is to first generate a list of categories for how people should be spending their time. A broad framework that can help you get started is to think about organizational work occurring in six broad categories:

1. Researching what to make or deliver
2. Producing products or services
3. Selling and marketing those products and services
4. Delivering products and services to customers
5. Supporting customers or clients with the products and services
6. Management and administration activities (i.e., monitoring and measuring performance, planning, recruiting, compliance, team member development and coaching).

You can then break down these larger categories into more specific categories. Here are some other categories to help jump start your process- time to think, innovation, developing a talent pipeline, analyzing data, reporting, strategy development, sales, debugging products, quality audits, training, product development, customer engagement, production and manufacturing, and patent development. The key is to identify categories that are closely related to your success.

I would like to highlight the category I mentioned first. Time to think is often the category we give up first, but it is the most important one for fostering creative and strategic thought. It helps us to broaden and expand our perspective. Be sure to include time to think in all of your time budgets.

After you have generated a list of targeted time categories, take the next step and put those categories in a prioritized matrix. Carefully analyze which activities are most important to your success in arriving at those priorities. Throw out anything that is not mission critical. I generally suggest keeping the list of categories small and manageable. Too many categories can become overwhelming and make the exercise less useful. Generally, between eight and twelve categories is a useful number.

After you have determined your priorities, assign percentages to the categories that support your most critical activities. It is a good idea to only budget up to an 80% total cap figure to make a 20% allowance for unpredictable delays and emergencies. While a number of the categories are daily or weekly in frequency, make sure to account for categories that happen on a quarterly or yearly basis (i.e., strategic planning or operational reviews). It is important to remember that activities will vary in frequency over the course of a year. For example, certain weeks might be heavy on planning whereas other weeks might be focused on training. The time budget needs to be seen as an average. Make the breakdown percentages reasonable and attainable or you will risk de-motivating your team by the exercise.

Here is an example of a STAB that I helped a VP of Engineering put together for his team:

- Design engineering: 55%
- Cross-functional team work: 10%
- Documentation: 1%
- Research: 5%
- Planning: 5%
- Training and development: 2%
- Recruiting: 2%

Step 2: Build Functional TAB's (Time Allocation Budgets)

The next step is drive time management down into all levels of the team or organization. I suggest you have your team create a time budget for their individual functions and responsibilities that are aligned with and support the organizational STAB. As I noted in the preface, alignment is a key element of the faster leader skill set.

I call these second tier time management budgets TAB's (time allocation budgets). Different categories and emphasis will show up in these budgets because they relate to different functional organizations, but they still need to be aligned with the STAB. You can use the process outlined previously to help your team members develop a TAB.

Once your team has developed their TAB's, be sure to check for alignment with the STAB. Have your team members share their budgets with each other to further collaboration and understanding between team members. Reinforce the idea that TAB's are targets that you want to achieve going forward. When you are finished with this process, you will have one STAB and several

TAB's for your organization that represent how you think everyone should be spending your time.

Step 3: Identify the Gaps.

After the time budgets are created and reviewed, the next step is to analyze the gaps between the current state and desired state. The quickest and easiest way to do this is to have your team keep a record of how they spend their time over a two week period. Two weeks is usually an adequate time period to get a baseline for your team. Be sure to pick a two week period that is representative of how the team typically spends its time.

You are trying to get a general idea of how far off you are from your desired budget and identify activities that sidetrack the team. Have your team members use the categories you have already selected and go through their calendars and categorize how they spent their time. Have them record and categorize time that is not aligned with your selected categories. At the end of the two weeks, each team will be able to compare how they actually spent their time versus their TAB. They will be able to identify problem areas in their budgets.

As a final step, you will aggregate the team totals and compare how the team did as a whole against the STAB you previously developed. This exercise will suggest changes you need to make at the organizational level.

Step 4: Build in Organizational Practices that Reinforce Time Management

The next steps in the time management process are to reduce activities that blow up your team's budget and improve processes to make things more time efficient. I suggest breaking your team up into several working groups to come up with solutions for the most egregious offenders. Here are ten of the more common problem areas to get you started:

- processes that don't work as they were intended
- too many ineffective meetings
- poorly defined strategy
- initiative overload- trying to do too much
- lack of prioritization
- inability or unwillingness to stop activities
- inadequate scoping of work to be done
- a reactive mindset
- a lack of value assigned to time
- unclear or overlapping team boundaries

Step 5: Put the STAB and TAB's into Practice
After you have put into place the changes your team identified, it is now time to put the STAB and TAB's into practice. I suggest that you treat the budgets as important organizational performance metrics and evaluate them on a regular basis. There is an old management saying that says what gets measured gets done. Pick a review cycle that makes sense for your team. Depending on the nature of your work, you might want to have your team review its actual versus targeted time budget on a bi-weekly, monthly, or quarterly basis. Don't let your review cycle be too long because it can undermine your ability to make needed changes on a timely basis.

Clients of mine who have implemented the STAB and TAB process have enjoyed improvements in productivity, team member engagement, and morale. By helping the team get faster, the speed gap between the leader and his team is reduced. I suggest you give it a try.

TIME BUDGET BUSTER #1: MEETINGS

The number one time waster in organizations and one of the biggest challenges for the faster leader is ineffective meetings. This problem is not new. We have known for a long time that meetings can be big time wasters, but because of the accelerating nature of work, we have to come up with better solutions for this historical nemesis. I have never encountered a leader who said he doesn't have enough meetings. Meetings are the top culprit for disrupting STAB's.

Research conducted by the Annenberg School of Communications at UCLA and the University of Minnesota's Training & Development Research Center shows that executives on average spend 40-50 percent of their working hours in meetings. The studies point out that as much as 50 percent of meeting time is unproductive and that up to 25 percent is spent discussing irrelevant issues.[9] There is even research that demonstrates that too many meetings lower IQ.[10]

The modern business meeting has evolved into an artificial life form that is a profound waste of time and company resources. Meetings have become a time to check your e-mail, check updates on social media, gossip, play games, take a nap, or get hypnotized by a progression of PowerPoint slides, presenters reading from those slides, and mind-numbing data. Don't allow these time leeches to suck out any more productivity from you or your team. Reducing the sheer number of meetings you attend, or actually making them more effective, is a challenge faster leaders need to tackle directly.

Here are eighteen common problems that contribute to a dysfunctional meeting culture and solutions to those problems. As a CTM, keep your eyes out for these problems in your organization and be ready to act. You'll need to practice vigilance because meetings continually spring up or get off course.

Problem #1: Poor meeting mechanics

The basics of good meeting practices are not followed. The purpose of the meeting is not clear. The expected outcome of the meeting is not clearly articulated. Minutes are not taken. Action items are not followed up on. Materials are not sent out ahead of time to help people come into the meeting prepared and with correct information.

Solutions: Institute basic meeting etiquette in all of your meetings. Help reinforce meeting protocols by participating and modeling good behaviors. Tie your participation to the practices being followed. Ask for an agenda before agreeing to attend. Have attendees grade the meeting's effectiveness and review these ratings on a regular basis.

Problem #2: The leader doesn't effectively exercise his role

This problem relates to the failure of leaders to do what they are supposed to do. They don't keep conversations on track, don't avoid rat holes, don't check to see that people are actively engaged, and don't close discussions at the appropriate time and move on to action. Leaders may not be clear on whether they are leading or participating, which contributes to confusion among attendees on how to respond to or treat the leader.

Solutions: Make clear to meeting leaders your expectations of their role. Many leaders have not received good training on meeting management and are doing what they have observed in other meetings. Give them concrete and specific feedback on how to improve the meeting. Ask them to send clear signals when they move between the roles of leader versus participant.

Problem #3: The leader tries to do everything

Managing a meeting means juggling several very distinctive activities. If the leader is trying to do all it himself, there will always be tasks that don't get done.

Solutions: Distribute important meeting functions among attendees. You can assign certain roles such as note taker and time manager to encourage participation from other attendees.

Problem #4: Lack of awareness around the true cost of a meeting

If attendees are fellow team members, their actual cost often gets taken for granted. Leaders just don't think about their coworkers in terms of cost. They can labor under false assumptions about what the actual employee hourly cost is, and that contributes to inefficient use of time. The result is companies are wasting millions of dollars a year on unproductive meetings.

Solutions: As a rule of thumb, an accurate reflection of the true cost for a mid-level manager would be 2.7 times their annual salary.[11] This estimate includes things like rent, utilities, computer costs, and infrastructure costs. Based on that assumption, the total costs for an employee paid $100,000 per year are about $270,000 per year or roughly $130.00 per hour. If there are ten people in this salary range in a two-hour long meeting, there is $2,600 worth of employee time spent during the meeting. Tighten up the meeting discipline in the organization by utilizing a cost calculator to measure the true cost of a meeting. Then evaluate whether or not the agenda justifies its ROI. If the calculation is not a good investment, either cancel the meeting or improve the agenda to increase its return.

Problem #5: No test or criteria established for creating a meeting
In most companies, *anyone* can create a meeting about *anything*. There is no gate keeping or clear standard that must be met before a meeting can be called. This is what I call the meeting reflex. When a problem is encountered, the first impulse is to call a meeting. Lack of discipline in this area can lead to an explosion of meetings, most of which will be unnecessary.

Solutions: Publish criteria for the establishment of any meeting (e.g., requires a group action, can only be thirty minutes long, etc.). Set up a meeting approval process and/or approval body that all proposed meetings must go through to be ratified. Have people submit their proposed meetings for approval. Consider limiting meetings to certain days, have meeting-free days, or set a maximum limit of meetings per week.

Problem #6: Meetings are a substitute for other things that are broken
Unclear or overlapping roles, broken processes, or lack of accountability can all contribute to meeting overload. Instead of fixing the core problem, people take the easy way around and set up a meeting. They learn to navigate around the institutionalized bumps in the road.

Solutions: Ask these simple questions to try and identify the real problem. Are there problems between roles and responsibilities? Are we dealing with a broken process such as decision-making? Are people willing to take ownership and responsibility? Set up a work group or team to start tackling the real issue once it is identified.

Problem #7: Control not exercised over membership
People are in the meeting who really don't need to be there, while others who should be present are not. As a consequence, things don't get resolved and more meetings are scheduled. A related problem is that the membership keeps expanding until the meeting becomes unwieldy and difficult to manage. A meeting beyond a certain size will evolve into just an information exchange.

Solutions: Scrutinize the invitee list. Un-invite individuals who don't have a compelling reason to attend. Alternatively, ask attendees to justify their presence or why they should attend. Meetings shouldn't be treated as a popularity contest. Invite people who need to be there and clearly explain the reason for their attendance. Keep the membership small when possible. An effective working meeting size is six to ten people. Beyond that range, plan to have meetings that are more communication focused.

Problem #8: Meetings have bad PR
Team members may think, "Any meeting is a waste of time. Can't I just go do my work?" If this is the situation at your company, meetings have acquired a bad reputation. They are framed as a necessary evil rather than an important mechanism for getting things done. People begrudgingly attend them, don't attend, or have low expectations. All meetings are seen in a negative light.

Solutions: Start a positive PR campaign about the benefits of well-run meetings (i.e., better communication and alignment). Solicit people's thoughts on how to make meetings better rather than just their complaints. Measure meeting performance and report the results. Although I'm not a big fan of meetings, they do have their place.

Problem #9: Lack of choice

Meeting attendance refusal is not sanctioned or there is no legitimate way for a person to opt out of a meeting. Meetings are defined as mandatory. As a consequence, people feel coerced and resent being there. They can demonstrate passive-aggressive behavior and contribute to the ineffectiveness of the meeting.

Solutions: No one likes to feel forced. While some mandatory meetings are unavoidable, keep them to a minimum. In the meetings, try to give people as many choices as possible. Add other rewarding activities to the meeting. Food, entertainment, games, and networking time help change the environment. Make it a point to end early whenever possible.

Problem #10: Lack of planning for disagreement

People show up at meetings with different viewpoints, perspectives, and needs. When it is time for a decision or closure, it is not surprising that many meetings get bogged down when disagreement raises its head. Often, the leader is caught by surprise when this happens and may not know what to do. He may try to force a decision, downplay the disagreement, or let the meeting end without closure.

Solutions: Anticipate disagreement. Whenever you get two people in the room, you will get different viewpoints. Solicit viewpoints ahead of time to get a sense of where people stand. Send out a brief communication before the meeting outlining the positions, pros and cons, the need for the decision, and ask people to send you any other feedback they would like to have included. Ask people to come prepared to make and support a decision, and let them know why the decision needs to be made at the meeting. Set up the agenda to allow for additional discussion as well as how the decision will be made (e.g., majority, consensus, etc.). Manage the meeting by raising the differences first, then moving on to options and tradeoffs. Keep people on track and employ the method for making the decision when the time is right.

Problem #11: Too much focus on info sharing versus decision making

With so much information to share, leaders use meetings as a default way to get a critical mass of people together and make sure they all have the same information at the same time. The sheer amount of information people deal with encourages the use of meetings as an information conduit. Unfortunately, these types of meetings engage people in a sequential manner. People's attention moves in and out depending on whether or not they see the information as relevant to them. At any point in time there will be people checked out and other people checked in.

Solutions: There are many better ways to share information than meetings. SharePoint sites, wikis, blogs, or other group collaboration software can be used to distribute information in an effective and efficient manner. Use them whenever possible.

Problem #12: Blended agendas

People set up agendas that blend too many different types of activity. One good example of this problem, which I see with regularity, is when strategic and operational activities are part of the same agenda. These types of activity require very different types of thinking and pacing, and people often have a difficult time shifting from one mode to the other.

Solutions: Try to break up meetings into different types and keep the agendas consistent. If you are having a longer meeting, break up the meeting into different segments and allow for transition time. For example, when holding a strategy-focused meeting, organize the agenda around break out time, time for brainstorming, and open-ended discussion. You might focus on only a few points or issues to get people thinking creatively. This type of meeting is very different from an operations review where you are basically reviewing results and problems.

Problem: #13: Unrealistic agendas

In this scenario, people set up agendas that try to accomplish too much. The actual amount of time required to accomplish a task is not calculated accurately and represents wishful thinking. The results are unfinished agendas and meetings that chronically run over the scheduled time. People end up getting meeting fatigue from these marathon meetings.

Solutions: Solicit multiple viewpoints from attendees before the meeting to get estimates of time needed per issue. Be sure to recognize that different activities require different pacing. Scheduling a brainstorming activity in a project review time frame won't work. Manage the allotted time slots aggressively. Identify people who consistently run over time and coach them on how to manage their time more effectively. If you work with a team over time, you should be able to get a sense of the team's pacing. Set the agenda to their pace, not yours.

Problem #14: Attendee bad behavior

Not coming prepared, expecting to be educated in the meeting, being disruptive, or expecting to be entertained are all forms of attendee bad behavior. Managing a meeting is made much more difficult when these types of behavior are present.

Solutions: Evaluate how these behaviors have come to be tolerated. Determine what you are doing that may be contributing to the behavior (i.e., not distributing information ahead of time) and change it. During the actual meeting or immediately afterwards, bring it to the attention of the individual(s) displaying the behavior that they are demonstrating ineffective conduct. Give them clear feedback on how you want to see their behavior change. Attach consequences to the bad behavior to encourage ownership and positive participation.

Problem #15: Discipline degrades over time
What was once a well-organized meeting gets sloppier over time. People start taking short cuts and meeting discipline gets worse. Meeting fatigue sets in and the leader has a harder time getting people to attend. People increasingly question the purpose of the meeting.

Solutions: This is a clear example of a meeting that needs to be revitalized or stopped. If the issue that drove the initial formation of the meeting is still active, look at refreshing the membership with a stretch break to get new perspectives. Look at transferring the leadership of the meeting to another person in the meeting. Help the meeting maintain its momentum by holding periodic meeting check up audits to get feedback from participants about the meetings purpose, how it is conducted, and how to make it better.

Problem #16: Meetings take on a life of their own
Leaders are good at starting meetings but not ending them. Meetings become a habit, and their charter can creep into other

areas outside of the original scope. New members replace original members and still the meeting chugs along. At some point it becomes difficult to remember who started the meeting and what it was supposed to do. As a consequence, meetings pile up like weight on a dogsled, eventually decreasing productivity to a dangerous level.

Solutions: I have found two basic meeting disciplines are useful in combating this problem. First, for a new meeting to be started, an existing meeting needs to be ended. In this way you'll keep the number of meeting stable. This will force people to be more discriminating about the meetings they start and will put pressure on existing meetings to be useful. The second rule is that every recurring meeting needs to have an end/evaluation date. Don't let meetings be open-ended; instead set a closure date at the very beginning. Manage the meeting to that date. A meeting can always be reinstated if there is demand for it. For meetings that are truly ongoing or mandated (e.g., safety, management reviews), establish an evaluation date where the overall effectiveness of the meeting is assessed. Be sure to evaluate the meetings at least annually.

Problem #17: Lack of continuity between meetings

Meetings are seen as isolated events that are not connected to the flow of work. Conversations do not occur about meeting themes between meetings.

Solutions: Meetings should be seen as part of an overall conversation about an issue, not as the only place where discussions about the issue take place. As you manage the meeting, think about activities and actions you can encourage members to engage in between the meetings. Assign actions, create homework, set up informal gatherings with subsets of the membership, and post communications about meeting activities as they are completed. Encourage members to interact directly to solve issues rather than wait for the meeting to solve them.

Problem #18: No transit time allowed between meetings
When back-to-back meetings get scheduled, there is often no time allowed for getting to your next meeting on time. The problem snowballs as the day progresses and you get progressively later. Meetings towards the close of the day end up having the worst attendance problem as a result. In part, this is a problem due to most meeting scheduling software which only allows appointments to be scheduled on the hour or half-hour.

Solutions: One very simple way of dealing with this problem is to set all meetings to a fifty-minute cycle. This allows for transit and transition time.

The ultimate goal for a leader to have regarding meetings is that they are seen as useful, productive, and engaging. By making sure people see their time is respected and valued, and tangible results occur, the leader creates an environment where people want to attend meetings, not dread them, and important work gets done. Review acceleration tool #2 at the end of the chapter to keep your meetings on track.

I'll pick up the thread of time management again in Chapter Six when I discuss the unique challenges a faster leader faces in managing their own time. Next up in Chapter Three, I'll cover resistance—the enemy of speed.

Acceleration Tool #2: Ten Rules for Better Meetings

To help you further improve the qualities of the meetings in your organization, use these ten guidelines. You can even post them in conference rooms to remind everyone to practice good meeting discipline.

1. Don't waste other's time.
2. Use meetings as a last resort. There are more efficient ways to communicate data or status updates than meetings.
3. If you add a new meeting, be sure to eliminate another meeting. Follow an add one, delete one philosophy.
4. Keep meetings small as possible. Every person you add increases the meeting complexity and cost exponentially.
5. Preparation is key. Give people the information they need beforehand to be productive in the meeting.
6. Keep meetings short. A good practice is to limit them to fifty minutes or less and break them up into ten to fifteen minute segments. This approach will give you time at the end to summarize.
7. Make sure that your meeting produces an output. It might be a decision or it might be a strategy, but you want people to feel that something valuable was achieved.
8. Although this may sound too obvious, start meetings on time. Don't restart the meeting to accommodate late arrivals.
9. Set an agenda that is realistic for the allotted time frame. Don't try to achieve too much or you'll end up rushing.
10. Make it a goal to end every meeting early.

CHAPTER 3

Resistance is the Enemy of Speed

❖   ❖   ❖

It is air resistance that finally prevents a road vehicle from going beyond a certain maximum velocity.

ALLAN STANIFORTH, *RACE AND RALLY CAR SOURCEBOOK*

FASTER LEADERS NEED TO UNDERSTAND their team will occasionally resist efforts to speed up the enterprise. While some of the push back may be deliberate, at other times it can be almost unconscious. The well prepared driver takes everything in stride and navigates the speed bumps and roadblocks that are part of organizational life.

Leaders should be mindful of the words of author Eckhart Tolle, who wrote, "Whatever you fight, you strengthen, and what you resist, persists." Individuals will fight you—only let that make you stronger. The organization may resist you—stay persistent in your need for speed.

Out of the many things a faster leader must deal with to be effective, the one that is the most difficult to manage is resistance.

While most leaders don't try to intentionally generate resistance, it happens nonetheless and can have a powerful effect on what you are trying to accomplish. It is helpful to remember for every action taken, there is a reaction. While a leader's intentions may be good, the law of unintended consequences maintains that the leader's actions will always produce reactions that can be difficult to anticipate or predict.

Resistance can be broadly thought of as anything that creates drag or works against the direction leaders are trying to go. Resistance slows you down and kills your momentum. It is the primary enemy of speed.

Resistance, at its heart, represents inefficiency. When you address resistance, you improve the effectiveness of the organization. You are engaged in activities that support **optimization**, one of the foundations of the faster leader model.

Leaders typically become aware of resistance when an expected result fails to materialize or when something happens that takes the leader by surprise in a negative way. To accelerate their leadership and remain ahead of the curve, leaders need to become familiar with resistance and master it to the best of their ability.

To illustrate the effects of resistance, let's turn to auto racing. Formula One drivers face a type of resistance called drag every time they get on the track. Drag is a result of the pressure created by the fast moving car being reciprocated by the air pressure around it. Drag slows down the car's momentum; therefore, physicists and engineers study it extensively in an effort to combat the effects. Yet, despite all that research, one of the best ways to reduce resistance was accidentally discovered by a driver in the late 1950s. It is a technique called drafting, which involves driving directly behind another car, sometimes mere inches away.

Drafting uses the resistance of the air pressure to the driver's advantage. The front car shields the second car from the bulk of the drag and creates a low-pressure area that acts as a vacuum that pulls the back car forward. This ends up being beneficial to both, since the rear car actually reduces the turbulence felt by the front car. It has been found that both cars can actually go five mph faster than either could driving on their own. The key lesson here is that you don't fight resistance, you use it and draft your way to success.

Resistance can take many forms, which makes it difficult to diagnose or understand. Any effort you spend in this area will be well worth it. Resistance can be direct or indirect, immediate or delayed. The signs of resistance can be obvious or subtle. Resistance can be passive like apathy or it can be aggressive like a team revolt. Resistance can come from an individual, a group, or an entire organization. Resistance can be in reaction to something you do or say, or it can be independently generated by others. Most important, resistance can be rational, emotional, motivational, or relationship-based in nature.

Regardless of its form or where it comes from, resistance is the antagonist of team member engagement and speed. While some leaders just try to overpower it (which almost never works in the long run), it is the failure to anticipate, understand, or value the power of resistance that undermines many leadership efforts and initiatives. Your skills as the **Chief Assessment Officer (CAO)** will come in handy in understanding resistance.

It is important to remember resistance is a force that can be managed. Never forget it's the leader's job to funnel resistance into constructive avenues. Like a race car driver, try to use the resistance to your advantage and turn it into a solution that is beneficial to you.

In this chapter, you'll learn about the differences between personal and organizational resistance, and how to overcome them. You'll also be introduced to eight resistance beliefs that act as roadblocks, and ten tendencies that form the foundation of most organizational resistance.

RESISTANCE AT THE PERSONAL LEVEL

"Punching holes in water" is an old Irish saying that captures the essence of futility. Every time you displace water it quickly fills back in again, leaving no evidence or impression of your efforts. Many leaders go through this same experience. Have you ever been in a situation where you invested considerable effort and energy to move an initiative forward only to have it dissipate, lose traction, or get sidetracked?

People can resist a leader and the direction the leader wants to take for multiple reasons. Through my consulting work, I have uncovered eight dominant perspectives that generate most of the resistance in people. Think of these perspectives as roadblocks because they slow down a leader and will stop a leader from accomplishing his goals.

Roadblock #1: Your Proposal Threatens Me

Fear is one of our most powerful motivations, and it is easily aroused. When confronted with something new or different, people can perceive it as a threat and resist it. Your position, or call to action, can threaten their perceived sense of safety, security, or predictability.

Roadblock #2: I Don't Agree with Your Vision

People can resist what you want to do simply because they don't agree with it. If you haven't convinced them it is the right direction, their commitment will be minimal or non-existent.

Roadblock #3: It's too Risky or is Likely to Fail

In this scenario, people evaluate the position or direction in terms of its probability of success; if it is seen as likely to fail, people will resist it. They think, "Why should I support it if I know will fail?"

Roadblock #4: It Represents a Loss for Me

What you propose can potentially take away a thing of value, such as perceived benefits or perks. When people value something and see your position as competing with or taking away this thing of value, they can resist quite strongly.

Roadblock #5: I Don't Trust You

Credibility and trust have a huge impact on involvement and engagement. If you are seen as not credible or your motives are suspect, people will resist you.

Roadblock #6: I Am Too Stressed to Deal with it

Stress has a profound impact on our ability to cope and deal with things effectively. When people are overly stressed, they can have a tendency to shut down and stop listening. In classic fight-or-flight mode, they either go on the attack or withdraw.

Roadblock #7: I Don't Care

The seventh roadblock of resistance is apathy. If a person has given up and no longer cares, it creates a barrier to action that is difficult to overcome. Apathy and passivity go hand in hand.

Roadblock #8: I Can't Change

This roadblock represents a self-limiting belief. A person can be so locked into the belief that it prevents him from thinking he can change.

Overcoming Resistance at the Personal Level

Since resistance is such a powerful force and one of the main enemies of the faster leader, let's start attacking it right away. For leaders to effectively deal with resistance, they must learn to recognize it and then respond appropriately. Here are seven tactics I suggest leaders follow to deal with resistance:

Tactic #1: Try to minimize resistance in the first place. By being mindful of how resistance is formed, you can take preventative action and decrease the likelihood it will be created.

Tactic #2: For every action you take, there is a reaction. Count on it. People will respond to or interpret your actions. Think ahead and try to anticipate how people might respond to you.

Tactic #3: Expect resistance—don't be surprised by it. Don't get caught up in the illusion things will go the way you want them to. Think about where you might encounter resistance.

Tactic #4: Respect resistance. It has a great deal of power and can easily make you fail. Rather than judging resistance as undesirable, try to appreciate its power and impact. You will be able to deal with it more effectively from a position of respect.

Tactic #5: Resistance is predictable. As seen by the eight roadblocks, resistance reliably springs from a small number of powerful forces.

Tactic #6: Get resistance out in the open. It is hard to deal with resistance if it is hiding behind the scenes. By commenting on it and bringing it to people's attention, you can address resistance more efficiently.

Tactic #7: Make room for resistance by allowing it to influence your plans and strategies. Sometimes resistance represents real concerns and can actually make your decisions better. Incorporate the resistance into your direction to quiet it down and make it more manageable. The more you try to ignore it, the more powerful resistance becomes.

ORGANIZATIONAL RESISTANCE

In addition to personal resistance, leaders can encounter resistance at the group or organization level. Resistance at this level is even more challenging to deal with because of its power and magnitude. Organizational resistance can stretch across different work groups and involve hundreds of people. Instead of dealing with an individual who resists, the leader is faced with resistance that is more widespread and powerful. In fact, many leadership and organizational change initiatives fail or stall out because group resistance is not adequately addressed or recognized at the start of the initiative.

There are dynamics and patterns in group behavior that feed resistance and are relatively consistent. These patterns reinforce different forms of organizational resistance a leader needs to fight against, contain, and minimize.

I have identified ten different tendencies of organizations and groups that contribute to resistance and inertia. Not all organizations have the same tendencies and the strength of the tendencies varies. Different parts of the organization can have different tendencies and respond accordingly. It is important to note these tendencies are not driven by a particular individual, but are instead generated by interactions within the organization and get more powerful as the organization grows. They all slow the organization down and cause problems for the leader.

1. **A tendency towards increasing complexity and differentiation.** Organizations love to add layers. More reporting levels, additional roles, staff functions, and administrative functions can grow by leaps and bounds. Unchecked, organizations will keep adding to themselves. This tendency makes it more and more difficult to get things done. Organizational complexity encourages the formation of resistance.

2. **A tendency towards local optimization.** Groups have a strong tendency to think of themselves as separate and distinct from other groups within the organization. They develop their own membership rules and identity, and approach their work in a way that is the best for them without considering the impact on other groups in the organization. This tendency is what creates silos and territorial thinking within organizations. Because internal teams are competing with each other, resistance is increased for the leader.

3. **A tendency to drift.** All organizations, regardless of their size, have a tendency to lose focus and get off track. I call this organizational drift. Given all of the choices, opportunities, and differentiation within organizations, it is not surprising organizations can get distracted and move in directions that dissipate momentum and compromise the mission of the organization. The leader must constantly

combat this tendency to drift and try to keep the organization on track. Distraction contributes to resistance.

4. **A tendency towards diffused accountability.** As a group gets larger, identifying who is in charge becomes increasingly difficult. Accountability gets more group-oriented and harder to track. Responsibility gets distributed, sometimes in ways that don't make a lot of rational sense. Uncovering the accountability matrix takes increasing energy and effort. Anonymity increases resistance because no one is taking responsibility.

5. **A tendency towards continued existence and self-interest.** An organization does not like to kill off parts of itself. Once an organization comes into existence, an instinct towards self-preservation takes over and the organization will act in ways to make sure it continues and grows. The organization becomes increasingly sensitive to perceived threats and will act to reduce those threats. A threatened organization is one that resists.

6. **A tendency towards more inward focus.** Organizations can develop a form of introversion where more and more of the available organizational resources are focused inwardly towards internal organizational needs. They can easily begin to lose touch with the outside world and become more isolated. They pay less and less attention to what is going on around them (i.e., competitors and other companies), and their thinking and decision-making take on a more limited perspective. This inward focus reduces an organization's ability to objectively assess its own functioning. This form of resistance is particularly difficult to surface and deal with.

7. **A tendency towards slowness.** Organizations can easily lose their sense of urgency and pacing. As they get larger,

organizations lose more and more of their ability to act or respond quickly. They become more and more deliberate, and processes like decision-making and crisis-management get slower. Organizational drag kills momentum.

8. **A tendency towards equilibrium.** One of the more unique and frustrating things about organizations is they continually seek equilibrium. They adjust and compensate to pressures and seek out a stable state. Every organization has its preferred range of stability, and if events move the organization outside of this range, it will take action to move back within the range. The more you push, the more the organization compensates. If a leader doesn't understand this tendency, he can create a reality opposite of what he desires. The more you push, the more you create resistance.

9. **A tendency to form habits and rituals.** Organizations develop activities that reinforce their sense of identity and convey stability and security. Varying little over time, rituals acquire meaning and drive more and more conformity in members. As the rituals become more ingrained, they influence a larger set of behaviors, and organizations become more resistant to change. Habits are among the most difficult things to change.

10. **A tendency to form limiting beliefs.** As organizations define who they are over time, they develop beliefs that drive behavior. In this way, organizational beliefs create the boundaries the organization lives within. These beliefs can become so powerful they compromise an organization's ability to adapt or grow. If an organization has a limiting belief, it will find it difficult to imagine itself differently and will resist attempts to move in directions that are not consistent with its beliefs.

DEALING WITH ORGANIZATIONAL RESISTANCE

Since organizational resistance is such an enemy of speed, the faster leader needs to get comfortable in dealing with it. Here are a few ideas for dealing with organizational resistance to get you started in your quest to become a faster leader. Get ready for flight school.

Identify it and Call Attention to it

The first rule in dealing with resistance is to recognize it and acknowledge it. Without judgment, call attention to the resistance and start having an open conversation about it. When you bring resistance to the surface and make it part of an open dialogue, you can begin to address it. If one team is not cooperating with another team, you can draw attention to it and get at the heart of the problem. By making the resistance public, you can begin to connect it to accountability.

Make it Part of the Solution

Rather than fighting resistance, enlist it in any potential solution. By including individuals, teams, or organizations in the process of moving forward, you channel the energy that is fueling the resistance into more constructive avenues. Inclusion is essential to getting people to participate and work with you. Another key to getting resistant parties to engage is to redefine the issues in terms that are less politically or emotionally charged, and more open to multiple solutions. Substituting language that is more neutral can help the dialogue move forward.

Attach Consequences

Consequences affect behavior. If you want to change a behavior, you will need to connect it to a consequence that makes the behavior less desirable or less likely to occur. If a behavior has no observable consequences, it will continue. You will want to select the right level or magnitude of consequence to stop the behavior: too strong and you create fear; too weak and nothing changes. I'll be talking more about applying consequences in Chapter Thirteen.

Dismantle the Outdated

Organizations calcify. To prevent this from happening, leaders need to periodically dismantle organizations and teams. Change the organization structure, move reporting relationships around, shift people and resources to different teams.

It is very important to recognize that every type of organizational structure has a life cycle. There is an interval of time where it is optimally effective and a point at which the structure becomes obsolete. Regardless of whether you are dealing with a matrix, functional, or geographical structure, identifying its half-life is a first step.

The half-life of an organizational structure is a useful indicator for beginning to plan for its next phase in the evolution process. The average half-life of organizational structures generally ranges from twelve to twenty four months. Establish a timetable taking into account the half-life and outline when you want to act. Be sure to give the changes time to take effect before moving on to the next reorganization. While you need to be careful not to do it too often, dismantling and rebuilding organizations contributes to the overall health of the organization. Even high-performing teams can benefit from change. Not every organizational change needs to be major, but plan on reshuffling your organization every two to three years.

Gain Better Control over Resources

To more effectively deal with resistance, you must gain control over the resources that sustain the resistance. Targeted resources could include people, budgets, access to information, and tools and technology. You can gain control over resources either formally or informally, through influence or direct exercise of your leadership power.

If you can't manipulate resources, you won't be able to impact the resistance. When resistance is starved, it generally goes away. Supply lines must be disrupted and shifted to areas the leader wants to grow or encourage. You need to be vigilant in this area because resistance can be quite creative in getting the resources it needs to survive.

Eliminate Bottlenecks

Bottlenecks can be people, processes that don't work effectively, areas of organizational ambiguity, or teams that don't work well together. Bottlenecks are areas in the organization that slow the organization down. They act as dams to movement, and they consume resources and energy. It is fairly easy to identify bottlenecks because they attract a lot of organizational noise and commentary, or they are characterized by puzzling silence.

People complain about them and work around them, or they are conspicuous because of their lack of contribution and visibility. After identifying the bottleneck, eliminate it by moving or coaching the individual, fixing the process or getting rid of it, clarifying organizational boundaries and responsibilities, and holding teams accountable to working together by putting linked objectives into place.

Focus on Simplification

Simplification is built on two basic principles. First, any addition needs to be accompanied by a reduction. For example, if you add a process, you should try to eliminate a process. While scaling to meet growth needs presents challenges to simplification, this principle is designed to help the organization focus on being more efficient rather than simply growing in a haphazard manner. By controlling the size and complexity of the organization, you directly focus on reducing resistance and improving efficiency.

The second principle of simplification is accountability needs to be defined for any action. By defining accountability before acting, you avoid introducing unnecessary ambiguity and confusion. Accountability should be clearly assigned to a specific individual or team, and the expectations that accompany the ownership should be clearly communicated.

Reinforce the Organization's Mission

To combat organizational drift, the leader needs to keep the mission in front of the organization and consistently reinforce it. Another way to keep the organization from drifting is to hold regular operational reviews to monitor the performance of the organization on key initiatives related to its mission.

By having the organization focus on its mission on a regular basis, drift can be minimized. Actions of sub-teams and individuals can be challenged to make sure they are in support of the organizational mission. Any activities that are off-line or tangential to what is important can be stopped or redirected.

Teach and Reinforce Systems Thinking

Silos rapidly and easily build up in any organization. To break down silos, you have to teach teams and functions to see themselves as part of the larger organization and you have to continually communicate and reinforce this perspective. Share how each team's work fits into the overall framework of the business.

Systems thinking reinforces awareness of how the actions of one team can affect another. Rather than letting each team focus on how it is different from others, reinforce commonalities and shared language. Be aware that siloing is an ongoing battle in organizations as there is a strong tendency to form local identities.

Introduce Change in Incremental Bites
Continually introduce a steady stream of incremental changes so your organization maintains a high state of change readiness and avoids calcification. Rather than avoiding or resisting change, your team will learn to expect and embrace it. They will become more agile and adaptive because they have had practice dealing with change.

The key is to make dealing with change familiar, and predictable. Break down any change you want to make into smaller pieces to allow the organization to easily absorb and internalize the change.

Bring the Outside Inside
To combat resistance that stems from organizational isolation and inward thinking, regularly expose the organization to what is going on in the outside world. Hold briefings where customer and competitor information is reviewed. Publish information on internal websites about key trends and happenings. Have external experts share their expertise with the organization. Encourage people in the organization to visit customers and attend industry events to enlarge their perspective. Make paying attention to the outside world an expectation of everyone's role.

In the next chapter, I'll cover engagement which is the opposing force to resistance. It is important to remember that for every force there is an opposing force, and engagement is your best strategy for combating resistance.

ACCELERATION TOOL #3: RESISTANCE MAPPING
Like a pilot mapping out a flight plan, you will want to practice the proactive discipline of anticipating resistance. By anticipating resistance, you can be ready for it and minimize the turbulence that is associated with it. The goal is to map resistance before you activate it.

Step 1: Assess the resistance
Here are some diagnostic questions that will help you to map out potential resistance. Be sure to identify specific individuals or organizations.

- What are the symptoms of resistance you have observed most regularly?
- What resistance beliefs have you observed in the past?
- Do you think resistance will be concentrated in one person or group, or will it be more widespread?
- Who has the most to lose by what you are proposing?
- Are there people or teams that have motivations to resist change?
- Who will be most impacted from a resourcing perspective?
- Who has been reinforcing the status quo?
- Who sees you as an enemy or adversary?
- Are there teams or individuals that you have had conflict with, and will this conflict spill over into what you want to accomplish?
- How strong is the silo effect in your organization and will it potentially impact what you are trying to achieve?
- What are the potential key themes of the resistance?
- Have you noticed any of the ten organizational tendencies operating in the organization?

- What is the most complex and challenging form of resistance you think you will encounter?
- What forms of resistance do you personally have the most difficulty dealing with?
- What are some of the consequences or ripple effects you think may occur?
- What strategies have you employed to deal with resistance in the past? Which ones have been successful? Which ones have been unsuccessful?
- What strategies are you planning to use going forward?

Step 2: Map the resistance and develop a plan of action

The next step is to actually map out the resistance and develop a strategy for dealing with it. Having a visual map helps many people to apply the concept of resistance. I use the following method with my clients.

1. Using a sheet of paper or drawing program, write down any person or organization who might be impacted by your plan. Spread out and use the whole sheet of paper and give yourself plenty of room. Try to be as comprehensive and inclusive as possible.
2. Draw circles around each entry. Vary the size of circle to capture the level of perceived impact of your plan on the entity. Use large circles for big impact and varying smaller sizes of circle to denote lesser impact.
3. Place +'s or −'s inside the circle to capture what you think will be their general attitude or orientation to your plan. The + is positive and the − is negative. Use multiple symbols to denote either a strong positive or negative orientation. Use fewer symbols to capture less intense orientations.

4. Color code the circles to capture the entities' current relationship to you. Green is positive, yellow is neutral, and red is negative.

5. Use lines to connect any entities that you think will form a coalition in response to your plan. It doesn't matter if it is a resistive or supportive coalition. You just want to capture relationships.

6. Draw another circle outside of the existing circle to identify those entities that you think will either actively support or resist your plan. The entities you expect to be most active will now have two circles around them.

7. Now, take some time to analyze your resistance map. After going through the assessment process, you should be able to easily identify different types of entities including: active supporters, active antagonists, allies, detractors, fence sitters, and players.

8. The final step is to identify which strategy you will use for each impacted entity. Here are some options to stimulate your thinking: create a rational and/or emotional justification, negotiate terms and conditions, persuade or influence using your personal currency, leverage an entity to influence another entity, employ a containment strategy to keep resistance from spreading, and distribute ownership for the project to others. Put your strategy into a triangle and connect it to the entity.

CHAPTER 4

Engagement is Your Gas Pedal

❖ ❖ ❖

You are going in one second the length of a football field.

FORMULA ONE CHAMPION DRIVER EMERSON FITTIPALDI

IMAGINE YOU ARE IN THE driver's seat of a Formula One race car as it approaches two hundred miles per hour. The force of acceleration feels like a 250-bound barbell against your chest. The roar of the engine drowns out all other sounds. The advertising signs around the track are nothing but a blur.

You can feel the heat of the engine through your jumpsuit. Your world is the steering wheel, the gear shift, and the cars immediately around you. Constantly you must look ahead and anticipate turns and road conditions. In your mind you visualize the race course and the finish line.

In a fraction of a second you glance at the gauges on your dashboard, check your rearview mirror for the position of cars behind you, and adjust the accelerator to keep the right distance between you and the car ahead of you. Through your hands on the steering wheel you feel the vibrations of engine and transmission working flawlessly together. You see an opening to pass the car ahead of you and make instantaneous choices. Accelerate to the outside, blow past the other car, and quickly cut back to the inside to take the lead.

After the next lap you turn into the pits to get more fuel and change tires. As you pull to a stop, the crew launches into frenzied activity. While it may look like chaos, everybody knows their roles and executes them flawlessly. The car is jacked up. Pneumatic ratchets whine as they spin off lug nuts. Old tires are quickly replaced with new ones. The hood is popped open and fluid levels are quickly checked. You smell the fuel as your tank is being topped off. The crew chief shouts instructions into your ear and updates you on the position of your main competitors. An assistant unbuckles your helmet, wipes sweat off, and pours cold water down your throat.

As the crew chief shouts, "Go, go, go," the process reverses itself. Helmet on, the car drops back down, hood is slammed shut, and the fuel hose is decoupled. When you get the thumbs up, you hit the accelerator. The tires smoke and the engine whines as you quickly get up to race speed, find an opening, and enter the course. Your world shrinks once again. You are a master of speed because you are tuned to your car and the track. You are engaged.

LEVERAGE PEOPLE

While gasoline is the energy that powers Formula One race cars, people provide the energy that powers organizations. Leveraging the energy of people is one of the foundations of the faster leader model I talked about at the beginning of the book. The fundamental question that needs to guide faster leader behavior is,

"What effect am I trying to have on the people around me and am I achieving this desired effect?"

This question gets at the essence of engagement. Ultimately, it is the productivity and results of your team that determine success, not what you individually accomplish. Faster leaders leverage the people and resources around them to achieve results that matter.

Engagement is where the rubber hits the road for you as a leader. The level of engagement you will be able to achieve is influenced by your words and actions. It is critical that you find a path to engagement that is reflective of who you truly are. Don't try to be someone you are not. Instead, identify those things that are important and relevant to you and bring them into the spotlight. Try to think of yourself as a CEO (**Chief Engagement Officer**).

This chapter will cover the building blocks that drive a faster leader engagement strategy including the six C's of credibility. I'll also touch on the RCI model which outlines how to communicate for engagement and the Ownership Formula.

THE BUILDING BLOCKS OF ENGAGEMENT
The building blocks that make up the faster leader engagement advantage include:

- Keep your eye on the prize
- Build credibility
- Distribute ownership
- Practice cockpit communication—keep noise to a minimum
- Get out of the way.

Let's examine each building block to see how the faster leader can leverage the energy of the organization.

Building Block #1: Keep your eye on the prize

A highly engaged workforce is an extremely productive workforce. But, team member engagement can be difficult to achieve. The main challenge the faster leader faces is how to get team members to move beyond cynicism and apathy, and commit to helping the organization grow and meet its challenges. Team member engagement is the prize every leader should be chasing. Here are a few things to understand about the engagement process.

The first thing to realize is **engagement is dynamic**. It is not stable and can change to disengagement very quickly. The dynamic nature of engagement is why you have to keep your eye on it at all times and not take it for granted.

The second thing to remember about engagement is it is built up through a series of interactions a team member has with the organization. I think of these interactions as touch points. These touch points continually move the engagement needle back and forth between a positive or negative orientation.

A third point to remember is there are multiple sources of engagement fuel and you want to leverage as many of them as you can. Here are several engagement sources you might want to tap:

- **The nature of the work**. Many people can get a sense of engagement from the work they perform. If they find it interesting, challenging, and gives them a sense of meaning, a team member can become more engaged.
- **Other team members**. If a team member feels a sense of connection to other members of his team, a sense of engagement is reinforced.

- **Products, markets, customers, or charter**. If a team member relates to the charter of an organization, or even the products it sells, a sense of engagement can develop.
- **Rewards and career development**. If a team member feels valued in a tangible way and they see their career progressing, they can develop a strong sense of engagement.
- **Success**. If a team member sees their organization as winning or meeting its challenges, they can experience a strong connection.
- **Management.** The leadership team of an organization and how they treat team members can have a large impact on engagement.
- **You**. Don't underestimate the impact you can have on a team member's engagement level. A team member's connection or lack of it to you can have a significant impact on their engagement level. One of the most consistent things found in exit interviews on why employees leave is their dissatisfaction with their boss. Let's turn our attention to other things you can do as Chief Engagement Officer to foster engagement.

Building Block #2: Build Credibility

Credibility is one of the faster leader's most important assets. It is what makes you believable, trustworthy, and is essential for keeping your people willing to follow your direction. Credibility cannot be forced; it has to be earned. Without credibility you can't lead. Once it is lost, it is difficult or impossible to regain. But, most importantly, **credibility enables leadership speed**.

Leading in challenging times can cover a lot of different scenarios. Organizational setbacks, late projects, business downturns, budget shortfalls, and loss of key personnel can all test the leader. How you behave in these scenarios influences the judgments people will make of you as a leader.

Faster leaders follow the six C's of credibility to maintain their speed advantage: character, commitment, connection, courage, competency, and convincing. Here's a breakdown of each:

Character: know what you stand for, what issues are important to you, define your code of ethics, and make it tangible in your behaviors and actions. Your values should be transparent to others. Trustworthiness and a concern for others are key prerequisites for a leader.

Commitment: do what you say you are going to do in spite of obstacles or barriers. Make sure your words and actions agree. Don't make promises you can't keep—no matter how tempting. Make the effort to ensure your message gets through consistently on the different communication channels in the organization.

Connection: roll up your sleeves; get involved in the details enough to know what the issues are. Connect with people at a level they find relevant. People love it when leaders take the time to understand what they are dealing with in their jobs.

Management teams and leaders can get disconnected from what is actually going on because they spend too much time with each other instead of with their people. Stay engaged and gather your own data rather than relying on second- or third-hand data.

As a general rule, it is a good idea to assume people know more than you think they do. Connect to them by treating them like adults and fostering transparency.

Courage: encourage truthful conversations. Create an environment where people are comfortable telling you what is really going on rather than what they think you want to hear. Be willing to listen even if you don't like what you are hearing. It is all too easy to shut down the flow of information. Don't take the easy way out or pull the fear trigger. Above all, don't abandon key values and principles you have established.

Competency: be good at what you do. Your credibility is tied to making good decisions that are proven out over time. Continually refine your skills and analyze your decisions—both good and bad—to learn from them. Have a personal learning and development plan to prevent your expertise from atrophying. Stay in touch with your industry and marketplace.

Convincing: win over a skeptical workforce. As a consequence of business practices and downsizings, the workforce has become increasingly skeptical about leaders. It is up to you to convince people that you are on the right track. A little persuasion is in order. Promote your position with passion and conviction. Disarm objections and concerns by having well-thought out answers and positions you stick to. Convey confidence and communicate with authority and command.

Although you may not always feel that way inside, your team needs to see you as strong, focused, and caring. Get your team to buy into your strategy or plan by formally asking for their commitment and support.

Building Block #3: Distribute Ownership
The next engagement building block is to get the organization's people to have a sense of ownership in the success of the venture. The higher the sense of ownership a person has for a task

or challenge, the more self-management that person will exercise. The more self-management someone has, the less management you will have to provide. Distributing ownership is key to becoming a faster leader. However, it is not as easy as it sounds.

Leaders must do more to combat the engagement problem by building or rebuilding a strong relationship with their teams and encouraging a sense of ownership. While ownership can involve a financial stake in the company, typically through stock ownership, leaders can do other things to heighten team member ownership.

Leaders can follow the **Ownership Formula,** which has six core principles to improve engagement. These core principles are:

1. Build a strong sense of social and task connectedness.
2. Select goals that are in the realm of the possible.
3. Create the capacity to affect, influence, or change a course of action.
4. Strive for consistency in the directions from leadership.
5. Give people as much choice as possible.
6. Get skin in the game.

Let's dig into each element of the Ownership Formula in more detail.

Build a strong sense of social and task connectedness. Share information about what is going on in the business and try to establish a connection to the organizational culture. Establish informal gatherings where people can connect and build interpersonal relationships. Create a personal connection by being visible, accessible, and stepping out of the "Corporate Speak" box.

Encourage cross-functional groups to interact and get to know each other better. Develop and maintain a feedback rich environment where people get feedback on their performance and how their work impacts others. Establish a connection to what people are doing and the key goals of the business, and reinforce this connection on a regular basis.

Select goals that are in the realm of the possible.
One of the more difficult aspects of goal setting is to set goals that are challenging yet attainable. If properly selected, a goal can be a motivating force in the performance and engagement of team members. If the goal is seen as unattainable or wishful thinking, it becomes a de-motivating force.

If the leader is too distant from the work being done, the potential for goal disconnect is even higher. What is critical for the leader to understand is how the goal is perceived by team members, not how the leader sees it. The best way to develop this understanding is to shop or float the potential goal in informal conversations with a few representative team members.

Create the capacity to affect, influence, or change a course of action.
A sense of ownership is directly correlated with the perception of being able to impact something. If team members feel their actions or input don't matter, they are much more likely to withdraw or become disengaged. If team members perceive their input is solicited and used, their sense of being valued is enhanced. Try to establish formal channels and meetings where team members can consistently give input and be heard. Actively manage these channels to make sure team members' experiences are positive.

Strive for consistency in the directions from leadership. Make sure there is consistency in the directions and messages from leadership relating to the goals of the company and to team members.

Team members are more engaged if they feel they have leaders who have a good sense of direction, align goals with that direction, and possess the fortitude to stay with that direction over time. Confidence in leadership is important to team-member engagement.

While adjustment can be necessary given the challenges of the marketplace, continually changing direction makes the leader look like he doesn't know what he is doing. Before you articulate a direction to your team, be sure to road test it for both strategic alignment and durability. Connect relevant goals to the direction and reinforce both the goals and direction on a regular basis. If a shift in direction is needed be sure to communicate why.

Give people as much choice as possible.
Mandates or commands create compliance, not commitment. Compliance leads to passive behavior and requires constant enforcement. Commitment comes from feeling you had options and you made a *choice*. A high level of commitment is desired in a team because people will actively take more responsibility and manage themselves. The more choice people have, the more ownership and commitment they will experience. Create choices for your team, and you will be able to lead in a more strategic way versus being more of a policeman.

Get skin in the game.
Ask people to make a commitment of time or resources and try to get them to do this early in the engagement process. Ownership is enhanced when people move from understanding to action. The goal is to get people to invest their time and energy because they will then have a sense of personal commitment. A personal

investment or sacrifice acts as a motivational device. The most direct way to get people to put skin in the game is for you to do it first.

Building Block #4: Practice cockpit communication—keep noise to a minimum

Using two-way radios, Formula One drivers are in constant communication with members of their car team and pit crew. The driver can receive crucial information from his team spotter about possible hazards or opportunities on the track that he may have difficulty seeing from his limited vantage point in the car. Drivers can report potential problems and strategize with their pit crews without needing to slow down.

These masters of speed keep chatter to a minimum. Only critical information is communicated. They have their own precise code which keeps everyone on the same page. There is no time for confusion.

Like a Formula One driver, a faster leader must be an expert communicator. An accelerating world places a premium on a leader's ability to communicate. Communicate effectively, and momentum and engagement are maintained. Communicate ineffectively and the organization gets distracted or confused. This often overlooked and taken for granted aspect of leadership is just too important for it not to be done well. How the leader communicates has a big impact on engagement, and getting a message across is not as easy as it used to be.

Many leaders find themselves in the position of competing for the attention and mindshare of people in their organizations, which significantly slows them down. It is like always pushing the boulder up the hill to get the message across.

An additional challenge is that people can misinterpret your message. People can read things into what you are saying, which means you end up spending more time trying to correct or contain stuff that isn't true, is distorted, or is tangential to the message itself.

On top of that, there is such a volume of inaccurate information floating around organizations that your message can easily get contaminated by hearsay. Have you ever played that game where a whispered phrase gets passed between people? Invariably, the phrase ends up being different at the end of the game than at the beginning. Interpretation is influenced by one's own filters. Miscommunication causes leaders a great deal of frustration and can have the effect of slowing everything down. Organizational chatter can have a lot of noise in it.

Your capacity to engage the organization is influenced by how well you communicate and **listen**. If you keep distraction to a minimum, focus on communicating what is really important, and listen well, you will win the race.

Your chances for success will be dramatically increased if you use the RCI model of communication: communicating **r**elevancy, addressing **c**ost and **c**onsequences, and communicating **i**mportance and **i**mmediacy. These three steps help you to become a faster leader because people quickly connect to your messages and stay focused. This kind of finely tuned communication is what allows a modern pit crew to change all four tires and refuel a race car in about thirteen seconds. Think of what that kind of efficiency could do for you as a leader. Let's dig into the RCI model in more detail.

Relevancy
We make decisions and judgments regarding whether or not something touches us, is connected to us, or is meaningful. Things we

define as relevant are things that impact us in positive or negative ways and touch us personally. Generally, we make time or commit resources to issues that are connected to us, and we ignore or minimize what we define as non-relevant.

Issues that top the relevancy list include such things as security, job satisfaction, the ability to impact outcomes, being included and valued, autonomy, work role and responsibility, family and personal life, recognition, and connection. When something passes our relevancy test, we make the decision that it is important to us and our well-being, and we respond to it.

Faster leaders understand that helping others establish a personal connection to a challenge is a critical aspect of team member engagement.

If a person sees an activity as personally relevant, he will supply more of his own motivation and be more self-managed and tenacious in pursuing the result. I recommend you follow a three-step process to establish relevancy. First, build an understanding of the framework and resonating themes of the people you are leading. Second, use this understanding and translate it into vision and action that speak to others by connecting to their desires, needs, and hopes. Third, overcome objections, resistance, and apathy by reinforcing the messages over time and modeling the behavior. Faster leaders formulate a powerful answer to the question that is in everyone's mind: "Why should I care?"

Cost and Consequences

There is no such thing as a free lunch. To accomplish great things, one must be willing to take risks and make great sacrifices. While leaders need to model this behavior, they must get others to follow them in making commitments and sacrifices. Too many leaders ignore or minimize the costs others pay to accomplish things. Other leaders throw one demand after another at people because that is all they know. They practice initiative overload, which ultimately generates burnout and team member flight.

Costs can be thought of either as expenditure (time, effort, energy) or as loss (a long-standing benefit goes away). People conduct a personal cost analysis on what leaders ask them to do. They think of the sacrifices they will have to make versus the rewards they will get. They basically ask, "What is it going to cost me and what will I get in return?" They evaluate whether or not the ratio is more tilted towards the cost side or the benefit side. They evaluate whether or not costs are equally distributed across the organizational hierarchy. They evaluate your ability to deliver on the promises you make.

Perceived cost is uniquely individual and can be emotionally charged. If what you are asking for involves investing a lot of extra personal time or losing a thing of value, people may feel threatened and openly resist acting on your request. People will tenaciously try to hold onto things of value to them. They will defend these valued benefits and, if they perceive you as trying to take away things of value, they will react negatively. They may resist in a more subtle, passive manner. The perceived cost can be related to opportunity cost. For example, what you are asking for may not involve a lot of time but it may compete with, or prevent them from, spending time on tasks that are higher in value to them.

Faster leaders understand people attach their own subjective costs to commitments, and these leaders make dealing with those costs a priority because missing the connection can lead to lack of commitment, outright rebellion, and a dramatically slower organization. They understand that leadership is not exempt from costs. Faster leaders treat the interaction between costs and achievements as a type of negotiation.

To address cost and consequences I suggest the following things:

- Develop an understanding of the perceived costs to any action.
- Build an accurate justification for the costs—connect them to a worthy goal or endeavor.
- Create an environment where costs can be openly talked about.
- Distribute costs equally. Make sure that management sets an example and claims its share of the cost.
- Minimize the cost whenever possible.
- Concentrate costs to allow the organization to deal with them and move on rather than stringing them out over time.
- Clearly identify and communicate the benefits/cost linkage.
- Provide incentives to balance out the sacrifices.

Importance and Immediacy

Priorities drive what gets done. A challenge for many leaders is that priorities can shift on an almost daily basis in times of economic uncertainty. It can be hard to establish a set of priorities that remain constant for an extended period of time. Stability and predictability have become more difficult to achieve. Market shifts, competitor's positioning, and resource shortages can force leaders to change tactics and strategies quickly and repeatedly. Individuals and teams can end up feeling jerked around or may abandon planning activities because they feel nothing sticks.

Compounding the issue for leaders is the fact organizations and individuals vary significantly in their abilities to adapt to change and shifting priorities. Some organizations and individuals are quite agile and adept at dealing with change. Others resist change and desire stability. While leaders can make adjustments to priorities on the fly, their organizations may need additional help, support, and coaching to keep pace with change.

One thing leaders can do to improve their effectiveness and engagement with their organizations is to communicate why something is important. When priorities shift rapidly, people want to know why and want to be assured the new course of action is connected to a larger picture or strategy and not just a knee jerk reaction. By communicating the reason for a change, the leader builds understanding.

Thinking through the relative importance level of a new action is a good discipline for you as a leader because it forces you to think about tradeoffs and challenges you to connect action to strategy. If the organization's plate is already full, something has to come off if you intend to add a new commitment. If the action can't be connected to strategy, then maybe you shouldn't do it.

Why something is important is not always obvious to others. Effective leaders understand this gap, limit their communication assumptions, and make sure to connect the dots for others. By establishing and communicating a connection to what is core to the business, leaders help people understand its importance and meaning. In this way, the leader fills another role: CPO (**Chief Perspective Officer**). They keep communicating the connection over time so people don't lose sight of it in the face of information overload.

Beyond importance, leaders need to communicate the appropriate level of immediacy or urgency that needs to be applied to an action. Because people are generally busy, the first question they invariably ask in response to a call to action is, "Do I need to deal with it now, or can I put it off until later?"

The level of immediacy people attach to an action is influenced by:

- The language a leader uses in communicating the call to action.
- Who is making the request and their history (i.e., are they a person who labels everything important and urgent?).
- The amount of work they are currently dealing with and how stressed they are.
- Whether or not there is a clearly defined prioritization framework for people to use in making judgment calls.
- Whether or not this tactic has been used repeatedly.

In my coaching work, I recommend leaders use the immediacy/urgency gambit sparingly because it sets off a mad scramble. When leaders pull the immediacy trigger, they instantly put your organization into action. It means this particular action needs to be done quickly and is of higher value than other things that are currently underway. People have to rethink their priorities and pick up the pace of their actions. Resources get reallocated and other things get shelved. If you do this repeatedly, fatigue sets in, and the performance of the organization starts to drop. People increasingly think it is one more fire drill.

But, connecting immediacy to a task is a powerful technique for a leader. People have a strong tendency to act on those things they perceive to be immediate and tangible, while they delay or put off things that are more long term or intangible, particularly in a fast-paced environment. Cause and effect are easier to observe with issues that are immediate or short term because there is little or no delay between the cause and effect.

People experience a sense of satisfaction by completing tangible activities. They can see the impact and results in a direct way. The larger the gap between the cause and effect, or action and consequence, the less immediacy they experience or attach to the issue.

To build immediacy, leaders can try the following things:

- Break up the action into smaller, incremental steps that people can easily execute.
- Create a sense of urgency around the action by showing how it is connected to other important activities, including the organization's strategy.
- Ask the individual or team to put the action into their scheduling framework to allow you to track activity jointly and in real-time.

If the leader consistently communicates the level of immediacy and importance attached to a proposed action, and places it into a prioritization framework, the organization will be able to respond more effectively. People will be able to set their priorities, plan their work, and be in alignment with the larger organization.

This framework provides consistency across organizations and reinforces alignment. Faster leaders are effective in their communication because they always make sure they have answered the four fundamental questions that drive performance: **Why should I care? What will it cost me versus what will I get in return? Is it important? Why should I do it now?** Review the acceleration tool at the end of the chapter to become a super communicator.

Building Block #5: Get out of the way

Once a course strategy is set, a Formula One driver doesn't try to keep telling the pit crew boss how to do his job. The driver focuses on what he does best and depends on the rest of the crew to do their job.

I suggest leaders follow the same course to build engagement in their teams. Set a strategy, make sure people know their roles, and let them do their job. Get out of the way. If you keep intruding on other's work, you will disrupt the momentum you have worked hard to create.

Getting out of the way is easier said than done for many leaders because they like control. The biggest mistake I see leaders make when it comes to building engagement is this tendency to be too hands on. Micro-management is another word for the same problem behavior. Team members invariably experience micro-management as a lack of trust. When team members don't feed trusted, they don't engage. When team members aren't engaged, the leader has to get more involved. The leader's ownership expands while the team member's shrinks. It is a vicious cycle.

The key is to be involved at the right level and not overstep your bounds. If you truly want to be a faster leader, you will need to give people the freedom and accountability to do their jobs but be close enough to give assistance when it is needed.

Engagement Wrap Up

Remember that momentum is your best friend when it comes to building engagement. If you are able to create momentum, it allows you to spend your time in more strategic ways rather than getting bogged down in a lot of detail.

The beauty about momentum is, once established, it can become self-sustaining. Rather than you supplying all the effort and energy, the team does it. Momentum feeds engagement as more and more people participate and get involved. Engagement becomes contagious. Keep these engagement strategies in mind:

- **Set a clear and compelling direction**. The direction you select should be seen as attractive and worthwhile rather than as just more work or more of the same.
- **Communicate so people will listen.** Don't forget to listen yourself.
- **Avoid being a micro-manager**. Let people own their work.
- **Enlist team members in the strategy.** Obtaining buy-in from team members is a necessary step.
- **Resource any key strategy appropriately.** Don't starve your organization or limit its success by not providing critical resources.
- **Enable the team to succeed early and often**. Create a pattern or habit of success that allows the organization to experience what success feels and tastes like.
- **Pick benchmark goals.** Set challenges for the organization in line with the organization's capability or potential.
- **Eliminate distractions**. Keep the team focused on the right direction.
- **Feed the momentum machine**. Momentum has an appetite. It consumes resources so keep feeding and reinforcing it over time. Give it plenty of fuel. Don't let your team stall out. The energy to pull a team out of a stall is huge. It diverts you from other things and disrupts your speed.

- **Eliminate roadblocks.** Identify and manage things that are obstacles to your team's success.
- **Plan the next race**. Be prepared by having the next challenge ready to launch.

In the next chapter, I'll dig deeper into building your self-awareness which is one of the components of the faster leader model. Get ready for flight school.

Dr. Arlen Burger

ACCELERATION TOOL #4: COMMUNICATION TUNE UP

It is important to continually keep your communication in top form so the engagement level stays high. To make sure that your communication engine is in great shape, follow these maintenance tips:

Tip #1: Always understand your audience

The message sent is not always the message received. When creating a communication, be sure to give some thought to the audience who will be receiving it. Think about what they want to hear and how they want to hear it. Customize the language to the audience rather than using a one-size-fits-all approach.

Tip #2: Use effective headlines

A good headline attracts attention and helps you compete with the large amount of information people are bombarded with. Are your headlines too wordy? The fewer words you use the better. Be sure to use powerful, evocative words that capture attention and convey emotion.

Tip #3: Use a storyline framework

People are programmed from a very young age to respond well to stories. Stories have beginnings, middles, and ends. Stories are told for a reason. Be sure the audience understands the point of the story. Like the storyteller Aesop from Ancient Greece, who created such fables as *The Tortoise and the Hare*, consider including the moral of the story in each tale.

Tip #4: Be clear

In chaotic environments, it is particularly important your communication is clear and unambiguous. Use language that has a low

86

probability of confusing others. Never underestimate the capacity for information to get garbled or misinterpreted. Avoid the use of jargon. Use everyday language that everyone on your team can understand. Simplify your messages. Complexity is the enemy of clarity. Make it brief and to the point.

Tip #5: Provide context and perspective

Context allows people to put your communication into perspective. Context is the set of circumstances, events, facts, and conditions that surrounds what you are saying and gives your message meaning. Context helps explains the why. Remember, you are the **Chief Perspective Officer**.

Tip #6: Stay on message

Repeat your message with regularity. Communications quickly get lost in the shuffle and lose their value over time. However, don't get too creative and continually reinvent the message. People need to be able to follow the theme. Vary the message slightly so you don't appear to be always talking from a script but stay on message.

Tip #7: Use different communication channels

Don't rely on one method; instead communicate using all of the media at your disposal. E-mail, voicemail, blogs and web pages, video, text and instant messaging, and face-to-face meetings are all different ways you can reach your audience and keep them engaged.

Tip #8: Get their attention and keep it

You can't mandate attention; it is a choice. Getting through people's filters and eliciting their attention involves persuasion and influence. Investing in these activities dramatically speeds up your leadership and improves performance. Use images and metaphors that grab people's attention and hold it long enough for your message to get through.

Tip #9: Master the art of the elevator pitch

The faster leader needs to be an expert in delivering an elevator pitch. An elevator pitch is based on the idea that you should be able to communicate your key messages in the time it takes to go up one floor in an elevator. This is not much time to get your point across. In most circumstances it probably boils down to five or ten seconds. Communicating under this type of constraint requires that you distill your key message down into a succinct, compelling, and clear statement. It is harder than it sounds.

The elevator pitch can be an important leadership behavior to master because it mirrors what people respond to. If you can capture my interest in the time it takes to go up or down one floor, I'll listen to the rest of your message.

Part II: Faster Leader Flight School

❖　❖　❖

CHAPTER 5

Do You Have the
Right Stuff?

❖ ❖ ❖

I feel the need…the need for speed.

MAVERICK (TOM CRUISE), *TOP GUN*

IMAGINE YOURSELF IN THE COCKPIT of a jet fighter as it approaches
Mach 1. The g-forces crush you back into your seat. You feel the
roar of the engines in every part of your body as the afterburn-
ers kick in. Lights flash in front of you: The Heads Up Display,
Integrated Control Panel, and Integrated Caution, Advisory, and
Warning systems give you real-time feedback on the performance
of the plane and your surrounding environment.

At 50,000 feet your world shrinks to the displays, the side-stick
controller in your right hand, and the chatter coming through
your helmet. You constantly scan the displays and the horizon for
threats or warnings. You make tiny throttle adjustments to maintain your airspeed. In your mind you visualize the flight plan and
your position. Your concentration is perfect and time seems to slow
down.

Flying an F-22 Raptor requires an immense amount of training, split-second decision-making, and focus. There is little margin for error. Operating in an environment where decisions are made every tenth of a second, the pilot has to maintain a rigorous focus and tune out distractions. In the face of large amounts of data, the pilot learns to focus on the small number of things that really make a difference.

Flying at high velocity magnifies everything. A small mistake can rapidly become a big one; a small adjustment produces a dramatic increase in airspeed. Splitting his awareness between what is going on in the now and what is coming allows the pilot to both react and anticipate. Concentration, skill, and state-of-the-art equipment allow the pilot cross the sound barrier and become supersonic.

While flight school is designed to teach pilots how to fly, its other main purpose is to test and evaluate pilots. To become a US Naval Aviator, there are a variety of training levels that take between eighteen months to four years to complete. The Introductory Flight Screening ensures that pilots have an aptitude for flying before they are admitted into the training program. The next step, Aviation Preflight Indoctrination, involves six weeks of extensive classroom instruction and tactical training. It is then six months of Primary Flight Training in the basics of flying before they can enter Intermediate and Advanced Flight Training.

At every step of the way, pilots are being rigorously examined to be sure they are fit to advance in the program. Those who pass the tests have the right stuff to go on to the next level, while those who don't have what it takes wash out. The majority of those who start on the path to becoming a pilot do not get their wings; but those who finish have been thoroughly trained and tested.

This fundamental process of testing and challenging individuals is relevant in the organizational world. Companies, universities, and non-profits all want to be sure they are selecting the best leaders to run the organization because the consequences of failure are high. As individuals move up the organizational ladder, their decisions have ever increasing consequences. The risks increase.

Since leadership operates primarily in the personal and interpersonal domains, the leader's personality, style of engagement, weaknesses, and blind spots determine his effectiveness and impact. The fundamental relationship that needs to exist between the leader and his team requires the leader understand how he is perceived by others. In this chapter, I'll be focusing on the important third element of the faster model; self-awareness.

In a study by Green Peak Partners, *self-awareness was found to be a primary driver of an executive's effectiveness.*[12] According to the authors, "A high self-awareness score was the strongest predictor of overall success. Executives whose interpersonal skill scores were low also scored badly on every single performance dimension." This study, among many others, emphasizes that self-awareness is a competency all leaders need to develop if they want to be effective leaders.

At the fundamental level, a faster leader needs to have a high degree of self-awareness in the following areas:

- Personal strengths
- Gauging one's impact on others
- Areas in need of development (both in the short term and long term)
- Weaknesses
- Behaviors produced when stressed
- Blind spots (areas consistently missed or overlooked)

What does the right stuff look like? During my past twenty five years in Silicon Valley as an executive/leadership coach, I have had the opportunity to work with hundreds of leaders. Over the course of my work, I noticed a sub-group within this population that had very different behaviors and very different results.

Because of their speed, productivity, impact on other people, and the type of results they were able to achieve, I began to study them with intensity to uncover their secrets and understand what they were doing differently so I could begin to coach other leaders on how to become faster and more successful.

I found them in all parts of the organization and at different levels of the organizational hierarchy. They were not exclusively in management or leadership roles. They worked on the receiving dock, in purchasing, or in sales. They were individual contributors, team leaders, and senior managers. They showed up in surprising areas. I found them with great frequency in some organizations and rarely in others.

MASTERS OF SPEED

I labeled these individuals **masters of speed** because they were both faster and better at performing important leadership behaviors than their peers. They were top guns of the organizational world and you never saw them sweat.

As I observed and worked with them across different environments, I was able to identify twenty-six behaviors that contributed to their success. While organizational culture had an effect on which behaviors where most important, there were patterns of behavior that had surprising consistency. While each master of speed didn't demonstrate all of the twenty-six behaviors, they demonstrated, on average, sixty-five percent of the success behaviors. Here are the master of speed behaviors:

1. **Self critical.** They are willing to take a hard look at themselves in the mirror. Rather than congratulating themselves on how good they are, they constantly look for ways they can improve.
2. **Open to feedback.** They are open to feedback from others and regularly seek it out. They use feedback to improve their behavior. They have an interest in understanding how others see them.
3. **Fast learners**. Masters of speed learn more quickly than others. There are several behaviors associated with this competency. They have an inquisitive and challenging mindset. They don't accept the status quo. They generate hypotheses and rigorously test them. They look for disconfirming evidence rather than data that just support their position. They consistently test their models and refresh their assumptions. They possess mental agility and are rapidly able to shift perspective. They don't fall in love with their positions, instead viewing them with objectivity. They are not prisoners of their experience.
4. **Highly productive.** They consistently produce more than their peers, both on a personal level and team level. They are often the first ones in and the last ones to leave. Their capacity for work is high and they possess large reserves of energy.
5. **Strong work ethic and disciplined**. They do the difficult things first and know how to delay gratification. They have a strong sense of responsibility. They continually practice and refine their craft.

6. **Simplifiers.** Realizing that complexity is the enemy of speed, they strive to simplify and streamline everything they encounter. Whether it is organizational structures or processes, their goal is to make things clearer and easier to use.

7. **Extremely focused.** Focus is a secret of their success. They resist distraction and keep their eye on the prize. They are purposeful in everything they do.

8. **Studious.** They are dedicated students of their business and organization.

9. **Efficient.** They work at a much faster work pace than others and with minimal wasted effort. They focus on getting the maximum impact with the minimum of effort.

10. **Edgy.** They possess a positive tension or edginess that demonstrates their passion and desire to get things done. They have intensity that other people pick up on.

11. **Bounce back quickly.** They are able to recover quickly from setbacks or defeat. They often treat these events as learning experiences. They absorb the lesson and move on.

12. **Fill the vacuum.** Aware of when leadership is needed in a particular situation, they willingly step into the role. They don't have to be asked, or told, or invited—they seem to recognize this intuitively.

13. **Optimistic.** They are positive, but not Pollyanna-ish, in their outlook. They have an inner confidence that almost any obstacle can be overcome.

14. **Respected.** Others treat them with high regard. They have high credibility and have earned it through their actions and results.

15. **In control of themselves and their environment.** One rarely sees them lose their cool, sweat (figuratively), or be stressed out.

16. **Scalable**. They easily absorb and digest additional role scope and demonstrate scalability.
17. **Strategic mind-set.** They are proactive and always seem to be one step ahead. With contingency plans in place, they always seem to be ready for the unexpected. They look for patterns in the data and connect the dots.
18. **Adaptive.** Flexible in their outlook and actions, they can quickly respond to changes in the environment. They are effective in a wide range of situations.
19. **Resourceful.** They are able to get things done despite being resource-limited. They seldom complain or ask for additional resources and find creative solutions to the problems they face.
20. **Talent magnets**. They surround themselves with talented people and top performers. They are constantly on the lookout for talent and are great recruiters. They create environments, where talented performers want to stay, and experience very little undesirable attrition.
21. **Always in the thick of things.** They gravitate towards the areas of highest impact and importance.
22. **High standards**. They aim high. They set stretch goals for both themselves and their teams. They have a strong achievement orientation. They don't like to settle for second best.
23. **Connector.** While always busy, they make time to connect with people. They are very good at linking people together, are effective team builders and networkers. People want to work with them.
24. **Not control freaks.** They seemed to "own" very little. While they might take on a challenge to help resolve it, they quickly hand it off to others.

25. **Compelling communicators.** Realizing that communication is important to engagement, they focus on compelling storylines and are able to convey messages in powerful, impactful terms. They can sell ideas and vision, and get buy-in from their teams.

26. **Organizational savvy.** While they are not inherently political, they understand politics exists and can effectively navigate through it. They don't get sidetracked or surprised by it.

How do you stack up? Do you have the right stuff? How many of the twenty-six master of speed behaviors do you demonstrate? The following tests will help you broaden your self-awareness, and assess your master of speed attitudes, beliefs, and behaviors.

TEST ONE: MASTER OF SPEED READINESS QUIZ

The following quiz is designed to help leaders assess their master of speed aptitude. Read each statement and decide whether you agree or disagree, then tally your score. At the end of the statements is a ratings scale to help you interpret the results.

1. Several people in my business life would lend me money.
2. I rarely experience fatigue.
3. I rely more on my intuition than my experience.
4. I am proactive and consistently ahead of things.
5. I am better at refining opportunities than seeing them.
6. I am an explorer.
7. I often acquire new knowledge that requires me to rethink my perspective.

8. I rarely get confused.
9. I am confident in my abilities. I am not a doubter.
10. I possess strong personal discipline.
11. My knowledge base is broad and shallow rather than narrow and deep.
12. I like surprises.
13. I am good at understanding human motivation.
14. I possess organizational and political savvy.
15. I am not afraid of failure.
16. People would say I am approachable.
17. I like to be in control.
18. I am a cautious risk taker rather than a go-for-broke individual.
19. I prefer to keep things simple.
20. I have hired several people who were more talented than me.
21. My work ethic is stronger than that of other people around me.
22. People would describe me as super focused.
23. People know not to waste my time and they come prepared.
24. I consistently ask the questions no one else has thought about.
25. I am self-critical and will admit when I am wrong.

Interpreting Your Score
20 to 25 agrees: You are a master of speed leader candidate
15 to 19 agrees: You have great master of speed potential
10 to 14 agrees: You have work ahead to become a master of speed
9 or less agrees: You need remedial master of speed help

TEST TWO: MASTER OF SPEED BASIC TRAINING TEST

The job of the leader is very different from that of a manager or individual. A leader's job is not to be a good engineer, marketer, or sales representative: it is to lead. A leader's primary goal should be to leverage people and resources to achieve the best possible *results*.

When all is said and done, the job of the leader can be summed up in thirteen core principles. Please rate yourself as a leader on the following baker's dozen of standards. For each principle, assess if you practice this rarely, sometimes, or usually.

1. Recruit and retain talent that fits your cultural system to give you the most options and chances for success.
2. Constantly improve the capability of your team. Get it the resources it needs to succeed.
3. Invest the time to manage key relationships well, whether they are internal or external.
4. Continually improve and fine-tune your organizational structure to make room for growth, change, scalability, and opportunity.
5. Establish core work processes that make your team's work more efficient.
6. Stays in touch with what is going on so you can respond quickly.
7. Establishes and maintains a high-energy work culture that is in sync with your core business. Feeds it regularly so it doesn't starve.
8. Never loses focus on producing high quality results—both short and longer term—in areas that have the greatest impact and matter most.

9. Is ruthless about aligning your team around key goals, strategies, and initiatives.
10. Quickly fixes anything that is broken or underperforming.
11. Get the team or organization ready for what is coming rather than always responding to what has happened.
12. Provide momentum and engagement through vision, strategy, persuasion, and personal connection to your team.
13. Show consistency between your words and actions so you will be seen as honest and credible.

Good news. Each principle that you rated yourself as practicing "rarely" or "sometimes" is an opportunity for improvement. Target one or two areas and develop a plan for improving your skills in each area targeted.

To raise your score, adopt the mind-set or perspective that it is not what you can individually do, but rather what you can accomplish with others. This is a challenge for many people because the nature of leadership accomplishment is very different from that of an individual contributor. Leadership results are collective, not individual, and can be more intangible. It is better to think of leadership impact as collaborative in nature rather than causative. A leader enables results to happen.

Test Three: Test Pilot Preparation Test

Flight school challenges you to prepare. It forces you to study, anticipate, and think ahead. Preparation is the foundation of success. Clarity of mind and purpose prepare you for the unexpected.

Doing your leadership homework and thinking through things will help you become a master of speed. I invite you to invest time and contemplate the following questions to boost your master of speed IQ:

1. How will I develop a vision or strategy for my team that is linked to success? Will I develop this vision on my own or include others? What process will I use?
2. How do I capture my vision and translate it into a tangible sense of direction that people can get behind and support? What language do I use to make it tangible and relevant to my team?
3. How will I know that my vision is resonating with people and being used to set priorities and strategy? A vision is not just a slogan on a coffee cup or tee shirt. It needs to be used.
4. How will I keep the vision and strategy alive and fresh over time? Like all other messages, a vision gets stale if not periodically refreshed and reinforced.
5. What kind of culture do I want to build and maintain? I need to think of myself as an organizational architect. The best work cultures are deliberately built around a set of principles or values.
6. How do I build and maintain an organization that generates great results? Organizations need to be continually improved or they stagnate and get distracted.
7. How will I make sure important financial and operational practices are followed? Best practices need to be communicated and monitored on a regular basis.
8. How will I get the best out of my team? High performance means is everyone doing their best. What mix of challenges and rewards will I use to get everyone performing at their best?

9. How will I know if there are issues or problems with alignment within my team? When the team is not pulling together, wasted energy and effort result.

10. How do I know or find out what is really going on in my organization? Being engaged with my organization allows me to quickly respond to challenges, bad patterns of behavior, or anxieties.

11. How will I maintain momentum towards our goals? Organizations are like ocean barges: difficult to get moving, but once in motion are hard to stop. How do I utilize the energy of my team to keep things moving?

12. How will I know when it is time for a change in personnel, organizational structure, or direction? Moving too quickly or too slowly can have a dramatic impact on performance. What signals will I look for that will tell me it is time?

13. How will I develop an accurate sense of what my organization is really capable of? I need to test my organization on a regular basis. These tests will give an idea of what my team is capable of.

14. How can I guarantee that my organization's successes won't lead to failure? Organizations develop a bad habit when they rely on their past successes to see them through. I will need to challenge my organization to look ahead and continually learn new behaviors. I will need to limit my organization's love affair with its past.

15. How will I know that my approach and engagement with the organization is in the sweet spot? (i.e., neither too challenging nor too supporting) My judgment of my organization's capability needs to be directly tied to the types of goals I set. If I am inaccurate, goals will not have the right

level of tension. Either too much or too little tension affects motivation in a negative way.

16. How will I know my messages are getting through consistently and accurately? When I have multiple organizational levels that a message has to go through to be communicated, the risk of errors in translation is high. I need to strive for clear, compelling language.

17. How will I know I am right? Conversely, how will I know I am wrong? I need to question myself rigorously and don't let my ego get in the way.

18. How will I gain respect and credibility, and hold on to it? I can't lead without credibility. It is the most important thing I can develop over time. Consistency between words and actions is its foundation.

19. How will I engage with others to foster a strong connection to me? I want my team to have a personal connection to me so I can earn their loyalty.

20. How will I know when I am getting in the way? I need to know the limits to my own effectiveness and find complimentary skill sets in others to cover for the gaps.

Thinking about these issues can help you to be purposeful and deliberate in everything you do. No wasted movements or distractions. Practice this self-assessment on a regular basis to keep yourself focused on what is important and relevant. Build your master of speed mindset.

TEST FOUR: EVALUATE YOUR WAKE

Just as a jet creates a wake as it moves through the air (akin to the wake a ship makes as it moves through the water), leaders create wakes as they interact with the organization. The decisions leaders make and their behaviors can create consequences that can last well beyond a specific event or interaction.

Here is an example from popular culture to illustrate this concept. In the 1986 film *Top Gun*, Lieutenant "Maverick" Mitchell, played by Tom Cruise, suffers a flameout caused by passing through the jet wash, or wake, of another aircraft. During a training mission, Maverick is caught in another Top Gun pilot's wake, resulting in an engine flameout that kills his plane mate and best friend, "Goose" Bradshaw, as they eject from the aircraft.

Was this just a danger created by an imaginative screenwriter? No, the danger is quite real. Here are just a few examples from a long list. In 1993, a chartered aircraft with five people on board, including In-N-Out Burger's president, Rich Snyder, crashed several miles before John Wayne Airport in Orange County, California. The aircraft followed a Boeing 757 in for landing, became caught in its wake turbulence, rolled into a deep descent, and crashed. In 1994, a USAir flight crashed near Pittsburgh in an accident that was believed to involve wake turbulence. In 2001, American Airlines Flight 587 crashed into the Queens, New York, shortly after takeoff from John F. Kennedy International Airport. This accident was attributed to pilot error in the presence of wake turbulence from a Japan Airlines Boeing 747.

Becoming aware of your wake, its size, and how fast it spreads is a critical master of speed awareness challenge. Too many leaders are simply unaware of their wake and, as a consequence, are unable to influence it. Leaders can be so focused on the task at hand that they don't consider how they are impacting others. While some wake is expected of leaders, too much wake has a disruptive impact on the organization. A large leadership wake becomes a drain of resources because of the amount of organizational attention it monopolizes or consumes. A leader with a large wake will have a huge impact on organizational functioning and create dependency in others because of their behavior.

But how can you measure leadership wake? Let's borrow a framework from the Federal Aviation Administration (FAA). The FAA is the national aviation authority of the United States. An agency of the United States Department of Transportation, it has authority to regulate and oversee all aspects of civil aviation in the U.S. The FAA uses a four-point classification scale to assess jet wake turbulence: super, heavy, large, and small. Use the following wake descriptions to identify your leadership wake.

How Much Wake Do You Create?

- **Super.** This is the type of wake created by a leader who insists on being the center of things. This kind of leader has created or reinforced a team culture that is strongly dependent on them. Nothing gets done without their say so. People don't take independent action. Turnover is high among top performers because they feel the environment is claustrophobic.
- **Heavy.** This is the wake caused by a leader who has a strong impact on those around him. Their personalities are forceful and charismatic, and they dominate the group environment. Everyone on the team exists in their shadow. They are not necessarily controlling, but their personalities are bigger than life. They tend to polarize people around them. Some people love them whereas others struggle with them.
- **Large.** This is the wake of a leader who is assertive and sets high performance standards for their team. They have strong people acumen and know how to get what they want

from others. While being forceful, they are transparent and forthcoming with their goals and aspirations. They are tolerant of those who have different approaches or style.

- **Small.** This is the type of wake caused by a leader who has created or fostered a leader-independent culture. They focus on developing other leaders and easily share the limelight. They strongly believe in empowerment and collaboration. People enjoy working for this type of leader because they have the opportunity to develop and grow.

A leader's wake spreads out though the organization and touches people with whom they may not have direct interaction or contact. People interpret these interactions and form perceptions about the leader that influences future interactions and expectations. The size of the leader's wake can be small, like a ripple, or large, like a tidal wave, depending on the significance of the leader's actions. The wake may be positively, negatively, or neutrally charged. Furthermore, the wake may generate unintended consequences and effects, and can have a significant influence on the willingness of people to work with you.

After spending the time to assess your master of speed behaviors and completing leadership flight school, it's now time to take the next step. To truly understand your impact and effectiveness, you'll need to take an in-depth look into how you manage time. The next chapter will explore time management as it relates to the faster leader and I'll introduce a number of strategies to help you manage this most important asset.

ACCELERATION TOOL #5: MASTER OF SPEED
FINAL CHECKLIST

Use the following checklist to do a final check on your master of speed readiness. Make note of any items that need additional attention.

1. Places a strong emphasis on time and how it is used-both for self and others.
2. Is consistently ahead of events.
3. Quickly deals with problems and issues.
4. Makes time to think things through.
5. Has a strategic mindset.
6. Focuses attention and effort on the most critical things.
7. Achieves results in a constructive manner.
8. Constantly builds organizational capability.
9. Actively engages people in the organization.
10. Minimizes resistance to goals, plans, and initiatives.
11. Challenges the organization.
12. Has a good sense of what people and the organization are capable of.
13. Builds and maintains personal credibility.
14. Has self-awareness and is self-critical.
15. Cultivates personal judgment through learning.
16. Is a quick study.
17. Has a strong personal network outside of the company.
18. Avoids building dependency on his leadership.
19. Embraces and uses leadership power.
20. Leverages the organization.
21. Creates momentum that sustains itself.
22. Focuses on making the organization faster.

23. Keeps his finger on the pulse of the organization.
24. Communicates messages that are clear and resonate with people.
25. Thinks about and plans for scalability.

CHAPTER 6

Win the Time Management Battle

❖ ❖ ❖

The bad news is time flies. The good
news is you're the pilot.

MICHAEL ALTSHULER

BASIC FIGHTER MANEUVERS (BFM) ARE actions a jet fighter pilot performs during aerial combat fighting. They can be offensive, neutral, or defensive in nature, and their goal is give the pilot maximum advantage over their opponent. Stall turns, barrel rolls, and yo-yo's are all part of the pilot's fighting repertoire.

In flight school, emerging pilots learn about these fighting techniques and other important concepts that are critical to winning a dogfight. Sight picture, rates of closure, and line of sight rates help the pilot understand the three dimensional environment in which they will be fighting. They also need to develop an in-depth understanding of their aircraft, its performance limits, and their enemy. Pilots learn to maintain constant aggressiveness when in combat. The enemy never sleeps.

BFM's require the pilot to make split second decisions about airspeed, altitude, and the plan of attack while in the air. The pilot is constantly adjusting his tactics in response to what the enemy is doing. Sometimes on offense, sometimes on defense, the pilot strives to achieve an advantage in an ever changing battlefield.

Leaders, in today's rapidly accelerating world, face similar challenges. Uppermost on your list of challenges is winning the time management battle.

In Chapter Two, I introduced the concept of how you can be the Chief Time Manager for your organization. Now it's time to shift gears and focus on how you manage your own time. As part of faster leader flight school, fine-tuning your personal time management skills is like practicing a BFM, and is an important step in progressing to the next level.

As an ongoing part of my executive coaching work, I constantly survey my clients on their time management performance. At least nine out of ten struggle with time management issues. Several of the trends I mentioned in Chapter One compromise a leader's ability to manage his time. I often hear my clients talk about the challenge of wanting to lead more but feeling like they don't have the time. It is a big problem and is only going to get worse as technology pushes us to be even more connected.

You can't lead if you can't manage your time. This point is at the very bedrock of leadership effectiveness and is at the heart of the faster leader model I mentioned in the Preface. There is no getting around this basic fact. Effective time management goes way beyond simply being organized or efficient, and it is not getting any easier. Organizational bad habits, demands from others, and fast-moving events all conspire to derail your daily plans and schedule. But keep this at the forefront of your awareness: you don't have time to waste because seconds matter.

If you let your time get out of your control, you *will* fail. It is not good enough to just manage your time; you need to become a master of it. As the time management guru Alan Lakein said, "Time = life; therefore, waste your time and waste your life, or master your time and master your life."[13]

What makes time management difficult for leaders? Leaders get the concept; it is the practice they have the most difficulty with. In the dogfight that is time management, leaders need help. I suggest you think of time management as a war you wage on a daily basis. In trying to win the war, I suggest leaders develop BFM's to help them succeed. This chapter outlines several important BFM's you will need to master if you want to get your time back under control.

BFM #1: Lock On to the Critical Path

A fighter pilot can't get distracted. They need to be able to sort through all of the information that is coming at them and quickly identify the most important data and then act on it.

In your ongoing battle with time management, you will need to practice a similar form of extreme focus. Borrowing a concept from the field of project management, I suggest that you utilize a critical path mindset to help you navigate the time management minefield.

The critical path is made up of a small set of variables that determine the success or failure of an activity. You need to sort through all of the things demanding your attention and identify which things to ignore and which to pay acute attention to. There are usually only between four and eight variables that truly matter, and these critical path variables don't vary much over time.

It is important to quickly identify the critical path for any domain—whether it is a company, a marketplace, or an area of functional responsibility. Leaders who possess a good sense of the critical path learn to recognize the most important variables in any situation they face.

The critical path forces you to approach your work from a disciplined perspective. It requires you invest your personal time on those things that have the biggest impact, not just the things you enjoy doing or are good at.

To kick-start your thinking about the critical path, here are a few variables that might go on your list:

- Resources in short supply
- Risks that might cause you to fail
- Opportunities that could allow you to leapfrog competition
- Interdependencies between important performance factors
- Decision efficiency and effectiveness
- Product or service cycle times
- Demand and adoption rates
- Sales trends
- Performance to schedule
- Morale and employee engagement trends
- Client/customer satisfaction rates and trends

BFM #2: Build a Personal STAB

After you have refined your critical path, it is time to convert it into a schedule you can monitor and manage. In Chapter Two I introduced the concept of STAB (strategic time allocation budget) and it is a relevant concept to the discussion here. To refresh, building a STAB involves determining relevant categories, assigning percentages to those categories, applying the percentages to your calendar management, and tracking how your actual time spent compares to your budget.

To maintain an adequate focus on the critical path, I suggest you convert it to a STAB and put it on your calendar. You can track your performance and identify any issues that consistently sidetrack you.

BFM #3: Limit Accessibility

Being accessible to your organization is an important aspect of leadership behavior. You have to be connected with people to engage and lead them. Being seen as approachable encourages people to communicate and bond with you. However, if you don't manage your personal boundaries in this area, people can either abuse your time or not value it sufficiently. You want to be accessible, but under your conditions. Here are a couple of suggestions for limiting your accessibility.

Practice Defensive Calendaring

After establishing the critical path and building a STAB to support it, you will find that you will be challenged on a daily basis to stick with your plan. As I've said before, the current work culture is one that disrupts time management. With linked calendar systems, anyone can schedule a meeting and request your participation. You may know very little about the meeting, aside from the fact that your presence has been deemed essential.

To maintain control over your time, you will have to practice defensive calendaring. Simply stated, you need to make it challenging for people to get on your calendar. You will have to establish several hurdles that people need to get over to get your time. One step you can take is to make it clear to your staff that you will not accept meetings that have not met certain criteria. Criteria can include a justification for the meeting and the desired outcomes. Other criteria could be meetings need to be used as a last resort. It will still require time on your part to make assessments regarding time requests. But you will have better information if you establish criteria from the start.

Additionally, do a post-mortem on meetings for their compliance with your criteria. If you think your meeting criteria were not met, be sure to give feedback to the organizer. You will want to hold people accountable for holding productive meetings and making good use of your time.

You can designate meeting-free days in your week. There are times when you and your team need uninterrupted blocks of time to strategize or complete a crucial project. This could be a regular arrangement (e.g., No Meeting Mondays). You can schedule days where you are working from home.

Kill Your Open Door Policy
The open door policy came into being when the empowerment movement was gaining momentum, and it was designed to combat the rising tide of employee dissatisfaction and cynicism that resulted from waves of layoffs and corporate restructurings. Over time, it became one of the sacred cows of leadership practice and was seen as one of the foundations of being an effective leader. Today, the majority of leaders have a version of an open door policy because they either think it is a good idea or it is expected of them by the organization and team members. Open cubicle environments encourage this type of behavior.

Like many leadership practices, the open door policy has good intentions. The basic structure of an open door policy is that team members can drop in on a leader and talk about whatever is on their minds. Leaders demonstrate their accessibility to team members by being available whenever team members want to talk. By making time for team members and listening, leaders demonstrate they value what team members have to say.

What could be wrong with a policy that has such positive aspirations? My fundamental problem with the open door policy is not with its intentions, but rather with its implementation and practice. I find that very few leaders can successfully pull off an open door policy and make it stick. The reality is that having an open door policy causes more problems than it is worth. It fundamentally undermines control of time and can lead to an erosion of leadership credibility. Here are four problems that plague the open door policy and recommendations on improving the situation.

Problem #1: Not enough time

The open door policy came into practice and gained popularity when the time demands on leaders were much less than they are today. The pace of work has become so great that many leaders have difficulty accomplishing what is expected of them and end up practicing triage—what is most urgent or loudest gets attention. Most leaders simply don't have the time flexibility in their daily schedule to make the open door policy work.

Imagine yourself in this situation. You are racing to meet a deadline and are really behind. A team member drops by your office to discuss an issue that is on his mind. You have an open door policy and feel the pressure to listen. You would like to put the team member off to another time but feel you can't. You allow the team member to talk, but your mind is elsewhere on the deadlines and tasks that are piling up. Or, even worse, your frustration and impatience show through. The team member picks up on your emotions or distraction and leaves your office feeling dissatisfied and dismissed. It is a no-win situation for both of you.

Problem #2: Inconsistency

A team member drops in when you are trying to meet a critical deadline and you need to put the conversation off to another time. Although you think you delay the conversation skillfully, you can tell the individual is disappointed. You've just lost points in the ongoing process to build engagement because the open door policy has an all or none characteristic. Team members will test whether or not you are serious about the policy and inconsistency sends the wrong message. It becomes an issue of credibility—do you really do what you say?

Team members are used to leadership saying one thing and doing another and are quick to jump on the distrust bandwagon. Even *one* violation of a stated policy starts to erode credibility. Once you formally commit to a practice, you must follow it to the letter. Think of it as the 100 percent rule. Don't commit if you can't practice it consistently all of the time. It is very difficult to be consistent when it comes to an open door.

Problem #3: Problems with Transition

The cornerstone of an open door policy is unstructured time. Team members can talk to you about what they want to talk about. The problem is you really never know from one conversation to the next what the team member will bring up. Unlike one-on-one time, which usually has an agenda, open door time does not. This unstructured quality makes it more difficult for you to manage the conversation and really challenges listening skills. Transitioning from focusing on work activities to a more open listening stance for an open door conversation is difficult at best.

Leaders are trained to be problem solvers and the open door policy works across the grain. Leaders often have a difficult time making the transition, instead bringing their problem-solving focus to the open door conversation. Team members generally want the leader to listen, not problem solve and assign action items.

Problem #4: Unproductive Time
While important issues do bubble to the surface, many team members use the time to vent, complain, or even gossip. Little constructive or useful information is communicated and the open door policy can easily legitimize ineffective behavior. The situation puts the leader in a type of double bind. If you listen to negative behavior, you reinforce it; if you challenge the behavior, team members see it as a violation of the policy.

Recommendations
One recommendation is to eliminate your open door policy and set aside a specific time each week where team members can bring in their issues. This approach allows you to better control access to you. Just like a doctor or teacher who has weekly office hours, you can set aside a time where you will be accessible outside of the normal communication channels. Generally, an hour a week is time enough to allow team members to raise their issues. This approach allows you to structure and control your engagement with team members. Set ground rules and expectations, and clearly communicate to team members to help them use time appropriately. Again, the key is to schedule open-door time consistently and hold to the practice.

Another recommendation is to hold ongoing and revolving open forum meetings with small groups of team members to solicit their feedback on topics they want to discuss. This practice will demonstrate your accessibility and give you better control of your time.

BFM #4: Maintain Two Calendars

Immediate or short term emergencies often knock your strategic activities off the calendar. Or, there are so many tactical activities that your leadership initiatives get buried. To combat this tendency and get better control of your time, I suggest you maintain a separate leadership calendar that only you have access to. You can use this leadership calendar as a timeline for the leadership actions you want to schedule. Having a separate calendar will help you to focus on important leadership actions that otherwise might get lost in the noise.

Here are some actions you might want to include in your leadership calendar:

- Review your vision and mission with the team on an ongoing basis
- Set target dates for delegating certain responsibilities to team members
- Establish check in times with your team members to give them feedback and coaching
- Take an engagement reading to see how the team is responding to your leadership
- Set up times for career development conversations with your team members
- Review your strategic plan
- Set networking targets
- Review your personal and organizational STAB to review your performance

- Set time for personal learning
- Allot time to refresh your perspective

BFM #5: Limit Your Ownership

Your time is priceless. As simple and straightforward as it sounds, I am amazed at how many leaders don't place enough value on their time and how it's spent. They give it away freely and openly. They jump in to help and will do others' work for them. They want to be seen as participatory and good team players. They believe an important aspect of their job is to support their team.

But if you play too much of a *supporting* role, you will end up neglecting important aspects of your *leadership* role. There is an opportunity cost to this type of choice. It's important to remember there are things that only a leader can do. No one else can do them for you. If you don't reserve your time or devote it to the leadership domain, those things won't get done. You will create a leadership vacuum.

Time is your most precious commodity. If you are too casual with your time, others can adopt the same cavalier behavior. It is important to remember you are a model for the rest of the organization. They will follow your lead. It is not arrogance to expect or want others to treat your time as a valuable commodity. You are not better than other people; you simply have a different job. By valuing your time, you teach your organization to value it.

The key principle to practice here is to **minimize your personal ownership of issues**. I know this position sounds contrary to many leadership approaches that emphasize ownership as an important leadership foundation. But, it is your job as a faster leader to avoid taking on too much ownership and becoming a bottleneck to your team. Instead, you want to make sure that ownership *is taken* by the appropriate people.

Get Comfortable Saying No

One of the bad behaviors that developed as a consequence of the time crunch is the evasion of responsibility. People have become very good at getting things off their plate and getting others to assume responsibility. Think of this as passing the hot potato. The goal of this activity is to minimize personal ownership by never taking it on in the first place. Leaders, because of their visibility, are easy targets for this type of behavior. If you are not careful, you'll end up owning or being responsible for things that require significant time to address. Before you know it, you will be bogged down in all types of things that have low value.

Don't fall into the trap of treating every request for your attention with the same level of urgency. It may feel impossible to prioritize all the demands that are constantly popping up in your inbox but you will need to try. If you are too busy putting out fires you don't have the time to assess the situation.

As much as it feels like an endless cycle, it is crucial you learn to stop being reactionary and evaluate what is truly urgent and worthy of your time. In a post on the *Harvard Business Review* blog called, "No is the New Yes," Tony Schwartz, president and CEO of The Energy Project, said, "Saying no, thoughtfully, may be the most undervalued capacity of our times. In a world of relentless demands and infinite options, it behooves us to prioritize the tasks that add the most value. That also means deciding what to do less of, or to stop doing altogether."[14]

Did you note the word "thoughtfully" there? Taking the time for reflection may not seem like a quality of a faster leader, but knowing when to pause to evaluate priorities will save you a good deal of time in the long run. As I said earlier, the paradox of the faster leader is sometimes you have to go slower to go fast.

Push Back

While it may not always be possible to say no, in most situations it is possible to challenge the handoff. If a person attempts to pass a task on to you, ask questions and push back. Why are they requesting that you handle this? Is the task really important? Should the task belong to another person? Evaluate the time commitments and whether it really is a good use of your limited time. Have reasons for declining the responsibility and be firm in your answer. Don't just take on a task just because it is easier than the alternative.

BFM #6: Practice Rapid Delegation

Fast paced environments require excellent delegation skills. If you are too slow with this management behavior, windows of opportunity will pass and you'll be left holding the bag. Don't let yourself fall behind. Take your delegation skills to the next level by following these steps:

1. The first step in evaluating a task for possible delegation is to ask if it is important enough to be delegated. If it doesn't pass this test, don't pass it on. You provide a very important quality control function to your team and need to be very discriminating in what you delegate. Be willing to kill something quickly rather than pass it on.

2. Keep in mind the workload of your team. An important faster leader behavior is to **continually take things off the workload plate** rather than keep piling things on.
3. Get things out of your hands as quick as possible and hand them off to the right people.
4. Be sure to match the delegation task to the skills and motivation of the individual. A mismatch will lead to failure or boredom.
5. Provide context to allow people to understand why an activity is important. This is particularly important with tasks that have low intrinsic motivation value (i.e., the stuff nobody really likes to do).
6. Connect delegation with career development whenever possible. You are providing stretch and learning opportunities that will help the individual grow.
7. Break up the delegation into manageable actions and deliverables. Try to minimize ambiguity or the possibility of failure.
8. Clarify the duration of the delegation. It could be a one-time event or could represent a more permanent shift in responsibilities.

By practicing these BFM's, you will gain better control of your personal time and have more time to devote to your leadership. You'll stand a better chance of winning the time management battle and excelling at the **Chief Time Manager (CTM)** role. In the next chapter, you'll progress to advanced flight school and tackle the challenge of improving your judgment.

ACCELERATION TOOL #6: DEFEND YOUR TIME

Leaders often find themselves in a situation where there are multiple and competing demands for their time. Meeting requests, 1:1 time, customer visits, and presentations are just a few of the time demands a leader has to make decisions about. Having a tool that helps you quickly sort through these requests is really helpful.

The DICED filter is the first decision tree that any request for your time should go through. I suggest you pass any request through it before taking responsibility or ownership for the request. Just like an oil filter that removes contaminants, the DICED filter is extremely helpful in screening requests for your time and attention. It speeds up decisions about what you should or should not do. What does DICED stand for?

Delegate: Share tasks and demands with others rather than trying to do it all yourself. Give people responsibility and accountability in line with their role and experience. In this way, you can effectively leverage your team and give them developmental opportunities.

Ignore: In challenging times, everything seems to become urgent. People can become very good at creating emergencies they want you to fix. Sometimes you have to ignore things to determine their significance. Some people overuse urgency and don't discriminate. If an issue you ignored persists, then it may possess more significance. If you ignore it and it doesn't come back, it may not have been important in the first place. One caution: Don't overuse this technique.

Challenge: Pushing back on demands for your time is an important leadership behavior. People can fall into the habit of wanting to avoid responsibility and accountability. They will try to get you to take ownership or escalate problems that they don't want to deal with. Avoid taking ownership for things you shouldn't by saying no. Keep the responsibility where it belongs by challenging and pushing back.

Eliminate: Get rid of things by shutting them down or cancelling them. Inefficiency and ineffectiveness constantly creep into workflow and the leader's time can suffer as a result. For example, a meeting will continue after its original purpose was exhausted and become an inefficient waste of time. Simply eliminate it.

Delay: Rather than acting on something immediately, delay it to another time of your choosing when you have more options or flexibility. Delaying things allows you to control your time and avoid the cascading effect that disrupts your schedule. If you are doing an effective job of managing your calendar, you will have established blocks or segments of time where you can drop time requests.

The DICED filter is a tool that can dramatically improve your time management and keep ownership from always ending up at your doorstep. An additional benefit is it teaches others to use your time appropriately. The more you use it, the more effective you will become.

CHAPTER 7

Judgment is Your GPS

*If a person does not know to which port he is
steering, no wind is favorable to him.*

SENECA, ROMAN PHILOSOPHER

GLOBAL POSITIONING SYSTEMS (GPS) HAVE made it easier to navigate unfamiliar terrain and keep you on course. Whether you are hiking a new trail or driving to a client's office, your GPS system can guide you every step of the way. If you make a wrong turn, the GPS makes minor adjustments to get you back on track. Most people are familiar with the GPS voice assuring you that it is "recalculating route."

For fighter pilots, navigation can be one of their most important skills. The more they can make it an innate part of their flying, the better pilot they will be. Dale Snodgrass is considered one of the best F-14 pilots in the world; the movie *Top Gun* is based on pilots like him. His colleague John Ellis said of him, "There are some pilots who seem to have a special sense of awareness of where they are at all times. Dale has that particular ability. His flying is smooth and aggressive at the same time. His senses are a little sharper than other people's."[15]

Like a fighter pilot, a faster leader needs to be constantly aware of the environment he is operating in and what is rapidly approaching over the horizon. Your sense of judgment is like a guidance system that enables you to quickly sort through information for the most important aspects, prioritize issues accurately and quickly, and make high quality decisions rapidly. If you must make a detour from the plan, your judgment will allow you to readjust your route and stay on track. Since judgment is critical, it is essential you make cultivation of your judgment a top development priority over the course of your leadership career. You must continually refine your judgment to be an accurate indicator of the right course. Your judgment skills make you an effective **Chief Guidance Officer (CGO)**.

One defining example of leadership judgment happened in January 2009 aboard US Airways flight 1549. Shortly after taking off from La Guardia airport, Pilot Chesley Sullenberger reported to air traffic control that the plane had hit a flock of geese, which disabled both of the plane's engines. After talking through the options with air traffic control, he made the decision that the best choice was to land the plane in the Hudson River. Under the extreme conditions of zero thrust and knowing he had the lives of 155 people in his hands, Sullenberger safely landed the plane. Even though he had a co-pilot, it was Sully's judgment and ability to remain calm and focused that saved the lives of his passengers. All of this happened over a span of six minutes, three of them without power.

While you may never be in the position where you have hundreds of people's lives in your hands, your leadership judgment can have a significant impact on the people around you. In this chapter, I'll examine how judgment is tied to self-awareness, one of the faster leader model components. You'll be introduced to the nine foundations of judgment and how to avoid common judgment mistakes. I'll walk you through the decision pre-flight checklist, a framework to improve your judgment as it relates to decision making.

What Is Judgment?

While it is tempting to think of judgment as a global attribute a leader either possesses or doesn't, a more accurate way of viewing it is as a combination of intuition, experience, critical thinking, and learning. Judgment is a master competency that a leader cultivates over the span of his career. It incorporates a bias towards resolution, clarity of thinking, openness to information and other viewpoints, a capacity for learning, a critical mind-set, and a capacity to discern patterns and relationships.

Judgment is the processes by which you arrive at decisions. While all leaders make decisions, those with good judgment have a pattern of consistently making better choices. Like other behaviors that require investment and refinement, judgment is a competency you deliberately cultivate over time.

An essential component of judgment is turning a critical eye on what you have done. Sullenberger's judgment and flying skills were honed through 19,000 hours of flight time. Speaking with news anchor Katie Couric, Sullenberger said, "One way of looking at this might be that for forty-two years, I've been making small, regular deposits in this bank of experience: education and training. And on January 15, the balance was sufficient so that I could make a very large withdrawal."[16] A leader's judgment needs to be evaluated regularly because the impact of certain decisions may take months or years to play out.

I consider judgment to be a master competency at the heart of faster leadership. It touches everything the leader does, from hiring and strategy, to team member engagement and management. It flows through decisions, choices, and the priorities the leader sets. The most critical thing a leader does on a daily basis is utilize his judgment to make choices and decisions that impact the organization on multiple levels. Cultivated over the lifespan of a leader, judgment determines how successful he will be. I have come to believe that judgment is the ultimate criterion by which leaders need to be evaluated.

Typically, there is no shortage of leaders willing to make decisions. The real question is: are they making good decisions? We celebrate leaders who make good decisions and criticize those who don't. Leaders with poor judgment can cause an enterprise to fail, whereas leaders who make good choices are often put on pedestals. Since judgment is important, I believe we need to understand what it is and what it isn't.

THE NINE FOUNDATIONS OF JUDGMENT

It is important to think about judgment being context dependent. What is good judgment in one situation might be a disaster in another. Good judgment in one environment doesn't automatically transfer to another. Judgment is multi-dimensional. For example, it can be applied to hiring people or making the right choice in a given situation. A generalized view of judgment is not very useful. Let's dig deeper into judgment. In my coaching work, I emphasize nine foundations of judgment that are important to understand, evaluate, and practice.

Foundation #1: Deliberate Decision-Making

When you are asked how you arrived at a particular decision, you should be able to describe the process you used. A sound decision-making process involves having correct data and making good use of it.

While you don't want to ignore emotion or intuition, what I look for is evidence you have analyzed and evaluated other options. Have you made a case for your decision? Can you present evidence and information showing how this decision was arrived at? Can you talk about the tradeoffs? Have you thought through the consequences and alternatives?

Before a pilot takes off, he conducts a rigorous pre-flight checklist where he evaluates the status of key fight readiness indicators. He takes a walk around the plane, looking for leaks or anything that is out of place or missing. He won't take off if anything is out of order.

Conducting a pre-decision checklist is a good practice for leaders to follow. It helps to discipline your decision-making process and can help you evaluate the decision making of other people. Since very few decisions happen in isolation, thinking through and not rushing a decision actually results in faster decisions because your decisions won't fall apart in the face of resistance.

Incorporate Decision Drivers

A deliberate decision making process only gets you part of the way to a good decision. You also need to incorporate what I call decision drivers. Decision drivers are values that are applied to the decision making process and they represent very deliberate choices a leader makes. Depending on what decision drivers are selected, very different decisions can be made.

A leader needs to be able to articulate why he is prioritizing certain drivers over others, and communicate them to his team.

Typically, no more than three drivers can be employed effectively in any one decision. For example, a leader may emphasize speed as a driver and make decisions that optimize speed over other options. He will select options or choices that allow him to get to his goal faster. He will sacrifice other variables in the name of speed. Here are nine examples of decision drivers:

- Speed- get to the market first
- Opportunistic- react to the environment and take advantage of opportunities that arise
- Strategic- focus on decisions that are consistent with your strategic direction
- Cost- make decisions that minimize cost
- Quality- make decisions that result in higher quality services and products
- Risk- make decisions that minimize risk and exposure
- Image- emphasize decisions that improve the overall brand or image of the organization
- Advantage- make decisions that give us an advantage over our competitors
- Customer- focus on decisions that place the needs of the customer at the top

I have included a checklist at the end of the chapter to help you review your judgment, decision making, and decision drivers.

Foundation #2: Know What is Important and be Willing to do it
Prioritization is the ability to rank things in terms of their importance, which makes it a crucial foundation of judgment. But prioritization in a judgment sense is not just about ranking; it is about understanding what is most important and where you should focus

your personal attention. You don't want to be solving the wrong problems; you want to be solving the right problems.

When I'm evaluating leaders, I want to see evidence of them having a nose for truth, an ability to cut through complexity to find what is critical, and an impatience for dealing with distractions. Because of the overwhelming amount of information and the speed of marketplace changes, leaders need to get at the essence or core of a situation and prioritize things quickly. They often don't have a lot of time to accomplish this. The critical path I talked about in Chapter Six is central to the leader's ability to prioritize quickly.

A challenge that many leaders face, is the critical path can force you out of your comfort zone. It may require you to do difficult things or make decisions in areas you are not an expert in. Judgment requires that you have a sufficient amount of courage to do what is necessary to do. A faster leader needs to get comfortable making the difficult, but right decisions. The critical path is not necessarily a comfortable one for leaders.

Foundation #3: Admit and Learn from Mistakes

Making mistakes is part of being a leader; it is how you learn and grow your judgment as a leader. The role of the leader involves thinking ahead and making decisions based on limited data. Because the leadership role involves ambiguity, uncertainty, and risk, the potential for failure or mistakes is high. Leaders need to become comfortable with admitting they were wrong and learning from their mistakes.

Acknowledging mistakes can be difficult because many organizations don't tolerate failure well. Leaders can be demoted, fired, or experience other negative consequences due to making a mistake. Leaders can engage in activities to hide their mistakes because of fear of repercussions. Fear blocks or interferes with awareness and understanding, both of which are important to learning.

The ego of the leader can get in the way. No one likes to be wrong, especially someone in a leadership role. People like to see themselves as competent and skilled, and being wrong can erode their positive sense of self. I call this phenomenon the competence trap. It takes a certain level of self-confidence to admit to being wrong and, as a result, some individuals have a real difficult time admitting a failure.

Needing to see yourself as successful, and needing to have others see you the same way, can impede learning and awareness. The competence trap can encourage you to engage in negative leadership behavior. You can blame others, blame the situation, or deny the mistake, which are all ways of not being accountable for your own behavior. If you can't internalize the mistake, you won't learn from it and, therefore, you will likely repeat it. In this way, ego can act as a barrier to learning.

As Oscar Wilde said, "Experience is simply the name we give our mistakes." For mistakes to become learning experiences, you need to take several steps to internalize the lessons. You must acknowledge the mistake to yourself. Then you should analyze the mistake to uncover what contributed to it. Ask, "What did I learn or what did this experience teach me about people, business, technology, getting things done, or myself?" Getting feedback and coaching from other people can give you a sense of perspective on the mistake. Try to develop alternate ways to deal with the situation or problem going forward. Modifying your behavior, beliefs and attitudes, and models to incorporate new insight and understanding will ensure the mistake was an educational one. You can then convert your experiences into judgment parameters and principles that form your personal GPS.

Foundation #4: A Bias to Action

When the world moved at a slower pace, we could easily take more time to make a decision. But since the world has sped up, the process of decision making has become more complex. Leaders can freeze when it comes to decisions because of the uncertainty that arises when things move too quickly. Other leaders are slow to make decisions because they over analyze and get lost in data and details. They are afraid of making mistakes. Still other leaders procrastinate when it comes to decision making because of the risks involved. What is right today could be wrong tomorrow.

I coach leaders to take the approach that **action is a diagnostic**. Taking action gives you additional information on which to make additional choices. Action informs you about consequences and gives you concrete feedback. A pilot uses action to understand how the plane is performing and the surrounding airspace. Based on this feedback, the pilot adjusts his approach to get optimal performance. Action acts as feedback and allows you to develop decisions and link those decisions into a decision chain. If you don't take action, you don't get the necessary feedback to make additional decisions. Don't worry about making a mistake. Things move so quickly that you can usually correct or compensate with the next decision you make.

Foundation #5: Don' be Afraid to use Intuition

Judgment incorporates the ability to understand and incorporate intangibles into the decision-making process. Not all correct decisions are simply logical and objective. Sometimes the right answer is not based strictly on facts but includes feelings. I think of this experience as using your intuition. Intuition is cultivated through life experiences. It is that subtle sense that allows leaders to know the right or wrong direction without tangible evidence and facts. It is more of a visceral kind of experience.

Have you ever had the sense a person is not telling you the truth? You may not have a concrete reason to distrust them, but your intuition is telling you they are deceiving you. Cultivating your intuition is a significant part of developing good judgment. Intuition can be cultivated by learning to read the subtleties present in any situation and by listening to your own emotions and reactions. Since intuition is not fail-safe and can be wrong, you want to avoid the extremes associated with it. Try not to over or under use it. But don't discount it either because intuition plays an important role in dealing with the intangibles associated with good judgment.

Foundation #6: Cultivate Perspective

Having perspective means being able to see the big picture, thinking beyond your own self-interest, and being aware of the implications and consequences of your choices on other people and other organizations. It involves being able to look at a situation from multiple viewpoints.

One leader I recently worked with was outstanding in this area. He had several direct reports, but felt some of his team would be a better fit in another organization within the company. He initiated the idea of transferring some of his people because he saw they could contribute more if they reported to another manager. Although he ended up losing a few people in the process, by exercising good judgment and doing what was good for the business, he improved his status in the minds of other leaders. By his actions, other leaders saw him as a leader who had the organization's best interests in mind.

This is not to say that leaders should abandon their own interests. An expectation of leaders is that they will defend the interests of their team or function; they need to support their team and protect them. Problems occur when the leader focuses exclusively on their own interests. What is needed is a balancing of self or team interest with larger organizational needs. The higher up you go organizationally the more it is necessary to think about all the parts of the system.

Foundation #7: Adopt a Challenging Mind-set
Faster leaders need to learn to ask tough questions because judgment involves questioning the status quo and avoiding the organizational tendency towards complacency. It is necessary to always challenge assumptions, screen out the bias of other people, be self-critical, and evaluate your own choices and motivations.

A leader's pointed questions are not asked just for the sake of gathering information but instead are focused on getting people to address the real issues. Leaders need to be assertive in their questioning and attentive in their listening, and be impatient with distractions. Assertive inquiry forces an honest evaluation of the issues. Leaders who are effective at this type of questioning are good at setting the stage and others do not take the questioning as a personal attack. Faster leaders are interested in finding the truth, not finding fault, assigning blame, or putting others on the defensive. Two tools that I have developed to help leaders adopt a challenging mindset are the core questioning technique and the BS detector.

The Core Questioning Technique
The core questioning technique is a framework for asking questions at three different levels. You often don't have a lot of time to

evaluate a decision and this technique helps to cut through the noise and chatter.

1. *Is it justified?* Typically questions that get at justification involve the use of why and its derivatives. Why are we doing this? Why does it need to be done now? What's the alternative? Why can't we do this?

2. *Is it focused at the right level?* Questions of this type are designed to get people to address issues at the root level rather than the symptom level. If you don't surface the root issue, you will keep solving the same problem over and over. Focusing questions include the following: Have we dealt with this problem before? What have we tried before? What is this problem/issue related to? How would someone who is not involved with the issue see it?

3. *Does it make sense?* Smart people can make bad decisions because they don't consider the ramifications. Questions related to ramifications focus on costs, benefits, and strategy. What are the tradeoffs? What are the costs associated with it? What is the financial impact? What benefit will we derive from it? What revenue will we see? Is the proposed action consistent with our strategy and goals? How does it further our strategy? What are the opportunity costs?

Turn on your BS Detector

Every leader should have a BS detector on their mental dashboard. This indicator should go off in your head when you hear information that is slanted or not objective. Just like a false signal on radar, biased data can lead you down the wrong course.

As a leader, you will consistently receive biased information. It is helpful to remember that **bias is predictable**. People can tell you what they think you want to hear rather than the truth. They can give you information with a certain spin on it, to further their own agendas. This is typically not malicious, but instead stems from their view of the world and their place in the work hierarchy. People in marketing see the world differently from those in engineering. Your work function influences your perspective. Leaders need to train themselves to be on the lookout for biased data and a good BS detector helps.

A leader is often in the position of having to make decisions using second or third hand data. The challenge for the leader in this situation involves recognizing truth in others' words and opinions, validating feedback, and discerning any personal or functional bias inherent in the data.

Most leaders rely upon key information sources within their organization. It is vital the leader be able to differentiate between bias, distortion, and truth in the information received from their sources. In order to root out the biases that may be contained in the information, use seemingly random questions and close observation of behavior to determine if the organization is on track.

Foundation #8: Build and Refine Models

At the core of judgment is the ability to create models which predict and explain results and behavior. These frameworks help to organize data into structures that give information meaning and context. A leader should be deliberate in building models and be able to explain those models to the team.

Many of the challenges a leader faces are predictive in nature. A leader needs to anticipate and think about what may happen in the future. They need to get their organization ready for the changes that are coming. Models help to accomplish this task. When I am coaching leaders, I encourage them to devote the time and energy necessary to developing robust models that capture key elements of the decision- making process.

The faster leader is continually taking in new information and testing it against his existing models. When he finds a discrepancy or has an observation that is not accounted for in the model, he modifies the model to incorporate the new data. The revising of models is a constant, never ending endeavor.

Leadership models can be built for any number of things. A leader can have a model that explains human motivation. A leader can have a model that articulates the key factors in business success. Faster leaders build models for the most important things in their environment.

When evaluating this aspect of judgment, I encourage leaders to get comfortable in articulating their models. If you can't explain your model, you can't test it. Communication of the model increases transparency and helps in validation.

I suggest a leader continues to refine his models. One of the big problems I consistently encounter is frozen models. In this situation, a leader has a model but has not modified it to assimilate new information. Instead, they distort new information to fit the model they already have.

Foundation #9: Achieve Results that Pass the Test of Time

Ultimately, leadership judgment must be evaluated over time. You have to establish a track record of making decisions that prove to be right when looked at retrospectively. What appears to be right in the short-term can be wrong when looked at over the long term.

It is important to have a large enough sample size and look at multiple decisions and their consequences. One or two decisions are not enough to evaluate judgment. Judgment is a pattern of good decision-making over time.

COMMON JUDGMENT ERRORS

As part of their training, aircraft pilots are exposed to many types of pilot error. The goals are to sensitize pilots, improve their awareness, and prevent lapses in concentration. In my work with leaders, I've found there are several judgment errors that consistently come up and limit a leader's effectiveness. You'll want to be on the lookout for these errors in your judgment process so you don't crash. Also, look for these judgment errors within your team.

The Halo Effect

Everyone has a judgment sweet spot. There is a range of topics and situations where your judgment is highly accurate. Outside of the sweet spot, your accuracy drops off. It is important to understand the drop-off effect to allow you to compensate for it and manage risk.

When you make an evaluation that a person has good judgment in one area, you can easily make a mistake and generalize that person has good judgment in other areas. Typically, people have good judgment in some areas and not in others. There are areas you can trust people in and there are areas where you will have to scrutinize their work. You will be a more effective leader when you can see others' judgment blind spots and weaknesses.

The tendency to generalize about a person's capabilities or attributes in either an overwhelming positive or negative way is called the halo effect. Either they can do no wrong or can't do anything right. People have a very strong tendency to make positive halo effect judgments of other people based on variables such as attractive physical appearance, shared values, shared background or experience, or general similarity. Negative halo effect judgments are often based on dissimilarities.

The truth of the matter is you will find that very few people make perfect decisions in all types of circumstances and very few will make poor decisions all the time either. Since everyone is a mixed bag, it is important for you to understand and avoid the halo effect. If you have a tendency to make halo-effect judgments, you will tend to not dig in and validate the decisions of people you give positive marks. Conversely, you may overly scrutinize the decisions of a person you judge negatively. If you take the view that everyone has positive and negative attributes, you will be far more unlikely to fall victim to the halo effect. A more balanced perspective will allow you to accurately decide when to test and when to trust.

An extension of the halo trap that is particularly important to be aware of is the confirmation bias. This is a phenomenon where people tend to believe data that confirm their position and ignore or deny data that challenges their position. This bias can extend to the halo judgments people make. People make positive halo judgments of those individuals who agree with them and negative judgments of those who don't. While it can be personally gratifying to have a person agree with us, falling prey to the confirmation bias exposes us to the risks of our own blind spots or weaknesses. Faster leadership involves being comfortable and encouraging disagreement to ensure the best decision gets made.

Missing the Decision Window

When we think about the decision-making process, we know decisions are made in a real-time dynamic context. There is an interval of time that is optimal for making a decision and taking action on it. Think of this optimal interval of time as the decision window. Demands in the situation and demands in the environment have a huge impact on how and when decisions need to be made, and the stakes are high. Leaders can miss the decision window by being either too quick or too slow.

Some leaders pull the decision trigger too quickly. Due to the pace of change in work environments, leaders can have a false sense of urgency. The speed of change and the rate at which new information is delivered in business enforces this pattern of quick decision making.

By making a decision too quickly, leaders may not thoroughly consider the entire situation; important information may have been ignored or not analyzed. Decisions that are made quickly can rapidly gain a momentum of their own. As a consequence, there is very little time to evaluate decisions and bad decisions can multiply. In this situation, decision-making that is too fast can actually make you slower because of the consequences of failure.

If you let your own sense of urgency drive your decision-making process, you can make big mistakes that could have been avoided if you would have been more deliberate and thoughtful. If you can realize not all decisions have to be made with the same sense of urgency, you can come to understand each decision has its own window.

The real decision window is determined by the characteristics of the issue and environmental variables, not by your psychology. When you make too quick decisions, you don't give yourself enough time to consider or capture those important variables that allow you to discriminate and be more effective. A faster leader knows that there are times when you have to slow down. You may need to let things play out a bit before you make your decision to pass the car in front of you.

The flip side of making decisions too quickly is delaying the decision. If you are risk averse, don't like being wrong, or have a perfectionist streak, you are particularly prone to this type of judgment error. The tendency is to delay making any decision until you feel you have all the information. You can be so focused on making the right decision and wanting it to be air tight that the result is delay and further delay, causing frustration with your team. **But the truth of the matter is you will never have perfect information.** When you do come up with the right decision, it is too late. It doesn't do a lot of good to be right and late.

You can't stop the world while you make your decision. As you go up the organization ladder and take on more responsibility, you will need to become more comfortable making decisions with minimal or ambiguous information.

You can be consistently too quick or too slow in terms of the decision window. This error in judgment is in missing the window either way. It is easy to fall into a pattern here—either you feel a false sense of urgency and react too quickly or you are overly cautious and delay the decision. The decision window is all about realizing there is a right and wrong time to make a decision based on the dynamics of the situation.

Falling Prey to the Complexity Error

Another type of judgment error relates to assigning the wrong level of complexity to a decision. Introducing too many variables can unnecessarily complicate a decision. It takes real skill to simplify things. The faster leader understands that complexity is your enemy.

One way leaders consistently overcomplicate the decision-making process is by including too many people in the decision. By having too many people participate, they slow the process down. The process is slowed even more when you have to educate individuals who may have been more peripherally involved. People can have opinions about anything; however, they may not be well-informed opinions. It typically takes a lot longer to arrive at a decision when there are ten people involved rather than three. I even have a coaching philosophy called the "rule of three." I am a strong proponent of the idea that most decisions should take no more than three people to make.

Another way you can overcomplicate things is by gathering too much information and incorporating too many variables in your decision process. Too much information can actually slow the decision-making process down unnecessarily because you get lost in the data. You can get so caught up in data analysis and presentation that making a decision becomes a secondary activity.

You can overcomplicate the decision making process by incorporating too many decision drivers. As I mentioned in the decision making section earlier in this chapter, three drivers is the maximum you can realistically employ on any decision. Too many drivers lead to confusion and poor decision quality.

On the other hand, it can be an error to oversimplify your decision process too much. The error of oversimplifying occurs when you do not think through the ramifications of your decisions, do not include critical stakeholders in the decision, or exclude entire classes of variables. Good judgment is all about finding the right range of variables to guide your decision making. Avoid over complicating or over simplifying your thinking process.

Local Optimization

Another bias to be on the lookout for is local optimization. This judgment mistake is about focusing on what you need or want to the exclusion of the needs of others. Short-term self-interest is the orientation of local optimization. You don't think about the bigger picture, or how others might be impacted by your decision.

You can make a mistake when you think a decision only impacts your own team and miss the fact that others may need to be informed or consulted. Very rarely does a decision only affect a few people. To counter this, you can ask yourself these questions: How will this affect other groups? Who else needs to be informed about this? What are the long-term consequences of this decision? Those who will be impacted may have to support the decision, be committed to it, buy into it, and give resources to it.

Falling in Love with Your Decision

The fifth type of judgment error is allowing a personal bias to influence a decision. I call this falling in love with your decision. It is easy to fall in love with a decision when you have invested a lot of time, energy, and resources into it. You begin to take personal ownership of the decision and invest your self-worth or esteem in it.

Personal bias colors ability to see a decision objectively and this creates the possibility of an error in judgment. One test you can take to see if you are overly attached to your decision is to ask: How willing am I to objectively look at alternatives? If you resist looking at other ideas, you can bet you have fallen in love with this decision.

I'm not an Expert

For some leaders, when they are challenged to make a decision that is outside of their area of expertise they can either delay or avoid making the decision. Feeling competent and knowledgeable is a position of strength and if you get outside of this zone, confidence can rapidly diminish. The fear of making mistakes or looking foolish can be a powerful avoidance motivation. As a consequence, leaders can gravitate towards areas they feel most competent in and ignore other areas that are not in their sweet spot. This behavior can lead to a leadership vacuum as decisions don't get made.

As leaders progress up the organizational ladder and take on more responsibility, this judgment problem gets even more problematic. Your increasing responsibilities erode your ability to maintain your expertise. You are no longer the expert and have less time to spend on details. You become more dependent on others to provide information and expertise. You increasingly need to leverage others to get the job done.

A shift needs to happen. Instead of being an expert in a content area, you need to cultivate your ability to evaluate the judgment of your team members. You need to shift from expertise-based decision making to judgment-based decision making if you want to be successful.

A Bias for the Short Term

Another judgment mistake a leader can make is to prioritize the more immediate things over the more long-term. I frequently see this type of prioritization mistake during the hiring process. A common scenario is a leader will have an open hiring requisition but they don't dedicate time to the process. The hiring process requires investment of time before seeing results.

The hiring process requires first defining the position, then publicizing it, screening candidates, interviewing people, and making the hiring decision. Because of the delay between investment and return, and the fact that many leaders don't like to interview, the hiring process can end up taking a backseat to other more immediate issues. This delay ends up putting a strain on current members of the team because they have to work harder to fill the gaps and the overall productivity of the team suffers. A talented new hire can dramatically improve the performance of a team, but only if the leader actually hires that person.

John Ryan, president of the Center for Creative Leadership and former US Navy pilot, reinforces the importance of not just focusing on the short term. In his more than three decades as a commanding officer in the navy, he realized how important personnel decisions could be, particularly on an aircraft carrier with a crew of thousands. In an article for Forbes.com, he said, "You must identify the most pivotal roles in your organization, play a key role in filling them and listen to what the people in those roles tell you…If we put the right people in the right spots, ensure that they have the appropriate resources and training, listen to them, and let them do their jobs, the ship will hum. If we don't, we jeopardize our ship's overall performance—and, quite possibly, the well-being of our women and men."[17]

Underestimating Emotions

A final judgment error to pay attention to is underestimating the role emotions play in decision-making. Your own emotions can strongly influence how you see a potential decision. If you are not aware of your emotions, they can bias your decisions. Emotions can create blind spots and cloud your judgment. The consequence can be quite dramatic.

Leaders can create an artificial split between their intellect and their emotions. As a consequence, emotionally based decisions can masquerade as rational ones. If you have a disconnect between thinking and emotion, your decision making can appear confusing to others. It will be difficult for you to evaluate the accuracy of your judgment over time.

If you try to suppress your emotional side too much, you will underestimate the impact of your decisions on others because you will be focused on just the rational aspect of the decision. Your emotions are an important aspect of your capacity for empathy. If you eliminate emotions from your decision making, you will be much more likely to generate the resistance I talked about in Chapter Three. Remember, emotions and thinking are both valid elements of judgment. Keep your radar on for this judgment mistake in yourself and others.

LOOK INTO THE MIRROR

Effective judgment is all about making refinements. While it is easier to look outward than inward, this chapter is not just about evaluating other people; it is about continuing to have discipline about refining your own judgment.

A good first step you can take is to look at your decision-making patterns from a historical perspective. Keep a decision log and take time every week to update it. At regular periods, you might go back and do an audit of your decisions over the last month, year, or three years. You might ask yourself these questions: Have my decisions been successful? Have I made decisions that have worked out as I expected them to and can I explain how I came to my decisions?

You can take time and really look at your decisions without ego involved in it. There are decisions that take a while to play out; it may take a couple of years before you know if it was a good decision or not. A good or bad hiring decision typically takes months to assess. Six months after the hiring decision, you can ask yourself, "Has this person successfully integrated?" A year later you might ask, "Has this person had impact and made real contributions?"

Refine your judgment by examining your choices. This involves self-questioning followed by honest answers: Have I learned from my mistakes? If a person I hired has not worked out, why hasn't he fit in? What can I, as a leader, learn from this mistake? If I had the chance to revisit or change a decision what would I do differently?

If you see you have a pattern in making a particular kind of judgment error, you can pay attention to it and work to correct it. With this perspective, you can identify your tendencies before they negatively affect you.

If you are usually quick to make decisions, remind yourself that even though you want to make this decision right now, you may have another week to let it progress. Or if you often delay until an opportunity has passed, you can make it a goal to make decisions more crisply. Remember to incorporate the decision window into your decision-making process.

You can talk out your decision-related thinking with a trusted advisor. That person will be able to give you outside perspective on the situation and help you avoid the types of decision-making pitfalls of the past. Ask this advisor what variables you may have missed that you ought to consider or what tangential variables should you be leaving out of your decision-making?

When it comes to falling in love with your decision, you can take a look at your attachment behaviors and ask yourself: Just how attached am I to this decision? How willing am I to look at alternatives? If you have a tendency to fall in love with your decisions, you must really consider other options, even when you don't want to. You can ask others to tear apart your idea and play the devil's advocate. Once you recognize you are prone to these tendencies, you can counteract them.

While it is vital to understand mistakes and correct them, it is important to understand why a particular decision was a good one. You can ask yourself these kinds of questions: Why was this decision a success? Why was it a good hire? Why did that person make it when others didn't? What did I do when I made this decision? Did I follow a methodology; what variables did I weigh heavily when I hired this person? Did I have a well thought out decision-making process? Did I follow it? Were the priorities I used the right ones? Have I demonstrated the ability to act in a more big picture way? Have I demonstrated the capability to focus on what is best for the business?

You can put the lens of judgment evaluation on others, and you can use it to take a look at your own judgment abilities. Just like a GPS helps you arrive at your destination, your judgment is the process by which you arrive at good decisions. In the next chapter I'll outline design principles that will help you build an organization that can keep up with you.

ACCELERATION TOOL #7: DECISION PRE-FLIGHT CHECKLIST

Use this tool to sharpen your decision-making skills.

- What is the decision to be made?
- What is the decision window? Is it minutes, days, weeks, or months?
- Who needs to make the decision?
- Who needs to be involved in the decision? Who will be impacted by the decision? Who has veto power? Who needs to be consulted before the decision is made? Who needs to own the decision after it is made?
- What is the magnitude of the decision? How significant are the consequences? How far-reaching are the implications?
- What information is needed to make the decision?
- What are the decision drivers?
- What does the risk profile of the decision look like?
- Look at the decision from at least three different perspectives (i.e., customer, stakeholder, and competitor).
- What are possible unintended consequences of the decision?
- Will the decision affect or compound other decisions?
- Can the decision be reversed or changed? What is the window for revisiting the decision?

Part III: Design It and Build It

❖ ❖ ❖

CHAPTER 8

Design a Fast Machine

❖ ❖ ❖

*"You don't have to worry about whether the car is
set up right or not; you know it is, and it's down to
you. Ultimately, that's what every driver wants."*

BOBBY RAHAL, INDIANAPOLIS 500 WINNER

REGARDLESS OF YOUR TALENT AS a driver, you must rely on your car to
carry you across the finish line. The maintenance performed by
the pit crew is vital in keeping the driver on the track. But if the
car malfunctions, even the best driver can lose the race.

Long before the race, though, that speed machine had to be
designed and built. Great care and expense goes into creating
these elite vehicles, and they are a crucial element in creating a
winning racing team. A driver does not want to be thinking about
the car's design as he is racing around the track. He must depend
on the mechanics and set-up being right so he can make second-
by-second decisions in the race with confidence.

Similarly, the faster leader must ensure his organization is a
finely tuned machine. Leaders are dependent on their companies'
cultures and the teams they have assembled. Having confidence

in the organization allows the faster leader to successfully drive the organization forward. To create a fast culture, a leader needs to play three very important roles: **designer**, **builder**, and **driver**. We'll be covering these roles in the next three chapters.

Let's tackle the role of designer first. To design a fast culture, it helps to have an idea of what one looks like. In my experience, fast cultures have several characteristics in common. Here are the top fourteen I have encountered:

1. There is a clear sense of direction and purpose in the organization. Goals and strategies are linked to this direction and team members know how they fit into the grand scheme of things.
2. Time is treated as a precious commodity. The importance of using time effectively and efficiently is a core foundational value of the culture of speed.
3. There is a focus on transparency. Leaders are open with their team to allow team members to understand how decisions are made. Leaders make sure the team has the information they need to make quick and accurate decisions.
4. There is minimal politics and unnecessary drama. Leaders try their best to create an environment where politics are frowned upon. When leaders encounter politics, they aggressively deal with it and minimize it.
5. There are well-honed decision-making processes. Ownership and involvement is clear.
6. There is minimal hierarchy. The culture is not bogged down with too many levels of bureaucracy. However, there is sufficient hierarchy in place to avoid chaos and drive performance. This allows the culture to adapt and be agile.

7. There is alignment across the different functions. Everyone is on the same page and pulling together.
8. Team members have productivity tools that work. For example, calendar systems, communication platforms, and project management systems are effective and efficient. Processes are kept to a minimum so people don't get overloaded.
9. Problems are solved quickly. Anything that distracts or slows down the team is dealt with aggressively. Needless distractions are not tolerated. The team is focused on winning the race.
10. There are high expectations and people work hard to meet them. There is a track record of consistently meeting those high expectations.
11. A priority is placed on learning. Mistakes are acknowledged, not punished.
12. Adequate resources are assigned to get things done. Projects are not starved and people have the tools to complete their tasks.
13. The environment is high on engagement and people want to be there.

THE ARCHITECTURE OF SPEED

How do you design an environment that has these fourteen characteristics? A fast organization is not an accident. It is the result of thoughtful design and it is the most important thing a leader creates. The best leaders spend considerable time thinking about their organizational architecture because it creates and shapes behavior. Your organizational architecture is a blueprint for the culture you want to create whether you are starting a new organization or changing an existing one. You are operating as the **Chief Architect (CA)**, one of the faster leader roles I mentioned in the Introduction, as you design a work culture that is optimized for speed.

I cannot emphasize enough how important it is to have a blueprint for building a faster organization whether you are starting from scratch or dealing with an existing enterprise. Your blueprint will map out what kinds of behavior you expect, the direction of the organization, what is important and what is not, and the strategies you will employ to meet your goals. It will touch every aspect of your organization. Be sure to give it a lot of thought.

As you read this chapter, adapt it to your unique situation. You may be building an organization from scratch, inheriting an intact team, or changing a team that you are currently leading. If you have inherited an organization, some of the design elements I am going to reference may already be in place. Be sure to leverage those things that are consistent with what you want to create and incorporate them into your blueprint.

Depending on where you sit in the organization, certain design elements may be more relevant to you than others. I'll be using the phrase, design elements, to encompass a wide range of factors that go into organizational design (i.e., vision, mission, charter). I would suggest you try to incorporate multiple design elements to strengthen your work culture foundation.

In this chapter, I'll cover five important design principles that will help you decide which elements to include in your organizational design. The key design principles include:

- Guidance
- Alignment

- Optimization
- Flexibility
- Obsolescence

Design Principle #1: Guidance

A driver never leaves the pit without a race plan that details his target speed, refueling strategy, positioning, and final sprint timing. Similarly, any organization needs a race plan that articulates its goals, direction, and aspirations beyond the next quarter. An organization, no matter what size, needs to have a longer term view that acts as a foundation for making short-term choices and strategies. Without such a plan, the organization will not have focus and clarity, and short-term issues will dominate its attention.

Think of organizational guidance mechanisms as existing on multiple levels. Just like an Indy 500 race plan, the focus can be on the finish line, lap 250, dealing with competition, or pit strategy. Guidance mechanisms are not optional; they are required for leaving the pit and entering the track. The main differences relate to the level of detail, the time frame, and ambiguity. The different guidance mechanisms in the leader's toolkit that I'll cover include:

- Vision
- Mission
- Charter
- Values
- Strategy

Vision

An organization's race plan is based on its vision and the leader needs to be in the driver's seat in creating a vision that is viable, inspiring, and enduring. But caution is in order.

The idea of having a vision and accompanying vision statement became popular in the '80s and '90s. As is the case with many popular management ideas, vision became over used and trivialized. It became somewhat of a cliché. I've heard leaders call it "the vision thing" in a dismissing tone. Having a vision has become so mechanical that companies and teams can think of it merely as an item on the to-do list.

In a popular scenario, a management team will go offsite for several days to craft a vision statement. They'll return with a vision statement that provides little substance and lots of rhetoric. What happens is the vision loses its power to be a viable race plan. It becomes only a slogan that no one can recall.

When working with an organization, I can easily tell when there is no vision. The organizational conversation is dominated by what competitors are doing. Without a vision, talk is focused on what is going on with other companies and not what is happening at home. Competitor behavior can't be the driving force behind your vision. Vision is about mapping the future and focusing on your unique values and advantages.

While many leaders and team members have had poor experiences with creating and nurturing a vision for their organization or team, it is important to remember that vision is exciting and powerful when done right. Poor execution does not invalidate the power of the vision concept.

One of the biggest differences I see between leaders who are less successful and those who consistently come in first is **discipline around vision**. Successful leaders not only create an engaging vision, they keep the organization focused on it over time. Every organization, no matter what size, needs a vision to be successful. Where to start?

Vision involves crafting a desired future on several levels and thinking about a time frame that is years out. Vision doesn't change every year, it has a long runway. It is aspirational in nature.

As I work with leaders, I try to find the limits of their vision and challenge them to see further. Much like eyesight, every leader has a different focus point. Some leaders can see out two years with clarity, whereas others can see out ten years. The keys to developing a vision involve challenging oneself, creativity, the ability to shift perspective, and comfort with ambiguity.

You get what you plan for and envision. Where you need to go is different from where you have been. A leader has to be on point, in front of the organization, anticipating, predicting, and forecasting. Vision takes time to develop and refine, and the end product needs to be a thing you can support with passion and consistency.

Getting Started

Creating a vision that is inspiring and will stand the test of time is not easy. In fact, more leaders fail at this activity than succeed. Why is creating a vision that is effective, useful, and successful so difficult? For one thing, the vision process itself requires a different way of thinking. It is easier and compelling to focus on the short term rather than the abstract future. We find it easier to focus on the tangible output in our day-to-day achievements. We reward companies and leaders for short-term thinking.

Vision is one thing you, as a leader, cannot delegate. While you can and will involve others, vision is one of your main outputs as a leader. Vision is a key element of your leadership legacy and your leadership platform. The final product of the vision building process is a vision that is enduring and powerful. The ingredients of a good vision usually incorporate the following characteristics:

- It targets a lofty goal, problem, or challenge that is relevant to your business or organizational space. It needs to stretch the organization. You never complete a vision.
- Vision needs to incorporate macro trends or patterns you think will impact the business.
- It is inspirational and needs to engage your team at a fundamental emotional level. Customers should find it attractive and respond to it. Be forewarned—inspiration is the most difficult aspect to accomplish in building a vision.
- It should be capable of driving the performance of the organization. You should be able to align your strategies, tactics, structure, and other processes to it.
- Vision should be clear, concise, and easy to communicate. It should not be full of jargon or trendy words.
- Vision should capture what makes your organization unique and stand out from the crowd.

An Inspirational Framework

Done well, an inspirational vision helps accelerate an organization and improve its productivity because people are energized by it, aligned to it, and will go out of their way to support it. An inspirational vision fosters high levels of self-management and self-leadership within team members.

However, too many organizations create visions that fail the inspiration test because they rely on clichés or "business speak" (e.g., empower, synergy, paradigm, out of the box thinking, etc.), or focus too much on just the financial aspects of the business. For vision to be inspirational, it needs to go way beyond the rational goals of business or work and connect deeply to core human experiences, needs, and, values. It needs to connect and engage people at the personal level and motivate them to do and give their best. While there are many options, I have found there are ten consistent inspirational themes that connect well with diverse groups. Here are the themes:

1. Making a Difference
This theme emphasizes that people's work matters and the goal of organization is to have a positive impact in the world. Altruism and helping others are consistently part of this theme.

2. Leadership
Forging a path forward rather than following others is at the heart of this theme. Organizations that adopt this theme take pride in setting their own direction. Values like integrity and credibility are often related to the leadership theme.

3. Reach Our Potential
This theme is all about growth and doing the best you can. You strive to continually grow, learn, and develop. You keep pushing yourself to improve.

4. Fun
Enjoying life is the foundation of this theme. Work is approached with a sense of play, enjoyment, and spontaneity. Creativity is emphasized.

5. Curiosity
Exploration and understanding fuel this theme. You value understanding the "why" and "how" of things. Following your instincts and interests is important.

6. Achievement

Striving and reaching difficult goals is the basis for this theme. Doing something that no one else has ever accomplished before is at the core of the achievement vision.

7. Innovation

Creativity and coming up with unique solutions and approaches underlie innovation. Innovation is more than just improving things; it is coming up with radical new solutions.

8. Responsibility

The responsibility theme is all about having a strong sense of duty and accountability. You protect, guard, nurture and serve.

9. Community

Having a strong sense of connection and affiliation with each other drives community. You will often hear the word family used in organizations that prize this theme.

10. Winning

Competition and coming in first is the goal of this theme. Beating out competition, overcoming rivals, dominating a market characterize the winning theme.

Do your homework and give thought to each of the desired vision ingredients. Refine the key inspirational themes you want to tap into (don't overdo it—one or two is all you need). You don't have to have everything all worked out before engaging your team, but you want to have given preparatory thought to each item to allow you to guide the rest of the process. Remember, vision is the foundation of your leadership and is the race plan for your organization. Faster leaders realize that the investment in vision pays off in building a culture of speed because everyone is following the same course.

The Vision Building Process
The next step in the vision process is to decide how you will refine the vision statement and complete it. I suggest you follow a three step design process. First, create a rough framework or straw man that captures key themes you want to emphasize. You will need to do this work independently and spend quality time on the effort. Second, engage a small group of people to help you flesh out and refine the straw man. Third, show it to the larger organization and get their feedback before finalizing the vision. You'll want to have a high quality product at this stage.

One of the most important questions to consider is who to involve in the vision process. You can make it a management team activity or you can include a cross-section of the organization. There is no one right way to do it. One suggestion I have is to keep the team relatively small to start. Between six and ten is a manageable group size. If the team is too small, you won't get enough different perspectives. If the team is too big, it will slow you down.

Pick a process that fits you, your style, and your preferences. The process has to engage and hook you before you can engage others. You have to have an investment in the vision and in making it real for the organization. You have to feel a very real sense of connection with what you are doing. You and your organization will live with the vision for many years. While you are the primary architect for the process, **you will want to use a process that allows others to experience a sense of ownership for the vision**. You can't be the only one driving the vision. You want to infect other members of your organization with it. You want people to have skin in the game.

Before launching the vision design process, map out the steps you want to take with the team. Here are a few suggestions:

- Determine how many sessions you want to target for the overall vision process. While you will need to be flexible depending on how fast the team works, you want to set up expectations about how long the process will last. Too many leaders try to rush the process. Give the team time to produce a great vision product.
- Decide on the working environment for the process. I recommend you take the team offsite to get them out of the day to day work mode. Trying to build a vision in the workplace doesn't work very well because of all the distractions and demands of work. If cost is a concern, you can use onsite facilities but take steps not to be interrupted or distracted. The vision building process can take several steps so make sure the working environment allows you to continue the process to closure.
- Create a set of pre-work actions and documents for the working team to complete before the first session. Pre-work will help improve the quality and speed up the process. This is where your straw man comes into play.
- Think about the ground rules you want to set to manage the process. Ground rules help you manage interactions and set expectations. I generally recommend that the leader create a few ahead of time and review them with the team at the beginning of the vision meetings to get the ball rolling. An example might be no cell phones allowed. It is important to allow the team members to propose additional ground

rules. When team members participate in the ground rule process their sense of connection and ownership is enhanced. Be sure to formally ratify the ground rules in the first meeting.

- Be clear in your own mind what role you will play and how you will conduct yourself. If you are too hands-on, you can stifle creativity. If you are too hands-off, the process can easily get off track.
- Think about what you want the end product to look like.

I like to suggest to leaders that they think about their roles as guiding and shaping the process, adding value through their insight and awareness of strategic influences and trends. Leaders can provide fundamental grounding in terms of what is right for the organization and what the organization is capable of doing.

Manage the Design Process

If you have people who are distracted and think the whole vision process is a waste of time, you are not going to get their best ideas. You want to set the stage so people come in excited and ready to go. It is important to remember that you cannot force a vision to take shape. It has to emerge.

During the process, you will want to challenge ideas until the team stops thinking at the superficial level and begins to consider the broader picture. You are looking for the right level of engagement and attention. You want to keep challenging the team to dig deeper and think clearly. What you want is a true vision. If at any time you see that your team is not engaged and you don't see the quality of thinking you need, you will want to refocus their attention on the core objective.

Help guide the process by asking thoughtful questions. What will our organization will look like in five, ten, or fifteen years? What are the key variables that might shape the vision? Will our customer base change, and if so, in what ways? What kinds of new talent or skills might we need? What forces might make the vision obsolete? What new technologies might come along? What new markets might open up? What things at the macro level do we need to think about? What untapped markets can we sell to? What new kinds of relationships do we need to establish with our customers and our partners? Will our collection of services and products need to change? Where are we going to be geographically? Where are we going to concentrate our resources? What do we want our legacy to be? These kinds of questions help fuel the building of a vision.

You will go through multiple variations of vision statements before you end up with a product you and the team are satisfied with. Remember the qualities of an effective vision mentioned previously and test your vision against those criteria.

Here are three examples of company visions:

- "PepsiCo's responsibility is to continually improve all aspects of the world in which we operate - environment, social, economic - creating a better tomorrow than today."
- "Our vision is to be earth's most customer centric company; to build a place where people can come to find and discover anything they might want to buy online." (Amazon)
- "Life is better when technology does what it's supposed to do. We make that happen for everyone by providing dramatically easier ways to solve complex technical support problems." (Support.com)

I'll talk about road testing your vision in the next chapter.

Mission

Dropping down a level of abstraction from the vision, an organization's mission defines why it exists. In other words, a mission clarifies the organization's purpose. It articulates how the organization will pursue its vision. Generally, a mission is achievable and more tangible than the vision. It has a "win the race" quality.

By developing a mission in support of a vision, leaders create a guidance mechanism that team members can translate into concrete goals and operational practices. Here are a couple examples of mission statements to spur your thinking:

- "To combine aggressive strategic marketing with quality products and services at competitive prices to provide the best insurance value for consumers." (AFLAC)
- "It is the Mission of Advance Auto Parts to provide personal vehicle owners and enthusiasts with the vehicle related products and knowledge that fulfill their wants and needs at the right price. Our friendly, knowledgeable and professional staff will help inspire, educate and problem-solve for our customers."

Charter

Still further down the abstraction ladder, the charter of an organization outlines its scope and reach. It defines the boundaries and responsibilities that it operates within. A clear charter will communicate what the organization will do and what it won't do. You should have a charter for the larger organization, and each functional unit within the organization should have its own charter.

Here is an example of a charter from Henry Schein, a company that provides health care products:

To Our Customers

We provide the best quality and value in products and services, helping our customers, as trusted advisors and consultants to:

- Deliver quality health care to patients
- Efficiently operate and grow practices
- Increase financial return and financial security

To Our Shareholders and Venture Partners

We endeavor to provide continued growth and profitability, resulting in a superior return on investment.

To Team Schein Members

We foster an entrepreneurial environment, offer exciting opportunities for personal and professional growth, and treat each individual with respect and dignity.

To Our Suppliers

Together, we create an environment that enables us to grow our respective businesses in the spirit of partnership, with each making a fair profit.

To Society at Large

We act in a socially responsible manner to:

- Further humanitarian relief and disaster response
- Increase access to health care among underserved populations
- Strengthen wellness programs and volunteer activities
- Enhance health care advocacy and education
- Positively address environmental concerns
- Maintain the highest standards of corporate governance.

Notice how the charter clarifies both the relationships that are important to organization and the responsibilities that go along with those relationships.

Values

Values are beliefs of an organization that produce a strong emotional connection or attachment. They articulate behavioral priorities and provide guidelines for how people throughout the organization should conduct themselves. They can serve as a decision-making tool in daily interactions. If you have been involved in a vision building process, you probably touched on value-based elements. I suggest you spin out values as a standalone guidance mechanism because of their ability to influence the behavior of your team members. Again, the end product will be a succinct, focused document.

When leaders create a values document, they are creating an organizational guidance mechanism that establishes standards for conduct in a variety of settings. An organization's values might be thought of as its moral compass for how it goes about its business. While circumstances may change, values do not. The vast majority of high performing organizations have a well developed values-based culture.

Defining and communicating an organization's values is not a process to be taken lightly. Once they are out in the open, they become a very strong accountability mechanism. Leaders who act in ways that are inconsistent with stated values can undermine team member's commitment and engagement. Here are some examples of values from companies I have worked with:

- Innovation
- Agility
- Partnerships

- Results
- Discipline
- Humility
- Teamwork

An important foundational element related to the expression of values is the existence of ground rules. I touched on this concept briefly before in this chapter. Ground rules are design element that is often overlooked by leaders. As a faster leader, it is important to remember you are the architect of the environment and you want to establish a desired set of behaviors within your organization. If you want to build a culture of speed, you must establish firm ground rules that encourage speed and then hold yourself and others to the same standards.

Rather than formal laws, ground rules are informal basic agreements about what is acceptable or not acceptable in a given situation. As a leader, there are many behaviors you may want to encourage or restrict. If you establish ground rules about what you expect, it can help to shape the organization in a profound way.

How do you do this, particularly if you've already been at the organization for a period of time? You have to be aware of what you want to achieve and how you impact those in your company. Ask yourself: What are the behaviors you really want to encourage? Is it proactiveness, openness, aggressiveness? List the types of behaviors you consider key to your culture. It is important you are deliberate and conscious of what you are trying to create.

It is a good idea to get your team involved and participate in the formation of ground rules. One way is to sit down with them and talk about what is important to the group and what it means to be on this team. This is a good opportunity to propose the values you would like to be part of your environment and get feedback on what team members think is important. It's important to get members of your team to buy into the rules and have them committed to the values. Once the team is in agreement, you can reinforce the rules and hold people accountable.

Some leaders prefer to have a written agreement to ensure everyone is clear and informed. Whatever you decide, it is crucial that once a ground rule is established, you must not break it. Don't be the type of leader who feels they are exempt from certain rules. As a leader, if you think the ground rules don't apply to you, be ready for toxic fallout. While it can be challenging, you should model the ground rules at all times. You must be committed to support any ground rule you establish 110 percent. You should be a good example that others would want to emulate.

Leaders who do not follow team rules can generate a lot of resentment within the organization. For example, a leader who establishes a ground rule that all meetings must start and end on time, but then is consistently late ends up compromising the ground rule. The rest of the team resents the double standard and the leader's credibility suffers.

Be on the lookout for unacknowledged ground rules that are problematic. For example, lack of openness can become an unstated ground rule. People feel they cannot bring in problems or challenge others because they will be punished if they do. The value of openness in this situation becomes compromised and the opposite value becomes the ground rule. This is what I call a dysfunctional ground rule and is very dangerous to your organizational culture. If you are not careful, dysfunctional ground rules become elements of the environment. Remember to be mindful about both functional and dysfunctional ground rules and you'll find the speed of your organization increases dramatically.

Strategy

Another organizational guidance mechanism is strategy. An organization's strategy articulates its formula for success and needs to support its vision, mission, and charter. There are typically two main elements to a strategy: identification of the target customer or audience, and the unique value proposition you bring to the table. Strategy provides a sense of focus by clarifying what you are going to do and what you are **not** going to do. A good strategy forces you to articulate how you are truly different and what is unique about your offering. The best strategies can be summarized in fifteen words or less, and should be easy to understand and communicate. A good strategy can be challenging to create.

Since strategy is dealing with the unknowable future, the process of developing one can make leaders anxious and fearful. As a way of compensating, leaders often create pages and pages of planning documents with lots of graphs and tables, and they tend to focus a lot of energy on the financials. It is important to remember that planning is not the same thing as strategy.

Rather than avoiding the anxiety that accompanies developing a strategy for the future, I suggest that leaders need to embrace it. Even the most effective leaders are not entirely comfortable in the strategy making process. Defining a strategy essentially means making a bet or decision that takes options off the table.

Keep your strategy simple and clear, and continually test whether your assumptions and data are correct. Don't be afraid to change it if you find it no longer works. To summarize, your strategy should have an objective or end goal, a clearly defined scope (review your charter and customers), and should emphasize your advantage. Here are a couple of strategy statements that fit the criteria listed above:

- "Everyday low prices for a broad range of goods that are always in stock in convenient geographic locations." (Walmart)
- "To provide for all the financial needs of our high-net-worth customers—those with liquid financial assets of more than $250,000—*through retirement.*" *(Merrill Lynch)*

Design Principle #2: Alignment

I introduced the notion of alignment in the Introduction and have been touching on it throughout the book. Earlier in this chapter, I highlighted how vision, mission, charter, values, and strategy need to be connected in a hierarchy of focus. Alignment is at the heart of faster organization design and all of your design elements need to be connected and supportive of one another. It helps to think about your organization as a system of interconnected parts that need to work together.

A Formula One race car that is out of alignment will shake, rattle, steer poorly, and burn through tires quickly. The driver will have to fight to keep it on the track and other cars will quickly lap it.

All of the parts of the car have a relationship to each other. Rather than acting in isolation, the parts of the machine have to work well with each other to win races. Additionally, each part that goes into the car has an optimal performance expectation attached to it. This expectation, also known as a tolerance specification, is a range of performance parameters the part is expected to operate within and is critical to the notion of alignment.

For example, the pit crew chief will select the optimal tolerance specifications for the car's tires before the race. By targeting camber, castor, and toe which are important tire alignment factors, he will try to get the most out of the tires. He wants to minimize wear and maximize maneuverability. He is looking for the sweet spot in the performance curve. If the tire's performance moves outside of the tolerance specification, it will need to be adjusted or replaced before it fails.

What might an alignment tolerance specification within an organization look like? A good example is related to an organization's mission. As an organization attempts to fulfill its mission, its behavior may dynamically change over time as it deals with new opportunities and threats. The risk is the organization may gradually expand its mission beyond its scope or lose focus. This phenomenon is known as **mission creep**. To combat this tendency, I suggest leaders specify how much mission creep is acceptable within their organization. A leader might specify that small situational deviations are acceptable while larger ones are not. Since level of alignment can change over time, leaders need to keep a close eye on it.

Beyond the concept of tolerance specifications, there are many things that need to be in alignment for the organization to perform well. To encourage leaders to think about alignment as a design principle, I ask them to consider the following questions:

1. What are the design features of your organization that serve as the foundation? What are the wheels and what is the chassis?
2. What are the secondary organizational features that rest upon the foundation?
3. How is each feature of the organization connected to other features of the organization?
4. What are your design tolerance specifications for each important organizational feature?

5. How will you measure whether or not features are performing within your desired tolerances?
6. If you change an organizational feature, how will it affect other parts of the organization?

Design Principle #3: Optimization

Wind tunnels are used to prove or refine conceptual designs. By blowing air and smoke at high speed over and around a car prototype, any flaw can be spotted. Excess drag or resistance causes ripples in the air flow that can easily be seen and design modification can then be made.

While you can't put your organizational design in a wind tunnel, it is important to think about how you can optimize your organization. In Chapter Three I talked about how resistance can interfere with the performance of the organization and how every attempt should be made to minimize it. I'd like to add two additional concepts to the optimization framework: efficiency and effectiveness. Efficiency entails no wasted effort or resources and effectiveness involves prioritizing the right things.

Efficiency

Because the demands on our time have significantly increased, being more efficient has become a critical organizational capability. The goal of efficiency is to accomplish the maximum with the minimum amount of effort and resources. A secondary goal of efficiency is to not waste anything. This includes time, resources, and people.

Efficiency is primarily concerned with the "how" and rests on the notions of simplicity, clarity and repurposing. The ongoing challenges for a leader are to make sure they reduce the unnecessary complexity that continually creeps into work and to keep reinforcing goals to ensure their team does not get confused or overworked. Leaders need to think about how to leverage the same resources in different ways to get the maximum impact. Like MPG (miles per gallon) the leader wants to think about designing a culture that gets the most mileage out of the least fuel.

I am often involved in helping leaders apply efficiency principles to organizational design. I'll touch on a couple of examples to illustrate the power of efficiency. In one organization, we analyzed how much engineering time was spent in meetings that were not critical to the product development process. By identifying and eliminating unnecessary meetings we were able to shorten the average design time by fifteen percent and make more efficient use of engineering resources.

In another organization, we were able to take outbound marketing messages and repurpose them for internal team member communication. The messaging content was slightly modified and was then able to be used for a different audience and purpose.

Efficiency tactics you might want to consider include:

- Measuring what you and your team do to establish a baseline for performance. Improvements are built on this baseline.
- Establishing standards (both in terms of expectations and practices).
- Establishing review cycles to reinforce the discipline of efficiency and to test that processes are being followed.
- Reinforcing the mindset of "no waste"
- Continually looking for ways to do things faster and better.
- Finding ways to continually repurpose and reuse resources.

Effectiveness
Effectiveness is all about focusing on the things that really make a difference: it is working on the "right" things. Effectiveness is

about things working correctly and doing what they are designed to do.

In terms of focusing on the right things, an important concept related to effectiveness is the critical path (those 3 or 4 things that make the difference between success and failure) which I have talked about previously. The challenge for the leader is to understand the critical path and to make sure that adequate organizational resources are focused on it as part of the design process. It doesn't matter what color you paint the car if the engine and transmission don't work well together.

What you put in place must work well and accomplish its purpose. For example, processes that don't work or aren't used add drag to the organization. In the quest to reinforce effectiveness, the faster leader needs to continually test that things are doing what they are designed to do. What may look good in the design process may not transfer well to the work environment.

One organization I was asked to consult with was having problems in its donor engagement process. They had an elaborate engagement methodology in place but were not getting the levels of donation they wanted. After spending time evaluating the process and talking to prospective donors, it became clear to me that the organization was actually targeting the wrong donor audience. When they shifted their target audience in a limited marketing experiment, the results were overwhelmingly positive.

Another organization I was working with was having problems getting traction with customers on its newly released products. After talking to customers and reviewing existing products, I came to the conclusion that the company had fallen into the trap of making product decisions based on what they could build rather than what the customer wanted. By changing the product decision making process to focus more on what customers wanted, the company was able to gain more sales traction.

When what you are doing is not getting you the results you expect, try an alternative. The correlation between action and results is at the foundation of effectiveness.

Here are a few questions to help clarify how you can build effectiveness into your organizational design:

- What are the things that most impact the success of your business and team? They could be strategies or perspectives, people, products, processes, or other resources. What things, if absent, would cause the organization to fail?
- What is the purpose of each of your design elements? What are you trying to achieve?
- What are the most critical things the organization should be spending its time on?
- What are the performance results you would like to see?
- How will you know the different design elements are doing what they are supposed to do?
- How long will you give a design element to demonstrate it is working as expected?

When optimized, effectiveness and efficiency can become important elements in your fast culture design.

Design Principle #4: Flexibility
Increasingly, organizations need to be able to shift and pivot quickly to respond to changes in the environment. If an organization is too rigidly structured, it will be too slow and will be outperformed by faster rivals. Flexibility, as an organizational design element, is becoming more important.

How do you design an organization for flexibility? Here are five design principles I suggest leaders use to optimize organizational flexibility:

- Minimize hierarchy and structure. Too many organizational layers slow down decision making and impede information flow. Resist the temptation to add layers as your organization grows.
- Incorporate autonomous work groups whenever possible. Autonomous work groups have greater self-direction and freedom to do what they need to do. Another important element of autonomous work groups is they have all of the necessary functions and skill sets to perform their mission. They are self-contained. For example, you can put sales, marketing, engineering, and support together in one group.
- Think about load balancing and make allowance for it. In most organizations, work flow changes over time. Some work functions can be idle while other functions can be overwhelmed with work. Overloaded work teams can act as obstacles as work backs up behind them. Load balancing is a strategy that focuses on shifting resources to where they are needed most. To enable load balancing, you will need to cross-train your personnel and get them comfortable with work rotation.
- Think about points of failure or vulnerability. If you don't anticipate breakdowns, you won't design for them. Expect things to break or teams to fail. Your organization will be stress tested by competitors and changes in the environment. By thinking through points of failure you can compensate for them by building redundancy into your organizational

design. That way when one part fails it won't stop the whole organization.

- Build in a radar detector. Too many organizations become isolationist in their thinking and fall prey to a speed trap they didn't see coming. To be flexible, you have to have a connection to the outside world. You will want to design in a type of organizational radar to pick up changes in the environment that might impact you. A Formula One driver always has a pit crew member on the radio giving information on what is ahead of him on the track. If you have an organizational capability that is paying attention to external changes you can more rapidly respond to those changes. Many organizations leverage their sales and marketing functions to get information about changes or shifts that might impact the organization.

Design Principle #5: Obsolescence

Everything has a life cycle. Whether you are thinking about people, organizational structures, or work processes, it is helpful to remember that nothing lasts forever. When designing a fast organization, it is important to keep in mind whatever you build will fail at some point in time.

To drive home this point with the leaders I work with, I have them assign a timeline to all of the important design elements of their work culture. I ask them to make a life cycle estimate for each element in their culture and to think about data points that would indicate it is approaching end of life. The acceleration tool at the end of this chapter is designed to help a leader think through the limits of their organizational design.

In the next chapter I'll cover how to take the design concepts I introduced in this chapter and put them into practice. I'll walk you through several important actions such as assembling your pit crew, building a performance dashboard, and rapid prototyping. Get ready to build your fast organization.

Acceleration Tool #8: Fast Culture Design
Use this tool to refine and assess your thinking about your organization or team.

1. What is the timeline of your current organizational design? How long do you think it will be effective?
2. Estimate the effectiveness timeline for your top five team players? How long do you think each will continue to perform at a high level? When do you think they might begin to plateau?
3. Think about your top three work processes. Examples would be planning, product development, or service delivery. How long do you think each one will continue to work well?
4. What are the lifecycles of your current product or service offerings? When will they reach the end of their competitiveness?
5. Think about the external trends that are currently affecting your organization. How long do you think they will continue to have impact and influence?
6. Where have you built in redundancy to protect against failure?
7. How have you incorporated flexibility elements into your faster organization strategy?
8. What kinds of efficiency and effectiveness measures are you using to optimize your organization?
9. Have you established tolerance specifications for critical parts of your organization? Have you taken into consideration critical alignment strategies?
10. What guidance mechanisms are you utilizing?
11. What characteristics of the faster culture have you tried to build into your organization?

CHAPTER 9

Build a Fast Machine

❖   ❖   ❖

*"I've got a great team of engineers behind this race
car. I've got a great bunch of mechanics that make
it reliable. This car is developed to go out there and
be better than the Reynard, and I feel that it is."*

AL UNSER

Now that you have your blueprint for building a faster organization, it is time to actually build it and make it happen. It's time to
assemble your tools and resources, and start to work. You will need
to drive your design concepts into reality and road test them to
make sure everything works as planned. The strategies I cover in
this chapter are designed to help you achieve your goal of building a faster organization. These strategies work whether you are
dealing with an intact organization or building from scratch, be
sure to adapt them to your needs.   The keys to building a faster
organization include:

- Become a continuous recruiter
- Put your best team on the track

- Create a retention engine
- Team building
- Build your action network
- Create your performance dashboard
- Install a knowledge pump
- Use rapid prototyping
- Perform test drives and time trials

Become a Continuous Recruiter

People are the foundation of the faster culture and one of the most important roles you play as a faster leader is recruiter. You have to think of this role as a continual one. **You need to constantly recruit new talent to your organization to replace people who leave and re-recruit important pit crew members to stay.** Regardless of whether you have inherited a team or are creating one, your primary goal is to build the best team you can and this is a pursuit that never stops. By constantly hunting for talent you fulfill the role of the **Chief Recruiting Officer (CRO)** that I mentioned in the Introduction.

The CRO role is a high impact role that you need to do well. If you recruit the right type of talented top performers, they can have a huge impact on the overall productivity of the team. If you recruit a person who becomes an under performer, that person can sap your energy and cause tension within the team. A pit crew member who doesn't execute his role can lose a race for the team.

What specifically do you look for, how do you find it, or how do you know someone has potential to be a great fit on your team? These questions are important ones you need to answer during your recruitment process. What made a person successful in one organization can cause them to fail in another. Finding the right person is a big challenge. Additionally, promoting a previously successful crew member to a new role can lead to failure if they get in over their head. There is probably no decision that causes leaders more anxiety than who to hire. In practice, talent can be an elusive quality to identify, attract, and retain.

While most leaders recognize how important talent is to their team, they often don't allocate enough time to the process of recruitment. Why is this so?

With work schedules already filled to overflowing, it is no wonder many leaders simply don't have the time to devote to talent search. While knowing that hiring is important, it often ends up at the bottom of the priority list because of the time involved and other priorities that appear to be more urgent.

The default position for many leaders is they end up outsourcing this role to internal or external recruiters. While this approach may be easier, it adds significant risk to your talent strategy. There are several factors that contribute to the risk of the outsourcing approach.

First, what you think may be saving you time is actually costing you time. Many organizational recruitment processes are just too slow and time-consuming. Developing a job spec, publicizing the opening, sorting through resumes, and interviewing all take time. Multiple internal functions can be involved, and it can take a long time to fill an open job requisition. Recruitment cycles can be as long as six months to a year for certain types of positions and that amount of time can mean disaster if you are under time constraints.

Second, if you are dependent on other people or organizations (such as HR or recruiters) to find candidates because of your limited personal network, you add to your risk. These individuals who you rely on may not know much about the challenges of your work environment and the chemistry of your team.

Third, the formal interview process that many leaders rely on is a terrible way to select talent. Certain individuals are simply very good at interviewing, others are not. It is important to remember interview performance doesn't always translate to on the job performance. A skilled interviewer is not necessarily a skilled team member.

The net results of outsourcing your hiring efforts are job requisitions staying open for extended periods of time, other team members having to pitch in to cover the workload, or even worse, the pressure builds to a point where you make a hiring decision built on desperation. Instead of top performers, the team gets populated with whoever is available and the overall performance of the team deteriorates.

There is a better way. To fulfill the role of the CRO you can become a talent magnet.

Attract Talent

A faster organization begins with you. In Chapter Four I covered how important engagement is to organizational acceleration and what a leader could do to foster engagement. Now we need to take engagement to the next level. Only leaders who are able to attract and retain talent will be able to build a faster organization. If no one wants to be in your pit crew, you'll never make it across the finish line.

A talent magnet is a leader who consistently attracts top caliber talent. A talent magnet acts as an attractor and pulls people towards the organization. The net result is people seek you out rather than you expending energy to go out and recruit them. Think of yourself as exerting a magnetic pull on people to get the talent you seek. If you invest the time and energy to become a talent magnet, your speed as a leader will dramatically accelerate, because you will always be surrounded by talent. Talent enables speed.

To become a talent magnet you have to do two things really well. First, create a favorable public presence or brand for yourself that highlights qualities people find attractive in a manager or leader. Think of this as building your great boss brand. Second, you need to continually communicate your great boss message to allow talent to find you.

A Great Boss

The key to becoming a talent magnet is to first become a great boss. You really can't be one without being the other. Everyone loves a great boss. A boss who encourages team member development, acts as a resource, and challenges team members to be their best is rare and valuable.

Great bosses never have a shortage of people who want work for them or are willing to follow them from company to company. The flip side is also true. People will always talk and there is nothing that gets talked about with more frequency than a bad boss. A bad boss reputation sticks with someone over time and actually acts as a talent repellant. Talent avoids bad bosses because of their negative effect on people.

There are several important characteristics of a great boss. They possess skills others want to develop and are good at coaching others on how to develop those skills. They are seen as credible and trustworthy. They create environments where people can thrive. They keep politics to a minimum and don't play obvious favorites. They take the development of people seriously and spend considerable effort and energy to make sure people get the tools and coaching they need to develop their potential. They place a high value on people and make time for them. They follow the basic tenet: **coach top performers and manage lower performers**.

Promote Your Great Boss Brand

Once you're on the path of becoming a great boss, how do you communicate this to other people who have no direct experience with you? This is a critical question because you want to extend your reach beyond people who know you. Think of the process as launching your personal PR campaign. You don't want to keep the fact that you are a great boss a secret.

As a starting point, you need to have visibility both inside and outside your company. If you don't have visibility, people won't be able to find you. This means you will need to be active in industry associations and events, serve on panels, speak in public periodically, and generate articles or opinion pieces. You need to be easy to find and accessible. Networking and staying in touch with people is critical. Let it be known that you are constantly on the lookout for talented people with certain characteristics and be specific about what you're looking for. You will know you are being successful if the number of people trying to contact you or connect with you increases over time.

Give thought to the image you want to project. It must be absolutely consistent with who you are because your credibility depends on it. Think of the words you want to use and the themes you want to communicate and reinforce. The image you construct becomes the brand people encounter when they connect with you. It has long-term consequences, so it needs to be good. The goal is to develop your reputation as a leader who people want to work with.

A good place to start in building your great boss brand is to think about people you would like to work with and why. What characteristics do they possess that make them attractive to you? Think about great bosses you had in the past and what it was that made them great. Ask yourself, "What characteristics do I share with them? Why should people want to work with me?".

Once you've identified what makes you a great boss, don't be shy about sharing it with others. Remember, recruiting is a continuous process and you need to be constantly filling your pipeline with people who'd like to work with you. Think about how you'll continue to cultivate the people you come in contact with and keep relationships alive.

Always Have a Short List

People leave organizations all the time. They find a better job or a better opportunity and move on. Typically, when a team member leaves you don't get a lot of advanced warning. When they depart, they can leave behind a performance vacuum that causes critical projects or initiatives to fall behind schedule. The vacancy creates anxiety and uncertainty, and considerably raises the performance pressure on other members of your team.

Hiring cold candidates (people you don't know) is risky. You end up making important hiring decisions based on a person's interview behavior and references they select. Even if you hire a good replacement quickly, he will still need time to get up to speed.

These risks are why I recommend leaders develop and rigorously maintain a talent short list. Building a short list should be one of the key goals of your constant recruiting.

I learned the importance of this concept from a leader I worked with who never seemed to miss a beat. If one of his key people left, he always had someone he could call upon quickly to fill the shoes of the person who left. He made it a point to have backup candidates for all his key roles.

The short list is a small group of people, usually between four and eight, who have skills you will need in your team either in the short or longer term. They need to be a good fit chemistry wise with your existing team members. Building a short list is one of those critical investment activities that enables speed, and it is a key element of your faster leader ecosystem. These people are individuals you will want to bring into your team when the time is right. The key is to spend time getting to know them, their skill levels, aspirations, and compatibility with your work culture *before* you need them.

It is important they get to know you and make a personal connection with you. They need time to become familiar with your business and work environment, and understand that you might want to recruit them in the future. Getting to know a person in a more relaxed manner reduces the risk of making a bad hire.

The short list is your safety net and allows you to minimize the negative impact when a team member leaves. Your ultimate goal is to have a zero time recruitment interval, which means when you have a need on your team, you have someone on your short list ready to jump in quickly.

PUT YOUR BEST TEAM ON THE TRACK

A Formula One pit crew is an amazing example of skill, coordination, communication, and performance. Take for example the crew members who are responsible for the wheels. There are four corner men who are responsible for removing the lug nuts from each wheel with pneumatic guns. There are two wheel men per wheel. One takes off the old tire and one puts the new tire on. What's truly amazing is the best crews can replace all four tires in less than four seconds.

With the fame and popularity of race car drivers, it can be easy to think of racing as an individual sport. But any driver will tell you he can only do so much without the help of his racing team. That team includes the owner, sponsors, manager, crew chief, car chief, engine tuners, tire specialists, engineers, mechanics, and many others behind the scenes.

As with the race car driver, talent helps you succeed. The more talent you have on your team that works well together, the more successful you will be. High-performing teams are populated with talent that works well with each other.

Earlier in this chapter, I talked about your role as a talent magnet. Now let's dig down deeper into what to look for in putting your pit crew together. Are you ready to step into the role of the **Chief Assessment Officer (CAO)**?

Think of talent as top performers who possess considerable upside potential and are compatible with your leadership culture. They mesh well with other members of the team. They are individuals who consistently demonstrate the ability to take on added scope and responsibility while maintaining high performance standards. They are highly scalable and demonstrate limited weaknesses and liabilities. Beyond these general characteristics, the individual qualities of talent can vary significantly from organization to organization.

It is important to note that not just any type of talent will work. Talent needs to fit in with your work culture, values, and your leadership style. Incompatible talent can be disruptive to your team and create a host of negative issues you will have to deal with. It's important to look for the right type of talent.

Not only must each member of the racing team be talented, but it is crucial they all work together seamlessly. Their work ensures the driver need only concentrate on driving that car across the finish line. Likewise, you need a team that keeps the engines of your business running smoothly allowing you to concentrate on the leadership role.

The faster leader needs a pit crew that can achieve similar success under the pressure of competition and change. You need to assemble a crew that is driven to win. What does your winning pit crew look like? Let's pop the hood and take a look.

Success Factors

Just like a professional race team, you'll want to give serious thought to the skills and profiles of people you want to have on your team. Not everyone with talent will be able to fit into your unique environment. Personal characteristics, as well as skills, are important to assess and evaluate. I have been involved in many coaching situations where a talented person was hired but didn't work out because of a mismatch with the company culture.

You want to pick winners and top performers that fit your system and culture. To pick the best pit crew members, ask yourself these questions:

- What are the most important values and characteristics of your work culture?
- What is your team chemistry like?
- What kinds of experience are you looking for?
- What are the current skill set needs of your organization?
- What skills sets will you need in the future, both short term and long term?
- What kinds of roles will you need in your team going forward?
- How quickly do you need people to get up to speed?

- Are there any impending changes on your radar detector that would affect your talent needs?
- What have you learned from past hiring mistakes?
- What types of individuals work best with you?

The Eleven-Factor Talent Evaluation

After giving thought to the pit crew selection questions, I suggest you develop a more detailed talent checklist and use it to screen potential new hires and evaluate your existing team members on an ongoing basis. A talent evaluation checklist will help guide your decision making about whether to focus on developing your internal talent or looking outside the organization to bring in new talent. Just like a Formula One driver performing a pre-race checklist, you will identify any potential issues early and avoid making a bad hiring decision.

To assist leaders in evaluating talent, I created the Eleven-Factor Talent Evaluation (EFTE). You will want to include other people in validating your perceptions and observations whenever possible. I suggest you use the EFTE to develop a profile on each of your pit crew members, as well as, potential new hires. It will take time initially to get familiar with the model and the questions, but the more you use it the quicker you will become in evaluating people.

As a first step in the evaluation process, observe a person's current behavior as it relates to the different factors. Do you see evidence to score them as strong or weak on a particular factor? When evaluating new hire potentials, you can modify the questions listed below each factor for use in an interview situation. You can review their experience to see if they have demonstrated the factor in the past. Use the questions under each factor to guide your assessment and evaluation process. For your current pit crew members, you can keep a log of your observations and interactions with them for each factor over time. Here are the eleven factors:

Factor One: Self-Concept

By understanding how a person defines himself, you can get a sense of how they prefer to live their life and what they value.

- Is their sense of self clearly defined, or is it more generalized? You can get at this question by asking them to describe themselves in a couple of sentences.
- Is their sense of self related to the roles they play or the affiliations they have, or do they define themselves in other ways? Look at their background and experience, and see what types of connections they sustain.
- Do they view themselves as capable of personal change or are they more set in their ways? Ask them to describe situations where they have gone through significant change and what they learned during the process.
- How robust and accurate is their self-awareness? This is generally validated by talking to references and other people who have had experience with them.

Factor Two: Skills

A skills assessment can help determine what kind of role you can put a person in and give you an idea of their upside potential. Certain skills are more scalable than others. For example, if someone is a skilled learner you can put them in a role they haven't performed previously because they can quickly pick up things.

- Are their skills broad-based or narrowly focused? Are they more of a specialist or generalist? You will want to look at their background and evaluate the kind of experience they have.

- What level of skill do they possess in the areas you deem important? Are they performing at the novice, competent, or expert level? Novice level is a beginner who operates by trial and error. Competent is a skilled individual who can handle most situations. Experts can teach others and perform well under extreme conditions.

- Are their skills relevant and up to date? Check to see that they have engaged in learning activities and courses to keep up to date in what is going on in their discipline.

- Are they quick thinking and acting? Ask them scenario based questions (e.g., what if...) that have no obvious right answer to get a sense of how they think on their feet.

Factor Three: Motivation

Motivation is one of the more difficult qualities to assess because it must often be inferred from behavior. As a general rule, people choose to commit time and energy to things that are meaningful and important to them. Motivation shows up in the choices people make.

- Are they more motivated internally or externally? Do they supply their own motivation or are they influenced by consequences and reinforcers? While most people are a blend, you want to get a sense of what side they tend to gravitate towards. Look for examples in their background where they demonstrated self motivation. How important are things like salary and recognition to them? Do they have examples of experiences where they succeeded despite opposition or lack of support?

- What are their primary motivational drivers? While you can ask someone directly about their motivations, you will get additional perspective by asking them about activities they choose to devote their free time to. You can ask forced choice questions that contrast opposite behaviors (e.g., would you rather work by yourself or in a group, would you rather do something new or something you have done before). Common motivational drivers include: achievement, autonomy, control, competition, creativity, order, recognition, affiliation, power, and fear.

Factor Four: Discipline

Discipline in a work context, can basically be thought of as an individual's commitment to the job and their willingness to put in the hours and effort to get a task accomplished. Discipline shows up in an individual's ability to avoid distraction and stay focused on the task at hand. Discipline is at the heart of self-management and the ability to work autonomously on things that are hard work. A strong sense of duty and responsibility go hand in hand with discipline. Here are a few questions to consider for assessing a person's discipline level:

- Have they demonstrated they are willing to put in long hours to get the job done?
- Do they possess a strong sense of ownership and commitment to their work?
- How much management and supervision bandwidth do they require?
- Are they capable of performing tasks that have little or no motivation value for them?

- Are they disciplined in how they use their time and responsible when it comes to utilizing company resources?

Factor Five: Learning Ability

Learning ability is one of the most important things to evaluate in terms of individual scalability. As a person progresses in their career, they constantly encounter new things that are outside of their experience. Additionally, what may have worked in the past may not work in new situations that place a premium on a person's ability to learn and adjust.

- How easily do they pick up new things that don't relate to their experience?
- How do they approach learning in areas that are not high on their motivational priority list?
- How do they perform when their existing model or framework no longer works?
- How curious and willing to experiment are they?
- How easily do they shift from one perspective to another?

Factor Six: Shortcomings

No one is perfect. Everyone has deficiencies of one type or another. It might be a skill deficit. It might be a personality flaw or motivation problem. It is important for the leader to look for flaws or shortcomings that may increase the risk of failure. Additionally, the leader needs to track the shortcomings over time to see if improvement is made or the weakness becomes more glaring.

- What deficiencies do you pick up in their behavior and thinking?

- Do they possess personal blind spots? How are those blind spots affecting people around them?
- Is there anything about them that poses a risk or threat to the organization?
- How do they deal with being confronted with a shortcoming or deficiency?
- What is the trend in their response to the shortcoming? Is the trend positive, neutral, or negative?

Factor Seven: Potential

Evaluating a person's potential is essentially a guess or a bet. It is very hard to predict how far someone can go in terms of broader scope or increased responsibility. You are essentially in the position of trying to use past performance to predict someone's future performance. Why even do it? Your evaluation of potential will help guide your strategy in developing and investing in people. With limited time and resources at your disposal, it is important to think about potential and place your bets where you think the return will be greatest.

- What kind of upside does the individual possess—limited, moderate, or great?
- How quickly do you think the individual can achieve that potential; what time frame or runway are you looking at?
- Is their potential limited to a particular job function or does it extend cross-functionally?

Factor Eight: Adaptability

A lack of consistency and stability is the hallmark of the modern work environment. Things change rapidly and organizations need to quickly adapt to survive and win. These environmental conditions require individuals who are able to adapt and respond to change and uncertainty.

- How well do they handle change?
- How do they respond to upsets in routine?
- How invested are they in historical approaches?
- How do they handle the unexpected?
- Can they fit into a wide range of environments or are they more limited in their adaptability?
- How willing are they to do things differently?

Factor Nine: Resilience

Resilience is the ability to bounce back from failure or setback. Some people are devastated by failure, others are strengthened by it. Working in faster environments requires willingness to experiment and fail, making resilience an important factor to assess.

- How long does it take, on average, for them to recover from a moderate to severe setback?
- What do they think about failure?
- Do they internalize setbacks and learn from them, or do they seek to blame others or factors outside of their control for the setback?
- How much mental toughness do they display when confronted with a setback? Or, are they more prone to emotional outbursts?

Factor Ten: Chemistry

Every pit crew has a different chemistry. No two pit crews are alike in how they bond and come together. When thinking about adding a person to your pit crew, it is important to think about how they will get along with other members. Many talented teams are sidetracked by individuals who are disruptive and don't get along with others.

- What are the top three behaviors someone needs to demonstrate to fit into your pit crew?
- Does the individual you are evaluating demonstrate those behaviors?
- How aware is the individual of the need to bond with other members of the team?
- How effective are they in picking up membership rules and behaviors?
- Do they make references to their previous role and/or company? Do they overdo it?

Factor Eleven: Stress Reaction
It is only when things become challenging that you see the best and worst come out in people. And, the modern work environment has plenty of challenge and stress to go around. How a person handles stress and pressure can have a huge impact on their performance and how they impact other members of the pit crew. While it can be challenging to evaluate how someone handles stress, particularly when interviewing new people, you'll want to try and get a sense of stress reaction because it can have such a large impact.

- What are their stress triggers?
- What are the dominant behaviors the individual displays when stressed?
- What kinds of coping mechanisms do they have?
- How aware are they of their stress reactions?
- How do they handle performance pressure?

CREATE A RETENTION ENGINE

Okay, you've invested considerable time and assembled a top-tier pit crew. Don't let all of that good work go to waste. You will want to create a work environment that is a retention engine. I would suggest you go back and revisit Chapter Four and incorporate as many high engagement practices as you can in your work culture. Here is a list you can follow to get you started in strengthening pit crew retention:

- Make yourself available on a regular basis. Set up regular one-on-ones to answer questions and stay in touch with how people are doing. If you are going to be unavailable for a period of time, assign others in the team to keep the connection strong.

- Communicate your performance expectations, standards of performance, hot buttons, and ground rules rather than keeping team members guessing. Let them clearly know what you value and what you find problematic.

- Introduce new team members to the organization and make them feel valued and connected. Hook them up with a work partner to show them the ropes.

- Foster connections within and outside of your team. Develop a list of people team members should be connected with and explain why those target people are important. Make the introductions personally whenever possible.

- Ensure the workspace is set up to reinforce productivity and interaction. A great workspace helps retention.

- Take the time to explain important organizational processes and procedures. Provide organizational charts to help team members understand who does what.

- Explain the nuances and subtleties of the organizational culture. Keep a conversation going with the team about the leadership code that exists within the culture—what is accepted and what is not.
- Hold mini performance reviews on a monthly basis to let team members know how you view their performance.
- Establish a longer-term career development plan for each team member that maps out potential career directions and skills they need to develop to move ahead in their career.

Perform Ongoing Talent Retention Inspections

Just like the driver who walks around the car before every race checking to make sure vital equipment is in working order, you'll want to make sure your talent retention engine is in great shape. You'll want to perform a retention inspection at least monthly because attitudes can change quickly. Here are several factors to monitor to keep your retention engine in top form:

- Remember that talent leaves first. Top performers are more proactive and aggressive in managing their careers than average performers, keep your attention focused on them.
- Check the loyalty meter. If people have a sense of connection and loyalty to you, the team, and the company, you are in better shape than if the connection is weak. People who are loyal will be more open, sharing, and forgiving of missteps.
- Monitor compensation and be proactive. You don't necessarily have to pay more than your competition, but you need to be close. Within ten percent is usually sufficient unless the team member's skill set is in high demand. Pay attention

to how often compensation comes up in conversation and if frustration is being expressed. Don't treat compensation as a taboo subject. By talking about it on a regular basis you demonstrate you value them and you make compensation less of a flash point issue.

- How strong is the personal connection and identification with the products or services the company offers? Do people talk about your products with pride or do they consistently downplay them? When people are proud of their work, they talk about it.

- Keep an eye on organizational performance. Top performers will often create their own scorecard to track how the organization is doing. If the organization's performance drops below a certain level, top performers are more likely to move on because they want to be associated with a winner.

- Watch out for work cliffs if your organization is a commercial enterprise. I think of a work cliff in a couple of ways: vesting and tenure. Typically, the first year of someone's employment is treated as a cliff in terms of stock or equity vestment. After the first year, the team member will typically be one quarter vested. After four years, an team member's initial options will be fully vested and they will have less incentive to stay. Another way to think of the cliff is how long a person has been in the same job. Three years in a job is often the limit for top performers. High performers are motivated by interesting and challenging aspects of the work and can get bored if they stay in the job too long. They like to be continually learning new things and growing their skills. Top performers want to see a clear path for advancement in their careers. You will want to keep track of the different cliffs and put them on a time line to stay on top of them.

- Check the frustration gauge. The higher the level of frustration, the more likely it is a team member will leave. People want a good working environment and the tools and resources to do their work. They want their work environment to be relatively free from politics, inefficiencies, and distractions.

- Watch for spikes in social media interaction. While top performers will typically be more active in social media, you will want to pay attention to unusual increases in activity. These spikes can be early indicators of a team member's growing restlessness and dissatisfaction.

As you monitor these retention conditions, pay particular attention to trends or significant changes in a person's behavior or orientation. If you are on top of things, you might be able to act quick enough to turn a person around. The key is to be proactive and use any of these retention alarms as an avenue for dialogue and conversation.

Since some of these conditions are beyond your control, it is important to focus on those you can impact. Things like compensation, work design, resources, career development, and recognition are all variables you can address to make the work environment a retention engine. Remember, when all is said and done, the keys to retention are great jobs, a great environment, and a great boss.

TEAM BUILDING

After focusing on talent and retention, what's next? You'll need to mold this collection of individuals into a team. Whether you are building a new team or trying to turn an existing group into a team, the same principles apply. Building an effective team is a very challenging process. It takes time, investment and luck to be an effective **Chief Team Builder (CTB)**.

How Much Team do you need?
Let's start off by considering the question of how much team you really need. Depending on the nature of the work and the challenges that need to be addressed, the level of team work can vary considerably. It is important to remember building a team can be an expensive activity in terms of effort and level of investment. As a consequence, I suggest leaders approach team building from an ROI (return on investment) perspective. The level of investment in building a team needs to match the return you expect to get. While many people don't think of team building and ROI as linked, I believe they are. If there is minimal need for a team, it doesn't make sense to invest considerable effort in building one. In Chapter Eight I talked about efficiency and effectiveness and those concepts are very relevant to the team building conversation. The faster leader wants to achieve the most he can with the resources he has.

Conditions that drive team level
As you think about how much team you really need, you'll want to consider several variables that strongly influence team building strategy. Start out by asking yourself to what degree do team members need to work together to achieve goals and objectives. What level of interdependency needs to exist between team members? If the nature of the work requires considerable communication and collaboration, then a stronger team will be needed. If the work is largely independent or individual focused, less team is needed.

You will want to evaluate the complexity of the work. If the work of the team is highly complex, you'll want to invest in building a stronger team to handle the challenges. Simpler work flows require less team work.

The level of available resources has an impact on team level. If a team has plenty of resources at its disposal to achieve its goals, less team is needed. If resourcefulness is an important element of team performance, more team will be needed. Resourcefulness requires initiative, creativity, and tenacity which are all characteristics of high performing teams.

Some work is episodic or situational in nature. Collaboration and team work are really only required at certain times of the year or on certain types of work. For example, the team work necessary to set yearly goals may only happen at a particular time. Other work is systematic in nature and requires ongoing team work. Launching a product involves many different functions over a longer period of time and requires more team work for success. The longer the scope of work, the more team work is needed.

The broader work culture has an impact on team level. Certain organizations are very team-centric whereas other organizations are more individually focused. You will want your target team level to match the broader work culture or you'll have an uphill battle. Depending on what type of organization you are in, you may experience a very different level of support for building your team.

The level of effort required to build a team can influence your team strategy. Strong egos and personalities can be more challenging to mold into a team because everyone thinks they should be the leader. Individuals or functional organizations that have negative history or animosity toward others make team building more difficult. The amount of work needed to build a team can make it untenable.

Finally, your personal preferences have an impact on team level. Many leaders value team work highly and strive to build work cultures that revolve around teams. Other leaders place less value on teams and focus more on the individual.

A Team Level Model

After walking through the analysis of how much team you need, I think it helps to have a model of team levels to guide your final team target. I think of teams as existing on a continuum, and I use a simple three point scale to capture the differences between team levels.

A level one team is a minimal team. The team focuses on work that is simpler and shorter in duration with a clear objective. There is some identification with the team, but other affiliations are more important. Communication and interaction are strongly task-focused. Every member of the team has a role to play and team members tend to stay within the boundaries of their role. Level one teams are often temporary or situational, and require minimal leadership investment. Most of your work will focus on making sure team members have visibility into what other team members are doing. By fostering visibility, you increase the level of awareness in the team and encourage team members to think about their impact on other team members. You will find you need to play an active and directive role.

A level two team is a mid-level team. The nature of their work requires a higher degree of cooperation. Team members need to actively cooperate with other team members to get things done. The work focus is more challenging and longer term. Team members identify with the team and have personal connection to other team members. Team members have a broader sense of ownership and are willing to go beyond their set roles to accomplish tasks relevant to the team. Communication is open and transparent. At this team level, your involvement is less than a level one team but still important. You will need to set goals and identify high priority tasks.

A level three team is a very strong team. The level of work integration is high. Team members actively collaborate to get things done. The team is often the main social affiliation for team members. Conflict is openly addressed and team members are comfortable taking risks with one another. Team members will do what is needed and are quite willing to go beyond their roles. There are multiple examples of members taking leadership roles to meet challenges. The work of a level three team is generally challenging, complex, and longer term. A level three team is highly collaborative and supportive. This type of team requires a high level of investment to build. You will find the level of direction you need to give is minimal because the team is self-directing and self-managing to a high degree.

Team Building Fundamentals

After setting your team building target, you'll want to develop a strategy for building the team and put it into action. Depending on the level of team you aspire to build, here are several building blocks you will want to incorporate.

Select a team task for the team to work on. Because of the work silos most individuals operate within, they often don't perceive a huge need to collaborate or work with others outside of their immediate work connections. This perception is often a significant obstacle to getting people to work together as a team. To combat the lack of perceived need for team work, I suggest leaders utilize a team task approach.

A team task is a task that every member of a team must participate in or the result will be failure. Within a correctly structured team task, it is impossible for an individual to succeed while the larger team fails. Everyone must work together.

The team task needs to have relevance for all team members and it must be achievable in the short to mid-term. You want to build momentum through early success. The team task should challenge team members to step out of their typical roles and take on new responsibilities.

Select team members that match your team target. There are three main characteristics I focus on: skills relevant to the work, interpersonal skills, and orientation to teams. Determine what job skills are needed in the team and whether you need specialists or generalists. I talked earlier in this chapter about the EFTE model for assessing people and you can use it in your team member selection process. For example, if you want a level three team, pick people who are high in affiliation and interpersonal skills. Depending on your situation, you may need to evaluate current members for fit with your target, coach existing team members to develop the necessary skills, or recruit new members.

Determine level of your involvement. Leaders differ in the level of involvement they want to have with a team. Some leaders like to be the hub of the wheel whereas other leaders want the team to be self-managed. Your level of involvement will strongly influence the type of team you build. You will want to determine how much leadership you will provide versus what you expect team members to supply.

Select the level of goal and objective linkage. One of the more important ways to encourage team work is to link goals between members. Linked goals are shared goals rather than individual goals. Linked goals encourage team members to work together because cooperation leads to successful goal completion. With linked goals, team members are evaluated on the same things and share equally in the risks and rewards.

Choose the level of work flow integration. As a leader, you have considerable influence over how the work is done. Your approach to work flow design can have a huge impact on team work. For example, if you design work to operate within functional silos you will get minimal team work. On the other hand, if you design a work flow that is cross functional in nature you'll get more team work. Work flow design is a critical component of team building.

Do you need a team contract? Higher level teams are often bound together by a set of agreements that mutually bind their members. I have talked previously about ground rules or rules of engagement which are examples of agreements that can be included in a team contract. A team contract addresses more subtle forms of behavior and outlines how team members should treat one another. While contracts can spring up organically, leaders can accelerate the team building process by having the team create a binding contract.

Determine how strong a team identity you want. A level three team will have a strong team identity. They will often have a unique name, shared workspace, a shared argot, and team rituals or disciplines that define them. Team members will often have passed certain membership trials that cement their inclusion in the team. A strong team identity builds chemistry and connection. If you want to build a stronger team, taking steps to build a team identity will accelerate your efforts.

Do you need team roles? Outside of the formal roles team members play, there are a set of roles that are focused on the team itself. These internally focused roles help the team to improve its performance and I think of them as team roles. Team roles are generally present in higher level teams. For example, a team mediator can help resolve conflict between team members. A team mentor can help team members work through difficult issues in private. A team conscience can challenge the team to stay true to its values. A team spokesperson can represent the team to the outside world. If you want to build a higher level team, you'll want to give thought to what team roles you want to incorporate and who you might want to draft into those roles.

After selecting your team building blocks, it will take time to put them into action. I'll talk more about translating your plan into reality in the upcoming section on test drives and time trials.

BUILD YOUR ACTION NETWORK

Over the last ten years, organizations have continued to flatten their management structures. With less formal chains of command to rely upon, leaders have had to learn to leverage the informal organization to get things done. With the increase in popularity of collaboration tools, work has become even more social. Newer forms of organizational structure such as the networked organization and the virtual organization have added to the challenge of being effective.

As a consequence, the level of interaction needed to get things accomplished has increased dramatically. The ability of leaders to navigate the maze of relationships and get things accomplished has never been in more important. As a leader, you fail or succeed by virtue of your relationships.

One of the things that separate effective leaders from those who struggle is the presence of an action network. The action network is not your direct team; it is the larger constellation of relationships within the organization you cultivate to accomplish goals. While some of these relationships are obvious because they are formally connected to your work flow or you have obvious dependencies on them, other elements of the action network are more informal. It is often these informal connections that are the most important because they can offer you speed advantages.

You can leverage your action network to solve organizational problems that have no clear ownership or build support for initiatives you are trying to get adopted. One leader I worked with used his action network to foster a higher state of urgency within a geographically dispersed organization. Another leader used it to get support for a large acquisition. Cross-functional challenges are ideal action network targets. You can use your action network to get behind the scenes information and guidance. Your action network can allow you to take short cuts and reduce the amount of effort needed to accomplish anything important.

The action network requires your investment and it is not created overnight. It is essential to being fast and effective. When I am working with a leader on building an action network, I have them target specific relationships to focus on. We put a plan in place to develop those relationships into ones that are responsive, helpful, and action oriented. Depending on the size of the organization, the critical threshold seems to be between twenty and forty relationships for an effective action network.

As you think about building or improving your action network, you'll want to review the chapters in the book on resistance and engagement to fine tune your approach. You'll want to make sure you allocate time on your STAB devoted to relationship building. You can modify the resistance mapping tool at the end of Chapter Three to map out your action network.

Rather than focusing on a group or function, I suggest you target specific individuals within groups. To accelerate your efforts, here are several categories of relationship you might want to target:

- **Formal influencers** are individuals who have the potential to have significant impact on your work. They are individuals who are formally connected to your work flow and are obvious targets to start with.
- **Informal influencers** are individuals who have built up considerable credibility and social standing within the organization. They may or may not be connected to your work flow, but could have impact because people seek out their opinions. They may be sprinkled throughout the organization and may exist at many levels. Their influence comes from their credibility, not their formal role.
- **Co-dependents** are individuals with whom you share a level of interdependency. You may share risks, rewards, or benefits. While the distribution of consequences may not be equal, you will want to make sure these individuals understand the interdependencies and have skin in the game.
- **Access controllers** are individuals who manage access to other key people and groups. They function as schedule gatekeepers and you generally have to go through them to connect with certain people. While they may have job functions that are lower in the organizational hierarchy, they often wield considerable influence. Ignore these individuals at your peril.
- **Resource controllers** are individuals who have a range of resources under their control. Those resources could be financial, people, tools, or technology. Target those

individuals who have intimate knowledge of the resources rather than individuals who may be connected to the resources in a more abstract way. The individual who schedules an engineer's time may be more important than the VP of Engineering.

- **Connectors** are individuals who have robust social networks. Because of their interpersonal connections, they are an important part of your action network. They are especially helpful in connecting you to people you don't know and providing introductions that get you through the access controllers.

- **Back channel experts** are individuals who know how to get things done outside of formal channels. They are experts in shortcuts and knowing who really controls things. By cultivating relationships with these individuals, you can cut down the amount of time it takes to accomplish your goals.

- **Historians** are carriers of important organizational knowledge. They are individuals who have been in the organization for a significant amount of time and have knowledge about organizational taboos and the origin of important organizational practices. They can help you avoid walking into quicksand or violating important norms and ground rules.

- **Publicists** are individuals who can help you position or sell what you are trying to do. They are experts at public relations and have an important role in shaping perceptions. They generally have good visibility across different parts of the organization and can help build momentum for your initiatives. They can give you positive or negative press, don't overlook them.

- **Judges** are individuals who evaluate, validate and test what you are trying to achieve. They are often involved in giving opinions about whether a strategy or initiative makes sense, is possible, or is financially sound. Their opinion matters and they can quickly and easily shoot things down. Make sure you give them the time and attention they need or they can become a significant obstacle.

CREATE YOUR PERFORMANCE DASHBOARD

Flying at Mach 1 requires almost instantaneous feedback and information. Clutter is dangerous. As defense analyst Carlo Kopp described it, "Critical information must be presented in the pilot's field of view, enabling him to concentrate on the external world. The form in which it's displayed must be easy to interpret and be arranged so as not to clutter up the area occupied by the target during gunnery. Status information demands organization. It must be easily accessible and again uncluttered, to minimize errors in interpretation. There is nothing worse than staring into a pile of figures which hardly make sense, especially when you're trying to find out what went wrong where."[18]

A tragic example of this was seen in 2009, when an Air France jet crashed into the Atlantic Ocean. The information from the flight recorder of the plane revealed that "the pilots became distracted with malfunctioning airspeed indicators and failed to properly manage other critical systems...The pilots apparently became confused by the alarms blaring from their instruments and despite trying to systematically respond to each warning, were unable to sort out the chaos and maintain a steady course."[19]

While leaders don't usually face consequences as dire as the Air France tragedy, the stakes are still high. There are important lessons to be learned about the dangers of being distracted by too much, or even incorrect, information. Leaders in today's complicated work environment are constantly faced with information overload. Social media allows people to constantly update everyone on the minutiae of their lives. On the Internet, highly inaccurate information can be distributed and taken for truth. The leader's feedback system can easily get compromised.

To be effective in navigating ever changing territory and dealing with poor information, I recommend that you build a performance dashboard. Don't run the risk of leading blind. Like a jet pilot, you want critical information at your fingertips. Think of a jet pilot's cockpit. Rather than having all the indicators in the same view for him to sort out, the most important information, such as air speed and course direction, is placed readily at hand, while other gauges, like radar or fuel levels, are placed to the side.

A performance dashboard allows you to improve your overall management of the organization by giving you feedback about what is going on. A good place to start in building your dashboard is with your KPI's (key performance indicators). Most organizations have metrics and tracking processes in place that allow them to get a picture of the organization's performance. But, I suggest you go beyond what is commonly measured to tracking those variables that drive the faster organization. As you start to engineer your custom dashboard, it is important to focus on the right things. I advise a fivefold focus on these key areas because this will help guide you as you decide what to track and how.

1. A focus on your team and how it is performing in critical areas. How much fuel is it burning to achieve results?

How is it doing in relationship to the STAB and TAB's you developed?

2. A focus on you and how you are performing. You are the pilot flying the plane and pilot error is a major source of concern.

3. A focus on what is happening in the environment around you. Is there wind shear, down drafts or inclement weather around you?

4. A focus on what you are trying to achieve. What is your flight plan?

5. A focus on what is coming. What is just over the horizon?

An effective dashboard is based on the guidance mechanisms you have established for the organization. I talked about the importance of guidance mechanisms such as vision, mission, and strategy in the previous chapter. You can't lead if you are always reacting to things as they pop up. Real-time feedback is great as you go along, but a pilot would never take off without a flight plan to serve as a guide. Faster leaders split their awareness and focus between the present and the future.

The faster leader needs to be purposeful in all things he does. By thinking ahead and planning, he minimizes his reactive behavior. The stakes are high. When a leader doesn't have a dashboard, he is flying blind. An effective dashboard is a dynamic feedback framework.

You will, of course, have certain elements on your dashboard that are crucial to your specific work. Your dashboard needs to be customized to your unique environment. I have developed a questionnaire that walks you through the different types of performance factors you might want to include in a dashboard (see Acceleration Tool Nine at the end of the chapter). Review the questionnaire to start creating your performance dashboard. Remember to keep the number of items on the dashboard manageable and tied to what is critical for your organization. There are several different types of software and online programs that allow you to quickly build your dashboard. You can check out Klipfolio (www.klipfolio.com) and Domo (www.domo.com) to start.

INSTALL A KNOWLEDGE PUMP

Jet fuel keeps the plane in the air. But if fuel is not mixed properly or delivered at the right pressure, it can cause a crash. Water contamination can cause fuel injectors in a jet to freeze. If the mixture of hydrocarbons is not right, the fuel becomes unstable and dangerous. Faster leaders understand that information is like jet fuel. If the mixture is correct and delivered at the right flow, the performance of the organization is optimized. If either the mixture or delivery is off, the organization's performance can become compromised. The quality and rate of information flow have a dramatic impact on decision making. Don't leave information flow to chance. I coach every leader I work with to build a knowledge pump. It is critical to speed and success. Think of it like a fuel pump that delivers high-octane information at a consistent delivery rate. In building an effective knowledge pump, you are fulfilling the role of **Chief Information Officer (CIO)**.

What specifically is a knowledge pump, and how do you build one? There are three key elements to keep in mind:

1. Get the mixture right
2. Refresh fuel because it degrades over time
3. Keep your injectors clean

Get the Fuel Mixture Right

In building a knowledge pump, it is important to understand the fundamental difference between information and knowledge. A simple way to think of the difference is that knowledge is chunked information. Chunked is a term from cognitive psychology that refers to information that is refined and organized into a framework, which makes it relevant, and easier to understand and apply. Knowledge has a how-to quality to it, and people subconsciously utilize it to make decisions and take action. Knowledge breaks complex content down into easily digestible pieces and is easily archivable in your mind.

Like jet fuel, knowledge has to be mixed right. The knowledge pump focuses on communicating knowledge (not just information) critical to the mission of the organization and the work of individuals within it. Its goal is to create a critical mass of accurate, shared knowledge that all members of the organization have access to and can utilize in their planning and decision making. It is an attempt to eliminate information islands where only a few have critical knowledge. I suggest including the following knowledge ingredients:

- Intelligence that impacts the team members' ability to perform their roles effectively
- New initiatives that are being rolled out
- Status of key projects across functions
- Critical recruiting needs
- Important trends observed in the marketplace
- Macroeconomic events and trends
- Key developments with customers and competitors
- Tracking of key business success indicators and metrics

- Surfacing and dispelling rumors
- Identifying new skills that will be needed to meet future demands

Refresh Fuel Because it Degrades over Time

Out-of-date information is deadly to a pilot. Weather reports that don't accurately reflect where storms actually are can put a pilot in the path of danger. The faster leader has to deal with the problem of information obsolescence, as well. This problem is becoming more acute because information is becoming obsolete at an accelerating pace. Experts assert that roughly 40 percent of what we know becomes obsolete over a two-year time frame.[20]

An important component of a knowledge pump is a mechanism for assigning a time value to knowledge. In other words, what is the shelf life of the knowledge and how long will it be relevant? Is the knowledge good for three months or will it still be accurate in a year? While it can be difficult to predict how long a particular chunk of knowledge will be relevant, you can develop a reasonable estimate by tracking the rate of change within your specialty or industry.

To get a sense of the rate of change, I suggest people look at how often new products or services are introduced, or how often innovation occurs within their field. In certain fields, knowledge becomes obsolete quickly, whereas in others, it happens more slowly. When communicating knowledge, I suggest leaders attach a time stamp (i.e., a specific expiration date) to the knowledge to give people a sense of how long it might be relevant. In this way, leaders can consistently challenge their team members to renew their knowledge base and stay up to date.

Keep Your Injectors Clean

The third element of a knowledge pump is its communication and updating mechanisms. Knowledge needs to be distributed in a consistent, frequent, and easily accessible framework. If you want people to utilize knowledge to inform their decision-making process, you can't make knowledge difficult to find. I suggest you start out by designing an overall communication strategy that includes all of the main communication channels you want to use. At the basic level, you will want an informational database where critical information can be saved and updated easily. You will want to utilize efficient and enticing methods for getting the knowledge into the hands of your team.

One company I worked with held weekly company briefings at lunchtime where critical information such as important project updates, funding efforts, and engineering breakthroughs were announced. Here are other communication suggestions:

- Performance dashboards that track critical performance data and render it in a graphical dashboard. Dashboards can be an effective component of your knowledge pump communication
- E-mail: the old standby
- Chat or instant messaging systems
- Group collaboration software
- Small group meetings
- Video broadcasts and video conferencing
- Wikis: web pages that can be edited by visitors
- Blogs
- Websites

In general, it is best to utilize more than one channel because people vary in their preferred means of communication. If you use at least two channels, you will reach most of the audience you are trying to engage. By building an effective knowledge pump, you will ensure that your organization gets high quality fuel delivered at a rate that it can turn into increased performance. Keep your knowledge pump in good working order, and it will help you to keep firing on all cylinders.

The leader must take on an additional responsibility to systematically combat bad information and information overload. Destructive additives can easily get in the mixture and contaminate fuel, thereby lowering its octane. Because the quality of decisions made in the team is directly related to the quality of information they have, the faster leader needs to pay a lot of attention to the information the team receives and acts on.

Too much information can be a contaminant. Think of information overload as putting too many ingredients in the mixture. Information overload contributes to bad decisions. These bad decisions have consequences that often need to be addressed or rectified. Importance gets lost in the shuffle and the team can focus on the wrong things. The team gets off course or they metaphorically fly into a storm.

Information overload can have a negative impact on the leader's credibility, because team members expect leaders to provide focus and clarity, not the fire hose at full blast.

Provide Frameworks and Context
Lack of filtering and lack of context are two of the main contributors connected to information overload that the faster leader needs to counteract to improve the speed and effectiveness of the organization. There is a pronounced tendency for people to ignore or

filter information when it becomes overwhelming or too complex. They can easily fall into the traps of relying too much on past experience or only paying attention to information that confirms their existing beliefs in their efforts to simplify.

While simplification is necessary, *how* people filter and simplify is the problem. What they pay attention to can be strongly biased by their own beliefs and attitudes and not necessarily what is good for the organization. As a consequence, their perspective and viewpoints can become isolated, narrow, and skewed over time. They focus more and more on the immediate and what is close to them. They can hold on to wrong information and make important decisions on this supposed knowledge. They can pay attention to the wrong gauges. Systemic thinking decreases, and symptoms, rather than root causes, are addressed.

Rather than allowing the individual members of the team to filter information according to their own criteria, the faster leader needs to build a shared filtering framework with them. This framework needs to simplify information in the right way to allow people to consistently get accurate information. Pilots understand there is a direct correlation between the information they are receiving and the performance of the aircraft. They know how to interpret the information to adjust the performance of the plane because they understand what the information means and how to apply it. They train their crews to interpret and act on data in the same way. In providing frameworks, you are acting as the **Chief Perspective Officer**.

The faster leader has to deal with the additional problem that much of the information we receive is broadcast without context and is packaged to grab attention. Its magnitude is manipulated to compete with all of the other information that is bombarding us. Everything seems immediate, urgent, or important. It is up to the individual to try and make sense of it, and the amount of information we receive is staggering.

Without context, it is difficult to determine importance or relevance in the information we are receiving. At an organizational level, lack of a shared context can contribute to misalignment and confusion. The crew on the plane can end up working at cross purposes. The faster leader needs to take additional steps to provide the organization with a contextual framework that gives meaning and application to information.

Given the time challenges that most people face, they simply do not make the time to refresh their knowledge rate. Increasingly, people are relying on information that is out of date and no longer accurate. Once information gets into a system (either personal or organizational), it is difficult to remove. The combined challenges of time pressures and the power of old information pose significant risks to the faster leader. To keep his organization from flying into an unexpected storm, the faster leader needs to make sure information is systematically flushed and updated.

RAPID PROTOTYPING AND ROAD TESTING

As you build your faster organization, you'll want to evaluate your construction as it progresses. You'll want to make sure your plane actually flies before putting a pilot in the cockpit. Two approaches that accelerate the building process are rapid prototyping and road testing.

Rapid Prototyping

To build a faster organization, you will need to develop a capacity to test ideas, processes, strategies, or concepts in a basic or rudimentary form before committing to more extensive development and investment. This bare bones strategy makes use of rapid prototyping. A prototype is basically a stripped down working model. I have worked with leaders to build prototypes of many different things including: products, customer engagement models, service offerings, team member feedback processes, sales campaigns, and organizational strategies.

This approach allows the leader to dramatically shorten the development and testing cycle. This minimalist approach allows the organization to adapt to rapidly changing conditions and cut costs.

By developing things quicker and with less investment, the faster organization can incorporate user, stakeholder, or customer feedback in the development process. The final result is a product or process that is more quickly and successfully adopted. To build a prototyping capability in your faster organization, try the following:

- Build prototypes with just enough functionality to test the idea. Avoid the tendency to over design or over specify. Good enough should be your guiding philosophy.
- Stay under the radar and take short cuts. Whenever you can, avoid engaging existing organizational structures or processes. The status quo is often your enemy and will try to slow you down. Don't build up a lot of fanfare about what you are doing. You don't want to be noticed too early.
- Treat prototyping as an organizational learning process. By getting feedback quickly and having an open approach to experimentation, you will accelerate the organization's capacity for adaptation and learning. Don't punish failure. The goal is to learn fast rather than get it right the first time.

- Make decisions quickly and discard prototypes that don't work. Don't become over invested in your prototypes and hang on to them too long.
- Identify your users/customers. Although this may seem obvious, you will want to have an accurate idea of who your target audience is.
- Since prototyping is user-centric, you will need to ensure users want to engage with you and can easily give feedback. Prototyping is a high engagement strategy.
- Manage expectations. Users need to understand they are getting a prototype rather than a finished product.

Road Testing

Before any big race, a Formula One car is put through its paces. The driver gets important feedback on how the car is performing and gets to do practice test laps to familiarize himself with the track. Adjustments are made to fine tune performance so that on race day the car and driver will be at their best. Putting a car and driver on a track without testing and practice would be a recipe for disaster.

Work teams also need performance testing and practice, but too often these things are neglected or sacrificed. Because of the time pressure most organizations are under, teams are often put into the situation of having to perform on race day without the necessary preparation. Performance suffers as a result.

In my work with leaders, I strongly urge them to take the time to put teams through their paces and fine tune their performance. Practice is the foundation of how you build and retain skills. Here are two examples of team practice activities you might want to utilize:

1. **Dry run**: A dry run is a practice exercise focused on improving performance. You can apply a dry run approach to almost anything. For example, you can have the team present to an informal audience to get feedback and refine a presentation. When it comes time to actually deliver the presentation, the team will be more ready. You can have the team do a dry run for rolling out a new customer communication process, launching a new website, or starting a new training program.

2. **Simulation**: A simulation is an imitation of a real world activity that allows for practicing and refining certain skills. For example, aircraft pilots spend many hours in simulators to practice and improve their flight skills before they ever fly a real plane. You can either develop or buy off the shelf simulations to improve team skills.

Road Test Your Vision

In Chapter Eight I talked about how important guidance mechanisms were to building a faster organization. Because guidance mechanisms are very important, I suggest you road test them to make sure they work before you do a full scale roll out. Let's walk through how you might go about road testing your vision. This same approach can be used for your mission and charter testing.

A vision that is not validated or road tested is just a slogan. If you roll out a vision and it doesn't engage the larger organization, your credibility as a leader will suffer. You will need to test your vision with a group of people and see if it resonates. Your vision needs to be scrutinized and tested. If it doesn't pass the test, you'll need to go back to the drawing board.

A key test of a potential vision is does it excite and inspire those who come into contact with it? For a vision to be successful, it needs to engage people at an emotional level. A vision needs to go beyond the rational and trigger emotions people identify with. When you are testing your vision, do you see evidence that it is touching emotions and generating excitement and engagement?

Just like a Formula One driver, you'll use your experience and practice to formulate the best approach to take the next step. You'll need a launch plan to roll it out to the larger organization. I recommend you think of this aspect of the process as a practice campaign. You'll need to decide how you are going to communicate it and what channels you will use. You will want to articulate the key talking points and messaging that supports the vision. You will need to decide who will act as spokespersons for the vision and what audiences they will engage with. All of this is done before you roll the vision out and you can use dry runs to perfect the launch process.

The launch plan will need to address how you will get buy-in and commitment from the organization. It should cover how you will sustain interest in the vision over time and how you will drive it into the organization's processes and decision making. The vision needs to become internalized into the organization and it needs to drive alignment.

The next big challenge to think about is how you keep the vision fresh and powerful over time. Like anything else, a vision can experience a sense of fatigue. A leader is continually challenged to find new ways to talk about the vision and keep people engaged. Think of the vision as an ongoing dialogue with the community of the organization. You can practice this dialogue with smaller informal groups and individuals to get feedback.

In the best of all worlds, your vision becomes a strong, integrating factor for the whole organization because you have sufficiently tested it and rigorously practiced all of the relevant push mechanisms.

Now it's time to get into the driver seat and drive the faster organization you have spent time and energy building. Get ready to take the pole position.

ACCELERATION TOOL #9: PERFORMANCE DASHBOARD QUESTIONNAIRE

You can use the following questionnaire to develop a set of factors to include in a performance dashboard. While all of the elements might not be relevant to you, pick the ones that best fit your unique requirements. You will then be able to monitor important variables on a real-time basis.

1. **Organizational Structure**
   Is your organizational structure helping or hindering? How agile is the organization? Is it too bureaucratic or too chaotic? What is the lifecycle for the current organizational structure?

2. **You**
   How are you handling the pressures and challenges of leading your organization? How is your engagement and connection to the organization? What is your comfort level with the direction you have set and the performance of the organization towards attaining the goals you have established?

3. **Time Focus**
   How efficient are your meetings? How are you testing out new ideas and innovations? What is the level of urgency? How is the organization performing against the STAB and TAB's you have developed?

4. **Accountability**
   Do you have to enforce it or are people embracing it? Is the accountability level high, low, and how is it trending?

5. **Competitor Comparison**
   Are you faster, slower, or about the same in terms of releasing new products or services?

6. **Emotional Climate**

   What is the emotional climate of the organization? How is morale trending? What is the rate of undesirable turnover? How well are teams working together?

7. **Execution and Discipline**

   Are your control and focus mechanisms working? How are you doing on key business metrics (sales, product ramp, manufacturing, production, profitability, burn rate)? Are your results in line or out of line with your plan and expectations? How well are your decision-making processes working?

8. **Strategic Alignment**

   How robust is your strategy? How well are the different functions aligned? Is there data that suggests lack of alignment or conflict?

9. **Innovation**

   What is the pace of new ideas like? Are you innovating in just parts of the organization or is it widespread?

10. **Leadership**

    Is leadership contributing throughout the organization? How is your leadership team performing? Do you have sufficient leadership bench strength in the organization?

11. **Risk**

    Are you focusing enough on barriers to success? Are you managing cash flow effectively? Have you accurately identified your risks and are you actively managing them?

12. **Engagement and Communication**

    Are key messages getting through? Are team members engaged and committed to the organization? Are you listening to team members?

13. **Talent Pipeline**

    Is the talent level of the team consistently improving? What is the status of your talent pipeline outside of your organization?

14. **Product and Service Pipeline**

    What is the state of your new product/service pipeline? Do you have any gaps in your product roadmap?

15. **Resistance**

    Do you have initiatives underway that might be affected by resistance? Are you seeing signs of resistance in the organization? What is the status of the resistance- is it getting stronger or weaker?

16. **Customer/stakeholder Engagement**

    What is the level of engagement with your current customers, partners, or stakeholders? Is it stable, improving, or getting worse?

Part IV: Drive It!

❖ ❖ ❖

CHAPTER 10

Take the Pole Position

*Take the leadership role, not out of ego gratification, but
because you believe passionately in what you are doing.*

THE POLE POSITION IN ANY Formula One race is the most coveted spot in
the whole race lineup. The driver that has it is in the front of the pack
closest to the guard rail. It is coveted because it is a leadership position
that allows the driver to control and set the early pace of the race. But
the pole position has to be won. It is always contested and the driver
who posts the fastest time in qualifying races wins the position.

A leadership role needs to be won. There are three important
trials a leader must master to win the pole position. First, you need
to learn how to navigate the leadership zone. Second, you need to
understand your role as a leader and how to leverage the power
that goes with it. Third, you need to articulate a leadership platform that helps the organization move forward with you.

NAVIGATE THE LEADERSHIP ZONE

Every engine has a peak performance zone where everything is
dialed in and output is maximized. Faster leaders have a similar

peak performance sweet spot, which I call the leadership zone. After working in the leadership field for over twenty five years, I have come to believe that leadership is a dynamic, transitory, and fluctuating state rather than a stable, static characteristic of a person. The leadership zone is a state that faster leaders constantly seek out and try to maximize. It is a peak performance goal.

When you are in the leadership zone you are able to get the best out of your team because you have your hands on the wheel. You know when to hit the throttle and when to back off. You can feel every bump in the road and are constantly adjusting to get every ounce of speed.

We have the capacity to move into the leadership zone and out of it on a day-by-day, minute-by-minute basis. Almost everyone has some capacity for the leadership zone. We can spend considerable time in the zone; at other times we step briefly into it or we may be outside of it for months at a time. Certain people are habitually in the zone, others move into it only under specific conditions or circumstances. Even the best leaders are not always in the zone.

It is important to realize the leadership zone is not related to job grade or responsibility. I have worked with senior executives who seldom enter the zone. I have worked with managers who are in the zone on a consistent basis. The leadership zone is different for everyone. It is very personal and is reflected in the choices people make and the principles they live by. It is affected by events and reactions to them. The conditions that move one person in or out of the zone are not necessarily the same for other people. For certain leaders, stress and crisis bring out their best while in others it acts as a derailer.

The leadership zone can be challenging to maintain. The stresses and distractions of modern day life make the zone elusive. That is why it is important to develop a real awareness of what the zone is like for you. Without self-awareness, it is much more difficult to manage and maintain the state. You can literally spend weeks and months outside of the zone without being aware of it and your capacity to lead becomes diminished. If you don't have a good feel for what it is like to be in the zone, it is hard to help yourself attain it. Ask any top performing race car driver, and they'll tell you the same thing. Being in the zone is critical to performance and it is challenging to maintain.

When I first raise the concept of the leadership zone, I am often asked the question, "What is it and how will I know I am in it?" While the leadership zone is slightly different for everyone, there are three elements of the zone that people consistently experience.

1. **A sense of purpose and direction.** Leaders often comment they feel particularly focused on something of importance or relevance when in the zone. They are decisive and believe what they are doing will have impact or make a difference. Doubt and uncertainty seem to slip away. They feel tenacious and are not easily turned aside. Obstacles are dealt with directly and quickly. Their sense of focus becomes extreme.

2. **An expanded sense of ownership.** People experience a deeply felt sense of responsibility that extends beyond their nominal responsibilities. They proactively take on responsibility, not for ego reasons, but because it needs to get done.

3. **Connection to others and something larger than oneself.** People in the leadership zone do not feel alone; instead they feel strongly connected to others. This sense of connection can go beyond people they know to include others they don't know. The connection can be to a company or

larger community. As part of the connection, they try to get others involved and participating.

Leadership Triggers

As a transitory state, there are three main variables that influence your movement into the leadership zone. Your beliefs about your leadership potential have a significant impact. If you believe you are not a leader, you will avoid or shy away from leadership opportunities. On the other hand, if you believe you are a leader, you are much more likely to embrace the leadership zone.

Your basic personality can have an impact. Since leadership is heavily interpersonal in nature, those personality characteristics that are social in nature (such as extroversion) can predispose you towards entering the zone frequently. If you are lower on these types of characteristics, you may have a more challenging time entering and staying in the zone. Certain people, by their very nature, tend to seek out and move into the zone and feel very comfortable in it. They have a history of taking leadership roles and find it gratifying. Others are more reluctant leaders. They may be shy or uncomfortable in the role.

Your skills can influence your zone. If you are strong in skills that relate to leadership such as influence or persuasion, you may enter and stay in the zone for longer periods of time. Again, if your skills are not well-developed in these areas, you may find yourself avoiding or minimizing the zone.

These beliefs, personality, and skills, are all areas you can improve or develop to increase your time in the leadership zone. I recommend individuals take the time to self-assess these three leadership zone dimensions and target those areas that act as personal barriers to leadership. I suggest being practical and focusing on a particular developmental area for a period of time to achieve progress and results.

There is a fourth variable relating to the leadership zone that is not as much under your direct control. It is the environment in which you operate as a leader. When I say environment, I am talking about the social, cultural, interpersonal, and physical context in which you operate. There are other forces and individuals that influence the dynamics of the leadership environment. Some organizations place a strong emphasis on leadership which makes it easier to demonstrate leadership. Other companies don't place such a high value on leadership, making it more challenging to lead. Likewise, there are individuals in positions of authority who can reinforce leadership or censor it in others.

While the environment can influence your leadership zone, faster leaders can expand their time in the zone by understanding the triggers that help them move into it. In my work, I found there are four situational triggers that influence time in the leadership zone.

1. **Invitation:** Certain people will move into the zone only when they are invited or nominated by another team member. They feel most comfortable when someone asks them or encourages them to step into a leadership role. Other people are self-nominating. They proactively put themselves into the zone by choosing to act.

2. **Expertise:** Many people step into the zone only when it relates directly to a perceived area of expertise or competence. For example, if they are technical experts, they step into the zone around technical issues. Others will step into the zone in areas in which they are not experts, or even in areas they may be uncomfortable with.

3. **Issue-driven**: People can step into the zone to solve a problem and then exit the zone when the problem is solved. Or, a particular kind of issue that is important to them can trigger their entry. Their zone is very transitory and tied to resolution of problems. For others, the zone is not tied to specific issues, and they tend to stay in the zone for longer periods of time.

4. **Other leaders**: The presence of others assuming a leadership role can affect whether a person steps into the zone. If another person else is providing leadership, there may be no compelling reason for anyone else to do it. Others feel the more leadership, the better, as long as there is good alignment between the leaders.

Moving into the zone and staying there is difficult. It takes energy, focus, and discipline. Distractions, stress, and work demands can conspire to keep you out of the zone or limit your time in it. Additionally, at times you are your own worst enemy. Your beliefs, behavior patterns, and basic personality can act as barriers to attaining and staying in the zone. Here are a couple of suggestions for extending your time in the leadership zone.

Strategy #1: Overcome self-limiting beliefs by disputing them

Beliefs are things we hold to be true. We develop them in many ways: life experiences, feedback from others, and through observing others. Many beliefs are helpful and constructive, others are negative and self-limiting. There are two main problems with most self-limiting beliefs. First, self-limiting beliefs are over-generalizations. They have an always true or always false quality. Second, because we believe them to be true, we don't really test their accuracy or examine them closely.

The dominant self-limiting belief relating to leadership is "I am not a leader." Typically, people who have this belief think of leaders as charismatic, self-assured, and supremely self-confident. When they compare themselves against this ideal they fall short. The truth of the matter is only a small percentage of leaders meet these criteria. I have worked with very successful leaders who were shy and introverted. While some leaders may not show their self-doubt overtly, they can be full of doubt on the inside. Being charismatic doesn't guarantee success as a leader. Indeed, charisma can contribute to ineffective leadership because it can be over utilized in dealing with others.

A key principle of the leadership zone is that there is no one-size-fits-all framework to apply to leadership. We all are capable of leadership and can demonstrate leadership behavior in our daily lives.

Strategy #2: Stay Connected

Leaders can get isolated. When you are experiencing challenging times, you can fall into a rut and do things repetitively that keep you out of the zone. One of the best ways to get back into the leadership zone is to focus on connecting to others. Networking with people, both inside and outside of your company, is a good way to keep your energy level high and to get exposed to other perspectives. I suggest you ask others about their zone strategies and then incorporate those strategies into your zone recovery approach.

TAKE THE POLE POSITION

In the age of employee empowerment, leadership authority and power have almost become dirty words. I find that some of the leaders I work with are ambivalent and reluctant to use the power of their role. However, leadership power plays an important role in organizational effectiveness. Leaders need to know when to grasp and use their power while avoiding the extremes of overuse or abuse. To be effective, you need to be willing to take the pole position.

The amount of power you have is related to many things. Your ability to get things done generates power. Your ability to connect and influence others has power implications. Your role may have power elements. This power can be formal or informal, perceived or actual, but ultimately you must choose to exercise it. A leader who understands and embraces his power is critical to keeping an organization running fast and smooth.

Not using your leadership power can create a leadership vacuum which can be very destructive, leaving an organization floundering and going in many directions. This is particularly true in talent-based organizations. Geoffrey Colvin wrote a classic article in a *Fortune Magazine* about dream teams, "The most important lesson about team performance is that the basic theory of the dream team is wrong. You cannot assemble a group of stars and then sit back to watch them conquer the world. You can't even count on them to avoid embarrassment. The 2004 U.S. Olympic basketball team consisted entirely of NBA stars; it finished third and lost to Lithuania."[21] With talent there often comes egos, and if you want to get talent to work together, a leader who knows how to use leadership power is critical.

How do leaders effectively utilize their power? There are all kinds of avenues in which leaders exercise power. Leadership includes the power to hire or fire people, the power to set a budget and determine how much money someone has to spend, and the power to hold team members accountable and to monitor progress. You have the power to set direction, to determine how tasks should be organized, and to designate who should do it. The use of power involves judgment, and it involves finding and using what is appropriate in a situation.

One of the more consistent problems I see leaders have in embracing their leadership power is an aversion to conflict. Many leaders don't like conflict and tend to avoid it. Too many leaders want to be liked and this need keeps them from developing the skills needed to handle conflict skillfully. When conflict occurs, they are not prepared to deal with it. The end result is conflict doesn't get resolved and becomes intractable.

You need to understand your leadership power may be tested or challenged at times. As you practice leadership, you will inevitably find yourself in a situation where you have to eliminate or contain an antagonist to protect the organization and reinforce your leadership position. You will need to get comfortable dealing with conflict and challenge. There is no way around it. In these situations you have to seize leadership power. It will not be handed to you and your team will expect you to step up to the bar and do what is necessary.

The first rule of owning your leadership power is to consolidate your position and your role. Consider the following steps as you work to consolidate your role.

Understand Alpha Behavior

One consulting experience I had was with a CEO who was also the founder of his organization. He was a scientist by training but spent very little time in the leadership zone. As part of my initial evaluation, I watched him interact with his team of direct reports at a staff meeting. Ostensibly, it was his meeting, but he was not able to focus the group and keep it on track. People on his team would hijack the meeting and talk about other issues that were completely off-topic. They were just short of openly disrespectful. There was an abundance of behaviors in that staff meeting that I would call borderline insubordination.

I was really struck by the fact that even though he was the CEO, it was in name only. No one treated him with the respect the title should have elicited. He was really puzzled by this dissatisfying scenario. It was not a one-time situation, and he had the sense that there was something wrong.

Analyzing the dynamics of the group, I came to the conclusion there were two people on his staff who thought of themselves as his rivals. Whether they had lost respect for him since he wasn't strong in his role, or because of their own need to lead and dominate things, they saw themselves as more the leaders of the organization than the CEO. He had not taken ownership of his role and it was creating problems.

You cannot be an effective leader if you have not consolidated your position. People will not see you as leader and, therefore, you will not be able to lead. Unfortunately, certain situations require you to put people in their place; this is what is known as practicing alpha behavior. When you practice alpha behavior you are establishing necessary order and hierarchy. This is not about ego, it is about effective leadership. In practicing alpha behavior, you have to recognize behavior in others that is a genuine threat to your authority and respond accordingly.

Assess Threats to Your Effectiveness

You have to have your threat antenna up. Part of evaluating a challenge to your authority is to observe people over a period of time to get a sense of what their intentions really are. I have worked with people who are so suspicious that they constantly overact and are always in a defensive mode. They are always putting people in their place and responding to people aggressively. This type of behavior from a leader will only create more problems in the long run. The key is to learn to discriminate between what is an actual threat and what is not.

Corporate cultures and individual personalities are all different. You must first evaluate what type of behavior is acceptable and what is over the line. For instance, say you are self-effacing and poke fun at yourself. If your direct reports do it as well, it is probably because you have sanctioned that kind of behavior. They are most likely not considering it a challenge to your authority. Even in these situations you should have your antenna fine-tuned to understand when someone is going too far.

It is important the organization accepts you in your leadership role. A worst-case scenario is you have a person actively or even subtly sabotaging you. If your team is not supporting you or even one highly influential person is not with you, you have trouble. They could be criticizing you in hallway conversations, breeding discontent in the ranks, and undermining your leadership. This type of behavior sets up a failure scenario. You will not be able to focus on the things that are really important because you will constantly be putting out fires and dealing with resistance. Your job as a leader has become ten times more difficult. It is critical that you learn to quickly assess threats to your leadership and deal with them effectively.

Understand Testing Behavior and Threat Containment

Testing the leader is part of human nature. In the world of Formula One racing, there is a technique called "trading paint." As a way of getting ahead, some drivers will deliberately bump or brush the car in front of them. This is highly dangerous and could result in a serious accident but that doesn't stop drivers from doing it. Even though the car in the lead may have to compensate as a result of this technique, a good driver will be able to maintain control and hopefully maintain his advantage. The best drivers expect trading paint behavior from other drivers and don't let it derail them.

There are whole classes of behaviors that are a genuine threat to your leadership. The most obvious is when a team member or peer overtly challenges you. For example, say you are leading a meeting and you say, "We are going to start the project on a certain date." A member of the team responds that he is not going to do that. Another example is a team within your organization tries to invade your turf and take responsibility for something you, or your team, are already managing.

Another form of testing occurs when people test the strength of your convictions or stated positions. They want to find out if you really mean what you say. They are trying to decide how much to trust you. You don't want to confuse an power-based challenge with a trust-based one. One CEO I worked with had always reinforced a special day where workers could bring in their daughters and sons to work. The CEO always made it a point to be there that day and bring his daughter to work. One year, he was going to be out of the office on that day. A long-term team member heard the CEO was not going to be there. He gently confronted the CEO and pointed out if he were not there people would wonder what the CEO's commitment level was. Why was he no longer supporting this special event?

Rather than being put off or challenged by the team member's behavior, the CEO realized the position the team member raised was a valid one. He thanked the team member for pointing out the concern and changed his itinerary for the day. As a leader, you have to understand that certain responsibilities come with power.

When you are in the role of leadership, you have to have your antenna up for consistency in your own behavior.

Leaders live in an environment where people will challenge, test, and scrutinize them. You have to learn to differentiate between challenges that are valid tests to address with normal behavior and those you need to assertively respond to. While you need to respond quickly to a team member being insubordinate or another team trying to take ownership over something that you are responsible for, you may not find it necessary to respond as assertively to other behaviors that don't really fit that mode.

The key is to respond to challenges to your leadership in an assertive manner and deal with it quickly. Ignoring, avoiding, or minimizing undermining behavior is a big mistake and only encourages the behavior.

Dealing with Former Peers and Prior Leaders

Just because you have the title and the role, respect for your leadership still must be earned. You earn it by your behavior, your skills, and by playing the role effectively. A particularly challenging situation to earn leadership power is when you have to lead what were previously your peers.

While a promotion may elevate you, your former peers may have difficulty accepting your new status. You may even have difficulty accepting the change in role yourself. There are generally two variables that strongly influence how the transition will go; the level of relationship you had with your peers prior to the transition, and how you handled the transition.

If you have respectful relationships with your peers and distinguished yourself through your performance, your peers will be less resistant to the transition. They will be more trusting of you and will acknowledge your role more easily. I always recommend leaders spend time building peer relationships because it is like putting money in the bank. When the challenge of leading people who were previously your peers happens, you will have currency you can draw on.

It is important to take nothing for granted. Some of your peers may have difficulty accepting your new role even if you have good relationships with them. Typically, the problem stems from them believing they were more worthy of the promotion than you. You will need to deal with this problem directly and quickly. The best approach is to have a direct conversation about making choices. Acknowledge they weren't chosen and point out their resistant behavior. Emphasize they have a choice about accepting the situation or looking for another opportunity, which you'll help them do. Establish the position that you can support them moving on but if they stay they will need to support you. Sitting on the sidelines, being non-committal, or actively resisting the transition is not an option.

Another challenging leadership situation is when you have to lead an organization when the former leader is still in the organization. Typically this situation occurs when the prior leader is demoted or steps down, and you are asked to step in.

The important variables to assess in this situation are: how does the individual feel about their change in role, what is their orientation to you, what is their level of support within the organization, and what options do you have.

Let's examine the last point first. You'll want to understand your options before moving into the role. You'll want to understand why the former leader is still in the organization, what value he brings, and why he wasn't let go. You'll want to understand how much leeway you have to deal with the situation if it is unworkable. If the individual is seen as still having a lot of value, you'll want to respect that position and find a way to leverage it. A worst case scenario is inheriting a person who is antagonistic to you and is untouchable.

Understanding how the individual feels and is reacting to their change in role will determine how you approach the situation. If a person is very negative and resentful, the opportunity for a successful transition is low. You'll need to make a determination whether you think the individual can get over the negative emotions given time and your support, or is it a lost cause you will invest minimal time and effort in resolving.

The individual's orientation to you is important. If you have had prior relationship, that can impact how the transition goes. They may or may not be able to separate you from the situation. You'll want to evaluate how the individual is reacting to you in determining your next steps.

Finally, you'll want to evaluate the level of support the former leader possesses within the organization. If the support level is strong and the organization feels the decision regarding the leader is wrong, you'll have your hands full. You will need to walk a fine line between establishing your leadership role and minimizing the resistance to you. You will want to try and enlist the former leader's support in winning over the team if possible.

Dealing with a previous leader in your organization is a challenging scenario to navigate. Assess the individual and your options quickly. As a leader, you don't want to be looking over your shoulder all the time or be embroiled in a no-win situation. Select a strategy that minimizes resistance and allows you to focus on your leadership and the goals you want to achieve.

Excel in Crisis Mode

There is no other time that demands more decisive leadership than during a crisis. It is during times of stress, setback, and challenge that your organization will have particularly high expectations of leadership from you and you'll need to use your leadership power effectively. You will need to recognize the signs of an impending crisis early and formulate a strategy for how you are going to respond. Get things right, and your leadership will be enhanced. Hesitate, appear indecisive, or make the wrong decisions and your leadership will suffer.

While I could write an entire book on leadership in times of crisis, here is a quick primer on what to do.

Step One: Recognize the signs of an impending crisis early.

- Continually scan the environment for changes that might impact your team
- Listen to the running commentary in the news and publications relevant to your field for increased signs of negativity
- Keep your finger on the pulse of the organization. Listen for signs of increased anxiety and fear
- Develop a causality matrix that links trigger events, relationships, reactions, and outcomes. For example, what would happen if a major customer dramatically cut back their forecast with you? How would you know about it early enough to do something about it?

Step Two: Remember, your role is to provide calm and focus.

- Develop a strategy ahead of time to prepare yourself for when you'll need to act

- Provide perspective and help people interpret events and consequences. Create a narrative that explains what is going on and how long it will last
- Remain calm and in control. Your team is taking its cues from you
- Be visible. Don't hide in your office. People want to see you make the rounds and walk around
- Don't fall into the trap of trying to provide all the answers. There are things you won't know, don't be afraid to admit it
- Use the rumor mill to your advantage. Feed it information that reinforces the messages you want delivered
- Deal aggressively with negative behavior that contributes to fear. Stress can bring out the worst in people, be ready to contain it.

By following these steps, you will be ready to respond to crisis and emergency in a way that reinforces your leadership role.

Establish a Leadership Platform

In addition to embracing the leadership zone and becoming comfortable with your leadership power, you can create a leadership platform to help you take the pole position. A leadership platform is the set of ideas, values, principles, and practices you consistently use to engage other people and organizations. It defines what others can expect from you as a leader. It forces your words to be consistent with your actions.

Your platform serves as one of your more important self-monitoring tools. By making it explicit and communicating it, you commit yourself to it. Your platform demands a high level of self-accountability and honesty. This is why it is important to only include things you believe in and can actively and consistently support. Anything that is trendy or true for others may not work for you. Don't sacrifice your credibility.

Your leadership platform is a short list of those things you will focus on and emphasize as important in your communication with others. In this sense, you are like a politician who is heavily into his campaign, communicating a platform of ideas and positions to capture the imagination of others and get elected.

The issues or themes that make up your leadership platform are those messages you will return to again and again. Your platform themes should remain consistent, and it is important you stay on message. Your platform should include your personal values, as well as the values held by the organization you represent. Not only that, but it must be consistent with the values of those to whom the organization is responsible: be it a group of investors, a board of directors, stockholders, customers, or the public at large.

One critical aspect of a leader's platform is there must be a strong link, an obvious association, between that leader's initiatives and the organization's success. If a leader is spending time and energy on something not core to the organization, the organization will not be on board and support it. There must be an obvious connection between what a leader is focusing on and its direct impact on the organization.

Initiatives on your leadership platform must not be reactive day-to-day type issues. They should be directly tied to building the organization and require a longer time frame to execute. I am not describing a quarter-by-quarter-strategy. Instead, I am talking in terms of at least year, or maybe even three. Platform elements should require sustained attention on the part of a leader.

Remember, these are things you cannot get distracted from. Once you pick them up, you must not put them down. When you have an initiative on your platform, you need to stick with it. Always carry it with you and find ways to continually make reference to it.

Your behavior and attitudes towards the platform elements must remain consistent, but remain fresh and alive. When an item is on your platform, focus attention on it, go after it, and build it. Go on the campaign trail with it. Put energy behind it. Stay focused. Keep encouraging it. Put into place the infrastructure to support it. It is only then people on your team will realize you are really serious about it. With every action, communicate, "This is important."

You can say you believe in something, but your actions and behavior must show support for those words. Be assured the people around you will look at your behavior and analyze how much you are budgeting in time and effort to support your platform proposals. If your actions don't line up with the messages people hear, they will soon conclude you are just paying lip service to the idea.

Let me give you an example of a leadership platform I helped create for one leader. Here are the key points she consistently focused on:

- Always come prepared to meetings and I'll do the same.
- If you want a quick response from me, leave me a voicemail and not an e-mail.
- Turn a critical eye on all of your proposals because I will be doing the same.
- Let's not take shortcuts on things that are critical, and instead, do it the right way the first time so we don't have to continually re-do our work.
- We need to resolve things quickly and with appropriate urgency because the marketplace and our competitors are moving quickly.

- Our main competitive advantage is the quality of our products and customer service. We are not the low price leader.
- Hire talent—don't settle for C-players. We'll always find ways to utilize talent creatively.

In developing your leadership platform, here are a few elements that you might want to consider including:

- The vision of the organization and what you are doing to support it
- The mission for the organization and how it is being realized
- Key strategies you have developed and deployed
- Challenges you want the organization to respond to
- Key opportunities you want to take advantage of
- The charter of the organization
- Key initiatives you are promoting
- Values that are important to the organization
- Your expectations and standards for performance
- Organizational ground rules
- Important business updates and forecasts
- Your personal leadership journey
- Customer success stories
- Examples of alignment and team work within the organization

Now that you have assumed the pole position, it's time to turn your attention to driving the machine as fast as you can. To get the best performance, you'll need to quickly diagnose problems that slow you down. In the next chapter, we'll dig into diagnosing problems at high speed so you can keep your organizational machine between the guard rails and win the race.

ACCELERATION TOOL#10: POLE POSITION CHECKLIST
Use the following check list to keep your leadership behavior in tiptop shape.

- Estimate how much time you spend in the leadership zone on a weekly basis. Do you want to keep it the same or increase it?
- What are your leadership zone triggers? For example, do you self-nominate or prefer to be drafted?
- What are the things that may be preventing you from spending more time in the leadership zone? What are you going to do to change the situation?
- What was your most recent leadership zone experience? What was it like and how will you recreate it?
- How conducive is your work environment to leadership behaviors?
- How supportive is your boss of your leadership behaviors?
- How comfortable do you feel taking a leadership role?
- Where would you place yourself on the continuum of using leadership power? Do you tend to under utilize it or over use it?
- What forms of leadership testing have you experienced? Have you ever had to deal directly with a threat to your leadership role? What would you have done differently?
- Have you ever had to deal with a crisis? If yes, what would you have done differently?
- What is your leadership platform? How are you communicating it? Is it resonating with your organization?

CHAPTER 11

Diagnosis on the Fly

It was my fear that made me learn everything
I could about my airplane and my emergency
equipment, and kept me flying respectful of my
machine and always alert in the cockpit.

CHUCK YEAGER, US AIR FORCE MAJOR GENERAL, THE
FIRST PILOT TO FLY FASTER THAN THE SPEED OF SOUND

IMAGINE YOU ARE A JET pilot screaming through the sky at 500 miles per hour. At that speed, everything becomes a blur. For a pilot, being aware of your position in the sky can be a matter of life or death. Without knowing information about airspeed and altitude, a pilot can't adjust the throttle and flaps to avoid stalling the plane. It's very dangerous to fly blind.

Thankfully, a cockpit is a feedback-rich environment. Gauges give the pilot immediate information on all the important performance systems. However, with so much information, a pilot could quickly be overloaded and in just as much danger as someone flying with no gauges at all. To avoid this problem, cockpits have been specially designed to minimize clutter and present relevant information in a well-organized and easy-to-read manner.

There are two kinds of information a pilot must pay attention to: critical and status. Critical information is the vital details a pilot needs at any given moment, including airspeed and altitude. Status information includes the types of gauges the pilot only needs to look at once in a while, such as fuel levels or radar. Modern cockpits have been designed in a way that organizes these various types of information to be easily observed. This is of particular importance when a pilot is trying to identify a problem on the fly.

In Chapter Nine, I discussed the importance of having your dashboard in top working order to get immediate feedback on the performance of your organization. Accurate real-time information is critical to the faster leader. Knowing what is going on in the organization and having clear feedback on key factors is essential to staying on top of things and making adjustments to optimize performance. Operating on inaccurate or out-of-date information dramatically increases the risk of making poor decisions.

A faster leader must be alert because things happen very quickly today. Things can rapidly escalate out of control and snowball because of the pace of change. This can lead to poor efficiency, misdiagnosis of the real problem, or an exercise in poor judgment. The recovery window can often be very narrow, quick action is paramount.

This chapter covers several important tools that allow a leader to diagnose problems and act quickly. I'll discuss a framework for quickly diagnosing different types of problems, how to build risk scenarios, how to recognize critical periods where your actions have greater impact, and understanding your team's redline. Your role as **Chief Assessment Officer (CAO)** is at the forefront of these activities.

ASSESS PROBLEMS ON THE FLY WITH THE PTAM

In the middle of a crisis, you can't call a time out while you figure out what is going on, what's not working, and how to fix it. Things can move so quickly that by the time you understand a problem it may be too late to address it. The window for fixing problems is incredibly small and the risks of getting it wrong are very high. Adding to the challenge are complexity and interaction effects that make problem solving more difficult. As you fix one thing, it can cause problems in other areas.

Leaders are often in the position where they know their organization is not performing optimally, but they are not sure why this is the case or what to do about it. The sheer number of possibilities or variables can be overwhelming. On top of that, the leader may be under significant time constraints and facing a sense of urgency to act quickly.

To help leaders quickly identify and solve problems, I developed the Problem Type Analysis Model (PTAM). The model articulates eleven different problem types. Each of the problem types can occur in any organization and they generally revolve around performance gaps between what is actually happening versus what is expected.

In certain cases you may encounter problems at multiple levels, or a problem at one level may be linked to another problem at a different level. Be prepared to use the model in a reiterative manner to fine-tune your diagnosis, as things may change over time. Don't fall in love with any particular diagnosis. Problem assessment is best approached from an objective standpoint. Diagnosing the problem accurately helps you pick an appropriate intervention. The types of problems covered by the PTAM include:

1. Task problems
2. Resource problems

3. People problems
4. Relationship problems
5. Process problems
6. Structure problems
7. Value problems
8. Direction problems
9. Alignment problems
10. Leadership problems
11. Culture problems

Task

The task category relates to basic work activities of the team. These activities are the nuts and bolts of organizational work. Tasks represent things to be done and are closely tied to goals or deadlines. Generally, problems at the task level will manifest themselves as missed deadlines, incomplete work, poorly defined work activities, and confused expectations relating to outcomes, goals, and deadlines.

Task problems are usually due to tasks not being clearly identified, not being defined in concrete terms, not being prioritized, not having a deliverable date assigned to them, or not being clear on who is responsible for them. Task problems are usually the easiest to identify and resolve.

Resources

Many projects and initiatives fail because they are under-resourced. In an environment defined by change and acceleration, it is easy to overlook this important performance variable. Because there is much to be done in organizations, a condition of **initiative overload** is often created. We try to do too much with too little. Another key contributor to the problem of resourcing is different levels of the organization have different views on the amount of effort or work required to accomplish a project. The executive team can fall into the habit of underestimating resources while the rank and file can over estimate what is needed. You can get into a vicious cycle where over optimism competes with pessimism.

Resourcing is an important, but overlooked variable to pay attention to because it has a major impact on morale and planning. Chronic under-resourcing leads to team member burnout and planning based on faulty assumptions about what can be accomplished. This approach contributes to predictable failure.

People

The people category of the PTAM relates to problems caused by individuals and/or a team or group. The primary issues are usually a performance gap or negative behavior. Symptoms of a people problem could include an individual or team who continually misses milestones, is self-centered and focuses only on what impacts them, has poor attendance or makes little or no contribution, deliberately tries to upset and antagonize others, creates us-versus-them dynamics, creates and reinforces rumors, is in over his/her head or in the wrong job, or has personal problems or dysfunctions that spill over into the work environment.

In particular, you will want to assess the specific types of people who are obstacles to change and momentum. I have identified the following types of problem people:

- **Poor performers**: Due to lack of skills, low motivation, or poor job fit, they consistently miss deadlines and goals. They act as a drag on momentum because their lack of performance impacts others. If you allow poor performance to continue, you will take a credibility hit because other higher performing team members expect you to do address it.

- **Saboteurs**: Actively engage in behaviors that are intended to derail or defeat any initiatives you start.
- **Resisters**: Anything new is bad or threatening to them.
- **Depleters:** Suck the air out of the room by verbalizing all of the reasons a thing can't be done. They dampen any enthusiasm and kill excitement through the use of excuses and over generalization.
- **Confusers:** Over complicate things or use tangents to stall momentum.
- **Controllers**: Have to be in charge, and if they are not, they will not play ball or engage.
- **Detail Addicts**: Distrust anything that is not defined at a detailed level. Any ambiguity is a bad thing. They slow down momentum by asking for tons of details.
- **Passive Aggressives**: On the surface they look like they are agreeing, but once you leave the room or the conversation, they change their tune.
- **Calculators**: Evaluate the costs and benefits of aligning with you on an ongoing basis. Their commitment is conditional as long as it is in their best interest.

In certain cases, a personal problem may initially look like a relationship problem, which I'll cover next. However, when you talk to other team members, you will find they have similar issues with the problem person or group. People problems tend to be one-sided.

Relationship

Problems at the relationship level revolve around interpersonal themes. Relationship problems impact how people interact with each other. This type of problem is different than a people problem because the interaction is the problem, not an individual or group. These problems can develop between two team members or between operational groups. When at the team level, problems of this type can manifest themselves in us-versus-them thinking and competition. Relationship problems can be holdovers from previous interactions. Generally the issues stem from differences in competitive agendas, interpersonal style, mistrust, missing or limited credibility, or lack of respect.

A team or organization experiencing relationship issues might have the following symptoms: withdrawal by members of a team, reluctance to attend meetings or participate in discussions, protracted conflict between individuals, conflict avoidance, coalitions, hoarding behaviors, and attack and blaming behaviors.

Relationship problems are more difficult to deal with than task problems because they involve affiliation, emotions, judgments, and interpretations of behavior.

Process

Problems at the process level involve *how* an organization accomplishes its tasks. Process relates to methods, workflow, and procedures. Important processes like setting strategy or direction, communication, and decision making are often negatively affected. Process problems can show up in areas that exist between functions or teams where ownership is unclear or ambiguous. Problems at this level often demonstrate themselves as protracted and confusing decision making, lack of unified direction, uneven information flow, communication lapses, poor handoffs between individuals and groups, and inconsistent practices (i.e., not following the formal product development process).

Structure

Structure relates primarily to how a company or group is organized. At a basic level, structure refers to who is actually a member of an organization. An organization's structure includes a definition of the roles in the organization and what those roles are responsible for. An organization that has structure problems might exhibit poor role definition, an absence of needed roles, accountability confusion, role confusion, conflict, and membership tensions (i.e., the right people are not on the team).

In every organization or team, there are areas of structural ambiguity where accountability and ownership are unclear. These areas are **gray zones**. They are where things fall through the cracks, get lost, or generate conflict between groups. The gray zones are where integration and handoffs do not occur. Gray zones are created when silos exist and there is a lack of systematic thinking.

In my experience, most organizational problems relating to structure happen in the gray zones. I always suggest leaders look first to gray zones if they are trying to diagnosis a structural problem. Resolving structural problems often involves negotiation, redesign, and reassigning resources.

Values

The values by which an organization defines itself, evaluates its performance, and makes strategic decisions need to be well-defined, clear, and agreed upon. If team members are not using similar value-based criteria to make decisions, then the organization's decisions will not be consistent. Value-based problems can be quite severe because they involve core beliefs. Poorly defined values generate competition between team members, individual-versus-team agendas, lack of commitment, values battles or arguments, and poor team member retention and low satisfaction levels.

Direction
Whether you call it vision or strategy, organizations need to have clarity about where they are going. While vision has longer-term connotations, the time frame is really not as important as articulating a desired future state for the organization. The direction communicated to the organization has to have the qualities of being engaging, desirable, attainable, and valid. Direction problems manifest themselves as confusion between organizations or teams, multiple or competing agendas, lack of team member engagement, distraction and lack of focus, and poor productivity.

Alignment
All parts of the organization need to be in sync if you want high performance. Goals of individual functions need to be connected and consistent with other functions, connected to the vision of the organization, and not compete with each other. Too often functional or team goals are shortsighted and do not take into account the impact on other teams. Efficiency and effectiveness are negatively impacted because teams are at cross purposes. The overall productivity of the organization is impacted.

Leadership
The leader of an organization exerts a powerful influence on organizational dynamics. The leader needs to help set and maintain boundaries, provide needed direction and clarification, and resolve conflict and disagreement. A leader who does not perform

the necessary leadership functions can impact a team in a negative way.

Ineffective team leaders let conflict go on too long, play favorites, avoid making decisions, do not provide clear direction and support, exclude important stakeholders, do not hold people accountable, and create environments that are political or uninspiring.

Beyond individual leadership, it is important to evaluate the leadership code that exists within an organization. **This code can be explicit or implicit, and it is a set of rules that governs what is acceptable and unacceptable in leadership behavior.** Leaders have a strong effect on the code, but the code takes on a life of its own over time and can have a profound effect on how leadership is exercised.

The leadership code of an organization is a cultural element a leader needs to be mindful of because it exerts an influence on the leader. The code binds the leader tightly. The code determines who will be promoted and given additional responsibility and who will be plateaued or passed over. The code is not always in agreement with what a company says it values in a leader, which makes interpretation of the code challenging. At times the code can actually contradict what a company says is desired leadership behavior.

Organizations are like people in that they create and tell stories about themselves. These stories are part fact, part fiction, a little exaggeration, some truthfulness, and a little propaganda. These stories, which are encompassed in a company's values and operating principles, are often more of a reflection of what they want to become, their aspirations, how they want to see themselves, rather than what they actually are.

Organizations have a much more difficult time talking about what they truly are. Self-criticism and honesty can be difficult or in short supply in organizations because organizational self-evaluation can be a very uncomfortable process. It is up to the individual leader to recognize this dichotomy and find the way through it, piercing the idealized veil to find reality.

Sorting through the many apparent contradictions between what is said and what is done in organizations to uncover the leadership code takes persistence and imagination. Many emerging leaders struggle to decipher this code through trial and error, following their instincts and intuitions, and by watching what other people do. It is like putting the pieces of a puzzle together.

While a few leaders end up in their positions because of political skills, alliances, or luck, others have figured out the leadership code and the secret that exists at its very core. Many of the most important things a leader must master are *not* those things that are openly talked about.

Why do these leadership secrets exist? It took me time to figure it out. First, the leadership code can be a test of sorts. It is the kind of test you can fail without even knowing you are in the midst of taking it. In Darwinian terms, it is like survival of the fittest. Those who figure it out survive and prosper. Those who don't crack the code get ignored or sidetracked.

In some companies, the code exists but it hasn't been openly talked about or discussed. It is simply there in the background. In these situations, a leader may not consciously be aware of the code but it can still have a profound effect on behavior.

Organizations generally are not deceptive on purpose. While there may be a few companies that send mixed messages on purpose, the discrepancies that exist are more typically due to the struggle that exists between what a company *is* versus what it wants to become.

In many companies, this gap is very small. They have made significant strides towards achieving their ideals. The leadership strongly supports key values and practices. In other companies, the gap is quite large. Where the gap is large, leaders will have a much more difficult time deciphering the code because greater inconsistencies will exist.

Culture

A final category to assess in solving problems is the overall culture of an organization. Think of culture as being the sum of its parts, yet having its own unique properties. Culture is the environment in which leaders operate. Ingredients like people, values in use, vision, and the leadership code help to create the culture of an organization.

Culture can be an accelerator or a decelerator depending on its characteristics. If the culture has serious elements of dysfunction like resistance to change, aversion to conflict, or a strong insular nature, it can present real challenges to the leader. Problems that are culture-based are the most difficult to assess and deal with because culture is like the DNA of an organization and is very difficult to change.

Assessing culture involves collecting information from several inputs and sources, connecting the themes, and organizing the data into an overall picture. In developing your assessment of a culture, you might want to investigate the following:

- The degree of gap between what an organization says about itself formally versus what it actually does in practice (we say we value diversity when the opposite is really true)
- The organization's orientation to newcomers/new team members

- Who it hires and why
- The organization's orientation to change
- It's orientation to time
- How it deals with conflict
- How self-reflective or self-critical the organization is
- Who rises to the top and why
- How well it meets its goals and objectives
- The organization's leadership code
- How quickly, or slowly it makes decisions
- The organization's orientation to risk, uncertainty, or ambiguity
- How it deals with customers, and/or other external stakeholders
- The organization's ability to stay the course regardless of distractions.

By using the Problem Type Analysis Model on a regular basis, you will be able to quickly identify what is going wrong in your organization and implement needed changes. I have included a checklist of actions you can take to rectify the different types of problems you might encounter in the acceleration tool at the end of this chapter.

RECOGNIZE CRITICAL PERIODS: MAXIMIZE YOUR IMPACT

Oftentimes leaders can pour considerable energy into an activity and have very little impact on the outcome. Try as they might, they simply cannot get the organization to respond to them. At other times, leaders can accomplish a great deal with very little expenditure of energy. It can seem almost effortless. Many leaders I work with struggle with this phenomenon and it can leave them frustrated, or bewildered. It can bring on a sense of powerlessness or an exaggerated sense of efficacy. Leaders can be unsure as to why they were successful in one situation and not in another.

Underlying this experience is a principle leaders need to understand if they want to be faster and more effective. It can be simply stated as: **"A leader's influence on his organization is not constant, but rather varies over time."** The leader's varying impact is strongly influenced by the fact that organizations regularly go through what are called critical periods. This is different than the critical path I have talked about previously.

A critical period is a concept borrowed from human development and can be thought of as an interval of time characterized by receptivity, accelerated learning, and change. Just as human beings go through critical periods, organizations do to. A critical period in organizational terms is an interval of time when the organization is particularly open and receptive to the influence of the leader. Critical periods are relatively short-lived organizational phenomena, lasting from a few days to a few months. If a leader recognizes a critical period and acts accordingly, it is like he injects super high-octane fuel into the system.

Whether it is a large-scale change initiative or an intervention in a problem scenario, the timing of the activity can have a huge impact on its outcome. If the organization is in a critical period, the progress can be great. If not in a critical period, progress can be slow or nonexistent. A critical period represents a window of opportunity and action for the faster leader. By understanding the concept of critical periods and learning to recognize them, the leader can dramatically improve effectiveness and speed. Critical periods can help leaders decide when to act and act quickly, when to move slowly and build momentum, or when to delay action.

Critical Period Indicators

Every organization, no matter its size, has a baseline level that represents its business-as-usual state. An impending critical period can be indicated by a trend away from this steady state. To assess whether or not your organization is entering a critical period, watch for the following trends:

- The level of confusion and noise increases. People seem less sure or confident, and may display more overt anxiety.
- People are trying new behaviors with greater frequency.
- The level of defensiveness decreases and more openness is observed.
- People increase the level at which they seek you out and want your feedback.
- People respond more robustly to your suggestions, direction, and guidance.
- The level of positive buzz increases.

If you observe any of these trends, the next step is to evaluate the receptivity and readiness of the organization through a series of probing actions. Generally, the probing actions need to be smaller, more incremental changes you ask the organization to make. The final step is to observe and monitor the organization's responses to your changes. In particular, you will want to watch for any signs of resistance such as the ones outlined in Chapter Three.

ASSESSING RISK SCENARIOS

Another element of diagnosing problems on the fly involves assessing risk and risk scenarios. Risk is assessed before a pilot gets into the cockpit and constantly during the course of the flight. Similarly, a leader cannot take his eyes off risk factors because they change dynamically and can cause you to fail before you are even aware of it.

A certain amount of paranoia in a leader is healthy. Many projects and organizational initiatives are technically complex and involve many people from different functions. There is a large potential for things to go wrong. Different projects can impact each other. Relying on subcontractors or outsourcing brings risk. Things rarely go as planned. Unexpected things *can* and *do* happen. Even when things seem to be going right, unforeseen events can quickly derail what you are trying to achieve.

Successful performance depends on accurately anticipating risks and developing scenarios to replicate risks that can occur. Don't try to do all of this yourself, involve your team. I'll talk more about how you respond to these scenarios in the next chapter.

As you and your team develop the scenario risk profile for any given situation or environment, it is helpful to review the issues and suggestions outlined below.

- Identify upfront the key scenario risks during the initial scoping and due diligence process of any project or initiative. Try to capture all the risks you can. Evaluate the likelihood, magnitude, and recoverability of those risks.
- Determine whether the scenario has potential for migrating or changing scope. Scenarios that include significant development or innovation are especially prone to migration and can easily impact other activities.
- Assess the team's ability to set boundaries around the scenario and stay the course. Certain organizations have a tendency to pull resources in multiple different directions,

which end up in stalled momentum. As a consequence, the schedule slips and team members have to work much harder to get things back on track.

- Evaluate opposition or resistance in the scenario. In certain scenarios, there may be a considerable lack of widespread organizational support. This lack of support can increase the risk of failure because critical resources may be withheld or offered in a token manner.

- Consider the level of interdependency between the scenario and other activities. If a linked activity misses a deliverable, it could impact your scenario. The risk from related activities flows into your work flow.

- Scenario risk and value-based decision drivers are linked. If your team has successfully identified its decision drivers (e.g., speed or time to market, quality, response to customer, cost, functionality, opportunistic), these same drivers can help the team identify scenario risks. For example, if the team has defined the scenario as a time-to-market initiative and developed decision drivers that reflect this theme, then the scenario risks will be related to schedule slippage and late deliverables.

- Evaluate team composition. Organizations consistently underestimate the risks associated with team membership. New teams, those with a high concentration of contractors or temporaries, and teams that have had significant membership changes, are more risky in terms of performance than established teams.

- Consider how many new processes your team must develop. More risk is involved if the team has to develop new work processes to fulfill its scenario objectives rather than relying on existing processes. Scenario risk is increased if existing work processes are inefficient.

- The loss of a resource (e.g., people, tools, and budget) can pose significant risk. Be sure to identify risks related to key resources. When considering people risk, evaluate things like flight risk or potential for burnout.
- Be sure to consider the risks that face individual team members. Team member career/personal needs, workload pressures, and new skill development requirements can stress individuals and represent additional project risks.

Finally, when evaluating risks, be sure to use a categorization system to quickly identify the magnitude of the risk. By differentiating between types of risk, your team will be able to respond and prioritize their responses. Here's a simple risk model you can use.

Category 1 Risk: The ability of this type of risk to impact the scenario is great and can cause failure. High risk variables must be managed and controlled at all costs.

Category 2 Risk: These types of risk can have a significant impact on schedule and can compromise milestones and key deliverables. Category 2 risks can result in major modifications to the scope or timeline.

Category 3 Risk: This type of risk is moderate and can result in schedule delays and cost overruns. However, these risks can generally be absorbed in the overall plan or approach as long as you don't let them get out of hand.

TEST THE REDLINE

With all this talk of speed, it is important for the faster leader to remember to not overdo it. You can only go as fast as your team allows you to. When a leader pushes too hard, the team performance begins to suffer. The team can feel like they can't win or no amount of effort is sufficient. Not understanding your team's limits is a mistake that many leaders make.

In the world of performance racecars, there is a concept called redlining. This is essentially the amount of RPMs a car's engine can handle before it freezes or blows a gasket. The term comes from the point on a speedometer where the numbers turn to red. It can be risky to push your car beyond the red line and, likewise, you shouldn't push your team to that limit either.

Pacing is a key aspect of being a faster leader and it is how you avoid exceeding the redline. The speed you set for your team is determined by a couple of factors. First, the competitive landscape or market you are in helps set the pace. Certain industries, like high technology, have a very fast pace. Any team that plays in this type of environment must equal or exceed the pace set by the industry. The second factor that plays into pace is the team's performance range. The leader has to hit the right pace by taking into consideration both the industry pace and the team's uppermost limit.

Think of the leader as a pace setter. The leader evaluates the team's uppermost performance limit by putting them through drills and challenges. I talked about using road tests in Chapter Nine to put your team through its paces. Some teams by their nature are sprinters—good at going very fast for a short period of time. Other teams are more like marathoners who can sustain a relatively fast pace for a long period of time. As a leader, you need to identify what works for your particular team. You'll need to test your team's redline to determine the pace you set. And remember that your own pace as a leader may not match the team's pace.

The problem solving tools I have discussed in this chapter are vital in setting up an effective work environment. With constant feedback at the ready, you will be able to make the various adjustments that will keep your team at the front of the pack. In the next chapter, I'll discuss how to make the best flight deck decisions you can.

ACCELERATION TOOL #11: THE PTAM QUICK ACTION GUIDE

The PTAM model is not just a diagnostic framework; it is also a guide for action. Here are some actions you can take when you have arrived at a diagnosis for your team.

Fix Task Problems

To fix a task problem try the following things:

- Define tasks in concrete action steps.
- Develop a tasks list with priorities.
- Assign due dates that are feasible.
- Assign clear task ownership.
- Review progress on an ongoing basis.
- Hold people accountable for the tasks assigned to them.

Fix Resourcing Problems

To fix a resourcing problem try the following things:

- When adding a project or requirement, be sure to remove or cancel something else.
- Build in a safety margin to allow for unseen risks or setbacks.
- Make sure to solicit the feedback of the people actually doing the work.
- Institute a transparent planning/resourcing process so that everyone is operating from the same information and assumptions.
- Ensure that the resources assigned to an initiative stay with the initiative over its life cycle.

Fix People Problems

To intervene with a people problem, try some of the following suggestions:

- Identify the problem behaviors.
- Assess whether the problem is due to awareness, skills, motivation, or resources.
- Clearly identify and communicate the performance gap.
- Evaluate the fit between the person and the job and move the person into another role if the gap is too large.
- Call the person/team on their behavior in a non-confrontational setting. Give visibility to the specific behavior so it is out in the open.
- Hold regular meetings with the individual/team to focus on the problem behaviors.
- Set up clear consequences for continued dysfunctional behavior.
- Institute formal performance management procedures such as a performance improvement plan.
- Remove or isolate the individual.

Fix Relationship Problems

When dealing with a relationship problem, try some of the following suggestions:

- Build trust and respect by having opposing parties work together on tasks that require cooperation to succeed. Hold both groups accountable for the results.
- Enforce ground rules or develop new ones to contain the problems.

- Challenge people to re-evaluate their assumptions and interpretations.
- Pull the involved parties together for mediation.
- Hold team-building activities.
- Set up mutual team goals that require both teams to cooperate and collaborate to succeed.

Fix Process Problems

When encountering process problems within the organization, try some of the following suggestions to resolve the issues:

1. Map out processes to uncover gaps.
2. Build in feedback loops to collect information about process performance.
3. Establish a method for creating and communicating a strategy to the organization.
4. Revisit and refine decision processes.
5. Plan for adequate handoffs and formal transitions between groups.
6. Ensure defined processes are followed or uncover reasons for noncompliance.
7. Re-engineer processes that are not working.

Fix Structural Problems

Suggestions to fix structural problems include:

- Redefine or revisit roles.
- Negotiate accountability and ownership.
- Redistribute workloads.
- Resolve conflict by minimizing role overlap.
- Evaluate structure to ensure it is consistent with the objectives of the organization.

Fix Value Problems

To minimize or resolve value problems in the organization, try the following activities:

- Translate values into operational and behavioral terms so they become tangible. Turn them into decision drivers.
- Reinforce decision drivers on a regular basis.
- Challenge the organization to focus on organizational values, not just functional values.
- Check for commitment before engaging in an activity.
- Make sure organizational values are fully communicated and understood.

Fix Direction Problems

To address direction problems, try the following:

- Make sure you developed and communicated a clear direction for your organization. Evaluate the assumptions you might be making—it might be clear to you, but is it clear to others?
- Check out the level of awareness regarding the direction across multiple levels of the organization.
- How well does the direction fit your operating environment?
- Review with your leadership team the specifics of the direction. Make sure they take the additional steps of communicating the direction accurately to their teams.
- Directly address any confusion and clarify the specifics of the direction.
- Review the direction with the organization on a consistent basis and reinforce its key elements.
- Recognize successes associated with the direction

Fix Alignment Problems

To address alignment problems, try the following:

- Establish a goal-planning process that establishes cross functional goals and fosters interdependence when possible.
- Link functional goals to the organization's overall direction.
- Define success as multiple teams working together and collaborating to accomplish a goal. Set up scenarios where one team cannot be successful if another team is not.
- Monitor performance and resource allocation for consistency.
- Deal with any misalignment quickly.

Fix Leadership Problems

If you are trying to minimize or resolve leadership problems in your organization, try the following activities:

- Make sure leaders understand the impact of their actions on the organization.
- Encourage leaders to deal quickly and decisively with conflict.
- Have leaders define their leadership platforms and communicate them to the organization on a regular basis.
- Encourage leaders to model desired behaviors.
- Encourage leaders to reinforce team ground rules and agreements.
- Have leaders solicit feedback on their leadership effectiveness on a regular basis.
- Distribute leadership functions throughout the organization so the organization is not dependent on one leader.

- Articulate the leadership code in more formal ways so leaders will have a clearer sense of what is acceptable and what is not.
- Try to close the gap between what the organization says it values and what it actually does in terms of leadership behavior.

Fix Culture Problems

To address culture problems, try the following:

- Establish a formal monitoring process to check how well the organization is actually following its values.
- When gaps are found, take action to bring the organization back in line with its stated values.
- Identify aspects of the culture that are dysfunctional. Develop interventions targeted at changing the dysfunctional patterns.
- Import new talent to help change the organization.
- Reorganize to break up groups that reinforce the status quo.

CHAPTER 12

Flight Deck Decisions

When you speed something up, the flaws become evident.

AMONG THE HUNDREDS OF DECISIONS leaders can make, there are several that rise to the top because of their significance. I call them flight deck decisions because they represent important decisions leaders make regarding how they will engage the organization and keep it on track. These decisions determine whether a leader lands the plane or crashes into a hillside. The flight deck decisions I cover in this chapter involve a choice by the leader to either let things play out or intervene and change course.

Like a pilot on the flight deck, the faster leader needs to know when to move from observation to action. Acting too early or too late can bring disaster or failure. The faster leader cultivates judgment in this area through practice, drills, and training.

At the heart of knowing when to act is the concept of an action threshold. An action threshold is a potential decision for a leader—a pivot point that signals a change in leadership involvement. Rather than thinking about thresholds in an impromptu fashion, I suggest leaders be deliberate and develop formal thresholds that can trigger a change in their behavior. This chapter reviews action thresholds for several key leadership decisions including: dealing with team conflict, getting a team back on track, deciding when to move to plan b, and deciding whether to coach or manage a team member.

TEAM CONFLICT: OBSERVE OR INTERVENE

Conflict between team members can be either constructive or destructive. The challenge is to understand the difference. Without a clear understanding, the leader can interrupt a healthy difference of opinion conversation or let destructive conflict go on too long.

A vigorous debate or difference of opinion can strengthen a team by getting the relevant positions out on the table. A personality conflict that goes unchecked can spiral out of control and pull other team members into the fray.

When is conflict between team members constructive and when does it become destructive? There are two factors that influence the action threshold for the leader. The first factor is the degree the conflict gets personal. The second factor relates to closure or resolution.

As long as the conflict does not become personal, the leader can chose to let the conflict play its course. Different perspectives can help the team to explore alternatives and come up with better decisions. When the conflict becomes personal, motives and emotions come into play. People interpret actions from a negative framework. They assume the worst of others. People's self-worth and fears get activated. Escalation of the conflict is often a consequence. Other people get pulled into the conflict and positions become intractable. You now have a big problem on your hands.

You cannot let personal conflict between team members go unchecked. This is one of the consistent mistakes I see leaders make.

Many leaders are uncomfortable dealing with conflict and the emotions it produces. They don't know how to resolve it. I encourage leaders to act quickly to resolve dysfunctional conflict. Watch for when the threshold is reached and then act.

I suggest you use your leadership power to resolve the conflict. Pull the offending parties together and have a boundary setting conversation. You want to establish the position they don't have to like each other, but they have to support and work with each other. They need to be professional. You need to make this position non-negotiable. Aggressively respond to conflict within your team when it becomes personal. Ignoring this type of team conflict only makes it worse.

Healthy conflict has predictable patterns of resolution. While it may change in intensity and volume, people will compromise and soften their position as their perspective is heard and incorporated into the solution. Positions come closer together. As things move closer to resolution, the noise level drops.

Unhealthy conflict gets stuck in a rut and things don't get resolved. People retreat into their positions and don't budge. The positions become rigid and inflexible.

As long as you see the conflict is moving and positions are changing, you can let the conflict continue. When you see that no new information is being offered, or people are just reiterating their earlier positions, you have reached a threshold and it's time to act. Don't let conflict solidify into immovable positions.

TEAM DECISION MAKING

While team conflict can lead to decision making problems, other factors at work put a leader in an act versus observe dilemma. Empowering teams to make decisions is a desirable leadership behavior. By pushing decision making further down into the organization, the leader fosters greater team ownership and reduces dependency on the leader to make decisions. When everything goes well the leader can monitor the team's decision process and the quality of decisions they make. The leader can stay out of the direct decision making path.

However, it is important to remember teams often get off course. This puts the faster leader in the position of having to intervene. If not done well, the leader's action can have a real disempowering effect. To prevent a negative interaction with the team or having the team fail to meet its objectives, the leader should communicate the concept of action thresholds ahead of time. By spelling out the conditions that signal a change in the leader's behavior, a leader can manage the situation in a way that doesn't alienate team members. The team will understand the boundaries that encompass its decision making.

The leader needs to be clear about the off-track behaviors that are associated with an action threshold being reached. By watching for and tracking patterns of behavior, the leader can intervene before it is too late. Here are a few of the more common behaviors that signal a team may be off course in its decision making:

- Delaying
- Revisiting or reopening
- Avoiding
- Rushing
- Excluding.

These patterns can be started by a single team member, multiple members, or even by a person not on the team. While each one of these patterns can be appropriate and not dysfunctional, the patterns become dysfunctional when no movement is happening and schedules are affected. Let's examine each behavior in more detail.

Delaying

While a certain amount delay can be valid, a team that is delaying too much can cause frustration and compromise schedules. Teams that delay will keep putting off decisions to be made and will talk it to death. The team may cite reasons such as not enough information or it may focus on the behavior of other teams or functions as reasons for delay (e.g., we can't do anything until Team X completes its key deliverable).

The faster leader needs to decide how much delay is right and when the delay exceeds the threshold. A certain amount of delay when critical information is absent is appropriate, but too much delay compromises execution. When the delay threshold is getting close, try the following actions to bring the team back on track:

- Give time frames for needed decisions.
- Continue to put pressure on the team and communicate consequences of the delays.
- Have the team focus on what it can control.
- Focus the team on what it can accomplish rather than on what it can't.
- Revisit and reinforce the decision drivers with the team.
- Require the team to report back on progress.

Revisiting/Reopening

When new and relevant information is received, it needs to be considered and assumptions need to be reassessed. This pattern becomes dysfunctional when decisions keep being revisited and questioned. A problematic revisiting process is often started by an individual or party not involved in making the decision or not buying into the decision.

Set your threshold to allow for a reasonable amount of questioning and challenging while still encouraging progress to be made on the team's objectives. Avoid having the team stall out on its work. When deciding how to intervene, consider the following actions:

- Establish a window of time for decisions to be challenged or questioned.
- Invite decision dissenters to re-engage and contribute.
- Provide context for the decision.
- Caucus other team members to validate the severity of concerns.
- Talk to dissenting parties offline to understand their issues.
- If sufficient information to change the decision is not forthcoming, reinforce the decision and communicate that revisiting behavior is no longer productive. Encourage people to stop resisting the decision and get on board.

Avoiding

A team that is avoiding will not make decisions. Decisions will be delayed in meetings, and the team will focus on other activities. There are reasons why a team avoids making decisions. The decisions may be hard to make, unpopular, or political. Ownership for the decision may not be clear, or the consequences of the decision may pose risks for the team/member.

The symptoms of avoidance show up in many different ways. Issues are not dealt with directly. Communication goes underground. Passive aggressive behavior is present. Once an avoidance response is learned by a team, it's difficult to overcome. The intervention threshold for avoidance behaviors needs to be set low because the resulting behaviors are more dysfunctional and harder to deal with. When the threshold is reached and you need to intervene, try the following suggestions:

- Get an accurate understanding of the reasons behind the avoidance behavior.
- Get things out in the open by creating an atmosphere of safety.
- Deal with and mitigate the feared consequences or risks.
- Offer support.
- Communicate the consequences of avoidance.
- Clarify ownership.
- Reinforce the timeline for the decision.

Rushing

Some teams can make decisions too quickly, often without considering key issues or the impact of their actions on others. They may have a false sense of urgency and immediacy, and may treat everything as a number one priority. They can get impatient with other teams and may not take the time to assess options before they decide. Their strong activity orientation means they are always busy doing things—but maybe not the right things. They are often in reactive mode and let short-term crises take over their decision-making processes.

The threshold for intervening with teams that rush needs to be low because the cost of undoing poor decisions can be high. Poor or reactive decisions can compound upon each other, leading to a confusing mess. One bad decision begets another, and the leader may find it difficult to manage or get control over the runaway decision process. Decisions gain momentum whether or not they are good ones. When intervening with a team that has a tendency to rush the decision-making process, try the following actions:

- Put into place formal delays or checkpoints to force the team to stop before moving on to the next decision.
- Implement additional sign offs on decisions.
- Challenge decisions early and test the team's response.
- Have the team examine the impact of the decision on other teams and organizations.
- Point out data that was missed, underestimated, or was not considered.
- Budget time to focus on longer term issues.
- Hold decision post-mortems to analyze decisions.

Excluding

If a team is demonstrating exclusion, it is not involving individuals or groups that should be part of the decision-making process. Stakeholders and customers get ignored or neglected. Teams can do this knowingly and at other times unintentionally. When the pace of work is fast, teams can get caught up and take short cuts. They can believe they don't have time to ask for other's input or build consensus. They can fail to understand the connection others may have to the decision. When key parties are not included in the decision process, they can feel angry, locked out, undervalued, and may not support decisions the team makes.

Establishing an intervention threshold for exclusion is important because teams that habitually exclude others can generate significant conflict, backlash, and resistance. Exclusion is at the heart of the us-versus-them dynamic that develops in many organizations. While overlooking a connection occasionally is not a dysfunctional pattern, doing it repeatedly is a real problem. If a team is getting close to the exclusion threshold, try the following interventions:

- Point out the exclusions and question the team on its behavior.
- Clarify why the excluded individuals/groups should or should not be included.
- Hold working sessions between cross-functional teams to drive home work connections and the impact of not working together.
- Mandate that the team include those excluded individuals in their decision-making process.
- Communicate the impact of the team's behavior on others.

Action/intervention thresholds are an important tool in the faster leader's toolkit when dealing with team problems. They allow the leader to intervene and act in a proactive way rather than being caught by surprise or being slowed down by having to do damage control.

KNOW WHEN TO MOVE TO PLAN B

If your radar is telling you that your original course is no longer tenable, you need to shift to your back up plan. Back up or contingency plans are created before you need them, not in real time. The risk scenario modeling I discussed in Chapter Eleven is a good first step in developing contingency plans. Contingency plans can be linked to the risk scenarios you develop with your team and will outline how you will respond to the different risk scenarios that unfold.

When you are moving fast, being able to shift directions is critical. The time spent upfront doing contingency planning contributes to speed of execution and makes your team agile. But, a note of caution is due. Too much focus on risk can paralyze a team from taking action and seizing opportunity. A leader can't anticipate everything. Effective contingency planning integrates caution, anticipation, and quick action.

When developing contingency plans, try to follow these guidelines.

- Approach the contingency planning process from a worst case, best case, and most likely case scenario framework. Integrate the risks you have identified in each of the risk scenarios you have created. Every leader should have at least three contingency plans for each important initiative. **A contingency plan follows this basic framework: if X happens, then we will do Y.**
- A formal contingency plan should be created. Spell out what the team needs to do and when. Individual roles and responsibility should be articulated. The impact of the contingency plan should be mapped out so affected parties can be identified and expectations managed.
- Create a set of leading indicators for each scenario to help you predict and anticipate what is coming. Scan the environment regularly for leading indicator changes. Leading indicators offer evidence a particular scenario is unfolding. They give you time to launch the contingency plan and respond to a negative trend.
- Identify specific events that will act as triggers for launching the contingency plan.

- When a contingency plan is launched, announce it, track it, and communicate it to organizations and stakeholders who will be affected by it.

COACH VERSUS MANAGE

Pilots make all sorts of choices including whether to fly around turbulence or fly through it. Their success in the air depends on the performance of their team and ground crew. Pilots rely upon their teams to support them, and everyone needs to do their job well. A pilot needs to apply the right touch to get the best out of their team, and they have to respond when a team member is not performing up to expectation.

Similarly, to get the best out of their teams, faster leaders have to know when to manage their teams and when to coach. Applying the wrong approach to the situation can cause a stall or spin out.

Leaders face this dilemma on a daily basis: do you manage an issue or coach a team member through it. At the heart of the question is ownership. Does the leader take ownership or give ownership for the issue to another person? Does the leader direct the activities of others or teach them how to do things better? Leaders rarely have very much time to make coach vs. manage decisions and the stakes can be high.

Management is essential to performance. A team may get off course and need a course correction. Company direction needs to be established and reinforced. Standards of performance need to be communicated so everyone on the team is pulling in the same direction. Poor performance needs to be addressed. Chapter Ten covered many of the important aspects of embracing your leadership power to manage situations.

Coaching is an important faster leader skill. While leaders see the value of coaching and would like to do it more, coaching is more time intensive than managing. Activities that are time intensive often end up at the bottom of the priority list. Coaching requires an upfront investment to reap its rewards. The time invested in coaching shows up in results later. This is the classic delay problem. Because of these issues, the default position for many leaders is to manage rather than coach.

The problem I encounter most often is not that leaders manage but they go too far. They are too controlling and they over manage. They teach people to depend on them. Regardless of the intent, the net result is everything slows down as the leader becomes the bottleneck. Rather than people making independent decisions, decision-making is deferred to the leader which generates delay.

In situations that appeal to your expertise or experience, the tendency to manage is exacerbated. It is quicker to do it yourself than take the time to coach someone else how to do it. This type of thinking is a trap you need to avoid. While it is tempting to manage, it is not always the best decision because people won't get the opportunity to build their skills.

Another variable at play is the potential consequences of failure. Coaching is a learning activity, and people need the opportunity to experiment and possibly fail. You want the consequences of failure to be minimal to encourage team members to keep trying. Don't put people you are coaching in high stress, high visibility situations unless you are confident of their success. Failure in a high visibility situation can permanently scar an individual's credibility.

Let's break the coach-versus-manage decision down further. When should you manage and when should you coach? How can you make this decision quickly? I suggest a three-step method to speed up your behavior in this important flight-deck-decision arena.

Step 1: **Examine your personal bias and understand the consequences of both approaches.** Do you fall on the side of management and control, or do you prefer the coaching approach? Do you have the temperament to be a coach (i.e., patient and understanding), or do you have a stronger appetite for taking action and being in control?

The following characteristics can predispose a leader to assume the manage/control position:

- They have a strong appetite for details and place a high value on how things are done. They can show a lack of discrimination for what details are important versus what are not. All details are important to them.
- A high need for being in control drives them. Easily shifting into micro-management behavior, they see threats at every turn. They feel if they don't do it, it won't get done.
- They have a strong need to be important and like being the hub of the wheel.
- Impatience and a strong need for action are at their core. A strong sense of urgency drives everything they do.
- An inability or unwillingness to see how their behavior affects others is another hallmark of their behavior. They either don't see, or don't care, how their actions can trigger emotions or dysfunctional behavior in people around them.

You'll want to step back and take a self-assessment break to see if you have any of these behaviors. Being predisposed to the management orientation can lead to you under develop your coaching skills. You'll miss coaching opportunities and the benefits of developing your people.

Coaching generates a lot of positive press, and management often gets a bad rap. Don't let the court of public opinion bias your self-assessment. Watch your behavior over time to get an accurate sense of what side of the coach vs. manage scale you gravitate towards.

As you self-assess, understand both approaches have pros and cons. Management is quicker but creates a state of dependency. If you give a team member a directive and tell them how to do it, you have retained ownership of the issue even though they are carrying out your instructions. The person may do what you tell them, but by specifying how you want it done, you get compliance. Compliance breaks down when pressure or stress is applied. Many a leader has been adversely affected by mistaking compliance for commitment.

Coaching improves the skills of people around you, but it takes more time than managing. By treating every situation as a coaching situation, you can fail to act when the situation demands action. Your team can come to see you as a leader who is unwilling or unable to take action or resolve disagreement. To be an effective faster leader, you have to display skill in both approaches and be able to deploy the right approach for the situation.

Step 2: Assess the person's coachability. A few individuals will not be coachable—at least not by you. They might not see you as credible or be open to your input. Or they may be resistant to change or feedback. People vary in their appetite for learning. Individuals receptive to feedback and open to learning opportunities are more favorable coaching candidates. Receptivity to coaching is an important attribute in your team members. It allows you to coach and get results faster.

While all of your team members have value—some have more value than others because of their skills, expertise, or the role they play. Everyone is not equal in terms of their impact. While you don't want to broadcast this fact, you want to remember it when making a coach/manage decision. Be sure to invest in your high-value team members.

Another important variable to consider when deciding your strategy is the size of the skill gap or discrepancy the individual displays. If the individual is performing at a basic level and your goal is to get them to perform at higher level, you will need to budget more coaching time. Where the gap is small, you will be able to do accelerated coaching. Also, think about the complexity of the skill or behavior. Complex behaviors are more challenging to coach and take longer to manifest.

Remember this important point. The biggest mistake you can make is spending large amounts of time coaching a poor performer and neglecting a top performer. This is the opposite approach of how you should be spending your coaching time. Don't let yourself get bogged down in a protracted coaching scenario with team member who is a low performer. Situations like this have a tendency to become a time management disaster.

Leaders can make the mistake of neglecting top performers because it is assumed top performers don't need or want coaching. This belief is wrong. Top performers are your best coaching candidates. **Remember, coach your high performers and manage your low performers.**

Step 3: Assess the situation. Sometimes the urgency of the situation demands quick action. For example, a crisis requires quick and decisive action by a leader to prevent events from spiraling out of control. You don't have a lot of time to decide and the consequences can be significant. At other times, the pace of events allows you to take a more measured approach. Every situation has its own set of unique demands. When deciding to coach or manage, be sure to assess the level of urgency in the situation.

Other people's expectations are another variable to consider when assessing the environment. Senior management may have expectations that you directly manage a situation versus you coaching someone on how to handle it. They may expect you to have a high level of involvement and to take control of the situation.

Think of the environment you operate within as your runway. You have a long runway at times and at other times you don't. Regardless, your goal is to get the plane in the air before you run out of runway. While you might coach a team member to a desired skill level if you had infinite time, realize you don't always have the time. Other factors outside of your control influence the length of the runway.

Consider the following questions in making your decision to coach or manage.

- What is your level of personal ownership in the situation? Do you have a strong enough personal investment in the individual to make coaching a viable choice?
- Do you have the personal bandwidth to devote to coaching? Will you be able to carve out the time to do a good job of it? Remember, coaching takes time.
- Do you have skill in the target behavior the individual needs to learn? Are you able to break the skill into teachable components?

- What expectations have you set about coaching? If you have made coaching part of your leadership platform, you will need to deliver on your promise or suffer a credibility hit.

POWER VERSUS INFLUENCE

A final flight deck decision to consider is whether to use power or influence in a situation. To clarify, power involves taking control or command; influence involves persuasion and subtlety. Misjudging when to use power vs. influence could lead to lack of commitment from others or conflict that spirals out of control.

Here is a quick checklist to help you make right power versus influence decisions.

- Make a determination regarding which approach fits the situation (power vs. influence).
- Assess how much power or influence is needed in the situation to achieve the desired result and how much power or influence you have at your disposal. If you try to use your leadership power and the level is not enough, you will end up looking weak. If you over estimate your influence, people will ignore you or discount what you say. You need the right level of influence or power to be effective in the situation. If your power or influence is not enough, leverage others who possess what you are lacking.
- Test the intentions of the people in the situation. If you decide their motives are negative, power tactics will be more successful. Positive intentions make influence possible.
- Situations that involve active threats to your business or organization are appropriate ones to use your leadership power.

- Is the issue at the heart of the situation within the boundaries of your formal role or charter? If so, use power to resolve the issue. Using the power that comes with the role is expected and legitimate. If ownership is unclear, or the issue lies outside of your formal role, use influence tactics to resolve it in the desired direction.
- Crisis situations high in urgency lend themselves to the exercise of leadership power.
- If a leadership vacuum exists, try using your leadership power to get the ball rolling.
- Is there a need for others to be committed to the outcome, and do you want ownership to be distributed? Use influence tactics.
- If the situation involves tactical issues, use leadership power to clear the decks. If the situation is more strategic, use influence to involve others and give them a sense of participation.
- In situations where the issue is holding others accountable because of missed commitments or deliverables, use power tactics to reinforce honoring agreements.

The Ten Minute Influence Drill

There is another level of decision-making you'll need to perform if you find yourself in an influence scenario. While a situation may call for influence, you may have to make a no-go decision if certain variables are not present. Alternatively, you may need to involve others or focus on building your credibility before proceeding.

I suggest leaders perform the ten minute influence drill to help guide their decision-making in potential influence scenarios. While influence can take a long time to develop, ten minutes is usually sufficient to evaluate the likelihood of your success in a particular situation. Here are the steps in the drill:

1. Once you've decided a situation calls for an influence approach, clearly identify the influence target. While this may sound obvious, many people make the fundamental mistake of picking the wrong influence target. You may have to look beyond first impressions to identify who really possesses influence in a particular situation.

2. Evaluate your credibility with the influence target before proceeding. A credibility judgment will typically involve perceptions about your intent or motivation, your expertise and results (either broadly or in a specific arena), and the level of connection and relationship you have with them. Think about your prior interactions with the target and how they responded to you to get a sense of their judgment of your credibility. You want all of these credibility vectors to be positive to proceed. You may need to develop additional credibility for challenging influence scenarios.

3. Evaluate the level of debt you have created with the influence target. Debt is created when you do favors for someone, give them assistance, or provide them with benefits or support. You'll want the accumulation of debt to be high to leverage it in influence scenarios. For future reference, you'll want to make influence deposits with key people on an ongoing basis to have the necessary currency to accelerate the influence process.

4. Review your intelligence on the influence target from your prior interactions with them. You'll want to have compiled a checklist of their pain points, values, motivations, and goals.

5. Determine your desired outcome in the scenario. Having a clear goal is critical to determining the right influence strategy. Think of your goal as a request because it will involve a request for action by your influence target. You'll want to make a decision at this point regarding whether you have sufficient credibility and debt with the target to accomplish your goal. You need to have attained the appropriate threshold to continue.

6. Identify a request that is in line with debt and credibility levels. To arrive at the right level of request, it is a good idea to first create a request ladder. A request ladder is a series of requests related to your desired outcome that vary by how much effort and energy is needed to complete them. For example, you might want a person to introduce you to someone else (mild), or you might want a peer to support your position in a high stakes meeting (strong). If your request exceeds the level of debt and your credibility, the likelihood of failure is high.

7. Identify a list of additional benefits, favors, or assistance you can give to the influence target to improve their orientation to your influence goal.

8. If your assessment of the seven steps is positive, you are in a good position to launch your influence strategy. Here are a few general guidelines to keep in mind:
   - Don't exceed your influence threshold
   - Emphasize your credibility and connection to the target
   - Break your desired outcome down into specific requests that are linked to each other
   - Pick a starting request that has a high probability of success to start with

- You must be able to re-frame or describe the request in ways that resonate with the target. You'll want to incorporate your knowledge and experience with the target to accomplish this activity. Emphasize the benefits to them
- If necessary, you can make subtle reference to the debt they have with you
- Consider what gifts you want to use increase the possibility of success
- Create a sense of urgency to get their agreement and commitment to move forward into action.

As you perform the ten minute influence drill, it is important to keep in mind that influence is not manipulation. You must approach the process ethically and with transparency. If an influence target thinks you are being insincere or are trying to manipulate them, you will encounter resistance that will undermine your influence.

In this chapter I covered several of the more important decisions you'll face on a day to day basis. Keep the information in this chapter handy and when you encounter a decision threshold you'll be ready to act. In the next chapter, you'll get to practice advanced pilot maneuvers.

ACCELERATION TOOL#12: DECISION MAPPING

To speed up your ability to make the right flight deck decisions, here is a decision mapping tool that will help you explore the different relationships to a decision. This tool will help you to think through a decision and figure out the right approach and strategy.

- Who thinks or believes they make the decision? Disputed decision making is a real problem and leads to high levels of conflict. If the dispute is at the peer level, others higher in the organizational will need to be involved.

- Who can overturn the decision? While these individuals may not be involved in making the decision, their position power gives them the right to stop or reverse a decision.

- Who needs to be involved before a decision is made? These individuals can offer important perspective, context, alternatives, and can influence acceptance of a decision. If you don't include them, your decisions could face an uphill battle.

- Who will the decision affect? Explore the decision's touch points and the consequences the decision will have on others. It is also important to look for perceived impact. Certain individuals may perceive a decision impacts them when in reality it will not. Don't ignore or minimize perceptions.

- Who needs to support the decision? There are individuals who have influence and can act as sponsors of the decision. They make getting a decision ratified and implemented much quicker. They often contribute resources vital to the decision. Without their support, your decision process can stall out.

- Who will resist the decision? Uncovering opposition to the decision is an important step in the decision mapping process. For individuals who are mildly opposed, you can use influence strategies to win them over to your side. Strongly resistant individuals will fight you every step of the way. Remember, resistance consumes a lot of energy and effort. Evaluate whether the decision will be worth the expenditure of effort you will need to make. If you believe the decision is worth the effort, galvanize your supporters and sponsors to close the deal.

CHAPTER 13

Advanced Pilot Maneuvers

❖ ❖ ❖

*If you are looking for perfect safety, you will do well
to sit on a fence and watch the birds; but if you
really wish to learn, you must mount a machine and
become acquainted with its tricks by actual trial.*

WILBUR WRIGHT

JET PILOTS ARE PUT THROUGH extensive training covering any potential situation they may encounter on the ground and in the air. The focus is on helping pilots to be able to handle any emergency or scenario. Pilots have problem-solving frameworks and emergency procedures in place because they don't have the luxury of figuring out things on the spot. They have to master incredibly difficult maneuvers and be able to withstand major g-forces.

For example, one of the most difficult aerial maneuvers to learn in a jet fighter is the Folov Chakra. When executing the Folov, the pilot performs a tight 360°loop about the length of the plane. The maneuver stalls the plane and dramatically slows its speed. In combat, the Folov can be useful in helping evade a pursuing plane or causing firepower to miss its mark. This maneuver pushes a pilot to the limit.

As you scale and take on more responsibility, you have to master more complex skills to keep the organization focused against a backdrop of increasing distraction. Like a pilot executing a Folov, you'll be pushed to the limit. In this chapter, I'll cover four advanced leadership skills that help you become a more effective pilot of your organization: shaping behavior, coaching, acting like a thermostat, and keeping the performance edge.

SHAPING BEHAVIOR: THE ART OF APPLYING CONSEQUENCES

The power you have to shape behavior in your organization is an important aspect of your leadership role (see Chapter Ten). You shape the behavior of others through your personal interactions with them, the systems and procedures you put into place, and the environment you create.

At its core, shaping is about applying consequences at your disposal to influence behavior in other people. Sounds ominous or manipulative? It's not. You don't control other's behavior, but as a leader you are responsible for making sure the organization works like a well oiled machine. You need to be an effective **Chief Focus Officer (CFO)**.

Regardless of what type of behavior you are trying to shape, you will need to master the art of establishing and reinforcing the relationship between actions and consequences. Shaping can help build accountability in your team, increase positive behavior, and reduce negative behavior.

The shaping of behavior is based on behavioral psychology and the key principle is straightforward. When you have a behavior you want to increase, you reinforce the behavior with a positive consequence when the behavior happens. If you see a behavior you want to diminish or extinguish, you remove what is reinforcing it or apply negative consequences to it. The concept of applying consequences to influence behavior is called the Law of Effect and it was developed by the famous learning theorist Edward Thorndike.

Sound familiar? Applying consequences is what parents do every day with their children. However, this important skill doesn't make its way into the workplace with enough frequency. Attaching consequences to behavior may appear to be easy but it is more difficult than it seems. Many leaders struggle with this important leadership behavior. The struggle stems from leaders assuming they have limited tools to influence behavior and not knowing how to pick the right consequence to influence a behavior.

A common work scenario unfolds like this. Imagine you lead a team and recently asked them to prepare material for an upcoming meeting. Because the team was very busy or didn't understand the importance of the meeting, they did minimal preparation that was not very well thought out. When you review their work the day of the meeting, you are unhappy with their work product. Because of the time pressure, you clean up the work and don't say anything to the team because you know they have a lot on their plate. You are still frustrated by their response and resent having to do the work yourself. The following week, you make the same request and the same thing happens. The group is again unprepared. You are now caught in a vicious cycle. Because you have not applied consequences, there is no reason for them to change their behavior. Your team has learned your requests are not important and they can ignore or minimize them.

Shaping behavior is how you get out of no-win scenarios that absorb your energy, attention, and focus. Depending on what you

are trying to achieve, your use of consequences in the shaping process can vary significantly.

Shaping Fundamentals

Here are a few fundamentals to keep in mind as you go about the
shaping process:

- Limit your focus to behaviors that are important and consistent with your leadership platform. Don't try to shape too
many behaviors because you will dilute your effectiveness.
- Consequences should be applied immediately after the behavior whenever possible. The longer the interval between
behavior and consequence, the weaker the connection or
association will be.
- Consequences need to be applied consistently. If you are
inconsistent in your application, you will generate confusion in others.
- Consequences can be positive or negative. Positive consequences are designed to increase the frequency of a behavior and negative consequences are intended to decrease a
behavior.
- Negative consequences should be used sparingly because of
their impact on others.
- The consequence needs to match the targeted behavior in
terms of intensity. If your consequences are too strong you
may create fear or embarrassment in others. If your consequences are too weak, they will be ignored or tuned out.
- Personalize the consequence because people respond differently to consequences. For example, certain individuals
react strongly to perceived criticism whereas others don't

take it personally. You will want the consequence to take into account the individual's motivational makeup. You can use the EFTE model I covered in Chapter Nine to help you get a handle on how a person will respond to a specific consequence.

- If a consequence changes the behavior in the desired direction, it is the right type and strength. If it doesn't change the behavior, try another tactic rather than continuing to apply the same consequence.

Shaping Methodology

Regardless of the type of shaping scenario you are dealing with, you will want to apply a consistent methodology to achieve the best results. I recommend a five step approach.

1. Develop clarity about the behavior you want to shape. Remember to limit your targets to behaviors that are important.
2. Assess the team or individual. You will want to establish a baseline from which to work and you'll want to get a sense of what types of consequences they respond to. Personalization of consequences is extremely important.
3. Develop a strategy for how you are going to go about shaping the behavior. The key is to be ready to shape the behavior and avoid having to come up with an approach spontaneously.
4. Put your strategy into action and apply consequences.
5. Monitor the scenario to see if the shaping is being effective and adjust your tactics if things are not progressing in the desired direction.

Shaping Scenarios

There are four primary scenarios leaders encounter that call for shaping behavior: accelerating the learning process, reinforcing guidance mechanisms, getting the best out of others, and eliminating behaviors. The types of consequences you use and how you apply them will change depending on what scenario you are dealing with but this methodology will work with all of them.

Accelerating the learning process

In this shaping scenario, you are in a teaching mode. Your goal is to help an individual or team learn a new behavior or improve an existing behavior in the shortest amount of time possible. The main focus of your shaping behavior will be removing negative consequences for failure or experimentation, reinforcing improvements in performance, encouraging risk taking behavior, and building confidence.

It is important to remember that when a behavior is learned it will be demonstrated consistently. When this threshold is reached, you can back off on the frequency of your consequences because the individual will have internalized the behavior. You will then shift to intermittent consequences which have a higher motivational impact with learned behaviors. Intermittent consequences help maintain the newly learned behavior.

Your personal involvement and investment will be significant in this shaping scenario so plan your time accordingly. I'll be talking about more about coaching later in this chapter.

Reinforcing guidance mechanisms

Most of your shaping efforts in this scenario will relate to reinforcing the guidance mechanisms you have developed and deployed (see Chapter Eight). You will want to make sure individuals in your organization are actively supporting your vision, mission, charter, values, strategy, and ground rules. By attaching positive consequences to behavior that is supportive, you build momentum and improve focus on what is most important.

Most of your focus will revolve around communicating expectations, reinforcing behavior that is supportive, establishing a personal connection between your team members and the guidance mechanisms, and quickly applying negative consequences to anything inconsistent or non-supportive. Consistency of consequences is especially important in getting your team to believe in and feel a sense of ownership for the guidance mechanisms.

Getting the best out of others

You get the best out of others by establishing a strong personal connection and creating a situation where they want to live up to your expectations. Another important aspect of shaping performance and getting the best out of others is creating a feedback rich environment which is systemic in nature. People want to know if they are succeeding, and how they can grow and progress. Too many organizations keep people guessing about where they stand.

Consistent consequences and feedback loops about performance help increase the motivation to perform. Clear expectations, feedback on current performance and effective appraisals, positive consequences for meeting performance targets, recognition, and opportunity for advancement and learning are all shaping tools you can use to accelerate the performance of your team. I'll be talking about performance later in this chapter.

Eliminating behavior

Shaping positive behavior is enjoyable; dealing with negative behavior is not. However, it is an important leadership behavior to reduce or eliminate behavior that is negative or dysfunctional.

In certain situations, the behavior you have to target is related to lack of support for your guidance mechanisms, but the list of behaviors can go beyond this scope. Challenges to your leadership or management, acting out behavior, mistreatment of others, unethical behavior, poor performance, and behavior that incites others are all targets for shaping. Using negative consequences, taking away something of value, and eliminating conditions that support the behavior are tools you can use to target negative behavior.

As I mentioned earlier in this chapter, you want to use negative consequences carefully because of their power. It is important to pick the right level of consequence. The consequence should be strong enough so you only have to use it sparingly. Too often, a leader will start with a low level consequence that doesn't work and then have to keep turning up the intensity. A risk is the person you are focusing on becomes habituated and negative consequences lose their power. You spend too much time and energy in a negative feedback loop which can be draining.

Build your consequence hierarchy

A consequence is your response to another's behavior and it is a good idea to have your consequences mapped out ahead of time rather than thinking them up on the spot. At the core of being a faster leader is constant preparation. If you want to effectively shape or influence behavior, you need to be prepared.

When thinking about consequences, it helps to have a framework to help with organization. There are important dimensions to consider when thinking about the consequences you will be applying. As I mentioned earlier, you will need to develop an array of both positive and negative consequences. Positive consequences are easier to identify so you'll need to work harder on coming up with a set of negative consequences.

Consequences can be tangible or intangible. Examples of tangible consequences include incentives, rewards, promotions, demotions, firing, putting a team member on a performance improvement plan, and attractive work assignments. Resources such as budgets, headcount, technology tools, and hiring approval can be part of your tangible consequence repertoire. Intangible consequences can include appreciation, rejection, verbal recognition, disapproval, empowerment, censoring, personal connection, and inclusion.

Consequences can be delivered either publicly or privately. You can take a person aside after a meeting and give them constructive feedback about how their presentation could have been better, or you could publicly acknowledge them for going beyond what was expected.

Feedback is one of your most powerful tools for shaping behaviors. To be effective, feedback should not be in the form of a judgment (i.e., you are not a team player) but rather descriptive and specific (i.e., you could improve your collaboration behavior by reaching out to other team members). Be careful of over using positive feedback because it can become less powerful. One leader I worked with was so positive and effusive in his feedback that he got a reputation as a "Sunshine Pump". His positive feedback became discounted because it was easy to get.

When thinking about consequences, it is helpful to remember they need to vary in intensity. Visualize a consequence continuum that ranges from very mild to very strong. Take the example of feedback. It can be delivered in either written or verbal form, or either formally or informally.

In my coaching, I encourage people to think about consequences that are clear and specific. As you build your hierarchy, be sure to focus on consequences you can visualize yourself actually delivering.

In your hierarchy, you will need to rank consequences in terms of perceived strength from weakest to strongest. An example of a low level positive consequence is, "Good job, Mary, on meeting the deadline" delivered in person. A stronger consequence would be to send an e-mail out to the entire team about Mary's accomplishment. A still stronger consequence would be to stand up at a meeting and say, "I want to thank Mary for meeting the deadlines. Let's all give her a round of applause."

Mapping out the different intensity of consequences is important, challenging, and well worth the effort. When you are faced with one of these scenarios, you can match the right level of consequence to the event quickly and efficiently. I have included a template at the end of the chapter to help you start building your consequence hierarchy.

Grade the behavior

Now that you have created a consequence hierarchy it is time to apply it to specific individuals, situations, and behaviors. There are five factors you'll want to consider in selecting a consequence from your hierarchy for a specific situation: motivators, outcome, difficulty, effort, and outside influences. Since these factors can interact, keep that in mind as you select consequences.

1. The level of consequence you apply will need to take into account the motivational makeup of the individual. Certain

individuals only need a slight nudge whereas others need a kick in the pants. Many people respond really well to public recognition, and there are others who are embarrassed by it. There are those who may respond best to your personal appeals such as, "Don't let me down, I'm counting on you". You will want to take into account how much energy and time it will take for you to apply the consequence.

2. Results matter. The outcome of a behavior is an important variable to evaluate in the shaping process. In general, if the behavior produces a major impact, then the consequences should be stronger than for a minor impact. This strategy is true regardless if the impact is positive or negative.

3. How difficult or challenging is the behavior? Does the behavior require high levels of skill? Is the behavior within the capabilities of the individual or does it stretch them? Your selection of consequence will vary depending on whether the behavior has positive or negative outcome. For example, if the individual attempted a challenging behavior but was unsuccessful, you could apply both a positive and negative consequence. The negative consequence should be very mild because even though they were unsuccessful, you want to encourage them to keep trying. If you select a positive consequence, it should be stronger because you want to reinforce the fact they took on a difficult challenge. If the individual successfully performed a behavior that was within their expected capabilities, then the positive consequence would be more moderate than for a person who tried a challenging behavior and was successful. The general principle with challenging behaviors is to be mild with negative consequences and stronger with positive consequences.

4. The level of effort a person applies to a task will influence your selection of consequence. Did they apply just enough effort to get by or did they go beyond expectations? Were they distracted or inattentive, or were they fully engaged? If the behavior had a negative impact and was the product of inattention, then the consequence needs to be negative and stronger than if they were fully locked on. In general, reward high levels of effort.

5. To what degree did factors outside of the individual's control play a role in the outcome of the behavior? Unexpected things happen and that can affect the performance of even your best people. In other situations, factors that should have been accounted for are missed. A few individuals look to make excuses for their behavior and fail to take accountability. In choosing your consequence, review the factors at play in the situation.

I have included an exercise at the end of the chapter to help you quickly grade behaviors as you encounter them. Coupled with your hierarchy of consequences, you now have a one-two punch for quickly shaping behaviors.

FAST TRACK COACHING

At the right time, coaching can have a tremendous impact on performance. In Chapter Twelve, I discussed how coaching is one of your most important flight deck decisions. In this section, I'll cover how to deliver fast track coaching as an advanced pilot maneuver.

I draw a distinction between planned coaching and situational coaching. Planned coaching is more formalized and structured, and it revolves around a plan you jointly develop with the person you are coaching. Planned coaching is a partnership between you and the person you are coaching. Situational coaching occurs spontaneously as you encounter behaviors you want to shape. Situational coaching can be much more subtle and the person you are coaching may not even be aware they are being coached. Both approaches to coaching have learning as their focus and the target audience is your high potentials. Here are a few ideas that will help you fast track your coaching process.

Step One: Focus

Zero in on a learning target that has relevancy for both the individual and the organization. I suggest you focus on one objective at a time. If you are taking the planned coaching approach, the individual who you are coaching will need to be an active participant in the selection process. People learn what they are motivated to learn, so having them be a participant in selecting the objective is a good idea. Rather than you supplying the motivational energy, you'll want to tap into the individual's intrinsic motivation. Situational coaching can target a competency that is under the radar of the person you are coaching. Because of your experience and knowledge, you may target a competency that is beyond the awareness of the person you are coaching.

Learning targets can be broken down into different categories. Here are the top four in ascending order of difficulty: awareness, skills, motivation, and self-concept. Some learning targets can combine the different categories.

Awareness

The focus on awareness is to improve a person's understanding. An example would be to help an individual understand how their behavior impacts others. Awareness skills are typically the fastest to coach.

Skill
The focus on skill development is to help someone master a set of behaviors. An example would be to improve presentation skills. Skills typically build upon one another. As an individual learns a skill, they can move up the skill ladder to take on increasingly challenging skills. Complex skills take longer to coach.

Motivation
Motivational coaching revolves around getting a person to attach importance or significance to an action or objective. The goal is to get them to commit energy and effort. You want them to put skin in the game. For example, many people don't like dealing with conflict because it makes them uncomfortable. Motivational coaching would focus on helping individuals overcome their reluctance to deal with conflict because it is an important leadership skill. Motivational coaching is more time intensive and difficult than either awareness or skill coaching.

Self-Concept
Self-concept coaching focuses on helping someone to change the way they think about themselves. This type of coaching involves getting a person to question self-judgments and beliefs that act as blocks to progress and fulfilling potential. For example, an individual may not see themselves as a leader while you believe they have a lot of potential. You'd want to work to unlock their potential by getting them to challenge their self-limiting belief. Self-concept coaching is the most challenging type of coaching.

Step Two: Assess

I recommend using a two-step assessment process. First, collect and organize your observations, experiences, and evaluations regarding the individual. It is especially important to assess their orientation to and appetite for coaching. Second, gather feedback from other people the individual interacts with. Their feedback will help validate your data, give you feedback on how they are perceived, and help fine tune your approach. Perceptual feedback is particularly important to collect because the nature of work is increasingly social.

Step Three: Establish a baseline

Using the information you have collected, establish a performance baseline. It is from this baseline you will start your coaching work. Coaching needs an accurate starting point. If you miscalculate the baseline, you can start the coaching process at either a too advanced or too basic level which will reduce your chances of success. I use a four level category system to help with establishing a baseline: non-existent, novice, competent, and expert.

- **Non-Existent**
  At the non-existent level, the individual will not display any evidence of the targeted competency. In most situations, the individual will have never been exposed to the competency or it has never shown up on their radar.
- **Novice**
  At the novice level, the individual will be operating by trial and error. They try different approaches without a clear understanding of what works and what doesn't. They might demonstrate glimpses of the competency, but they will not have a good handle on why they succeeded or failed.

- **Competent**

  When a person is at the competent level, they are performing at an acceptable level. They are regular and consistent
  with their behavior, and it will meet the expectations of
  people around them. They are generally able to demonstrate the competency but won't wow everyone with their
  performance.

- **Expert**

  When a person is at the expert level they have mastered the
  competency. They can demonstrate it under difficult and
  challenging situations, and can coach others on developing
  the competency. They operate at an intuitive, almost unconscious level when performing the competency.

Step Four: Gap analysis

Gap analysis involves evaluating the difference between the current state and the desired state. You can use the baseline assessment framework I just covered to plot both the current state and
the desired state. For example, you might want to coach a team
member to move from the novice level to the competent level.

Step Five: Determine the runway

If you had infinite time and resources you could coach anyone.
The truth of the matter is you don't have infinite time. The environment you operate within injects urgency and limitations into
the coaching process. There are limits to how much of your personal time you can devote to coaching.

Factors outside of your control can determine how much coaching runway you have in any given situation. You will want to understand these limitations and incorporate them into your coaching
runway. In a few situations you may find coaching is not possible

given the restraints. For example, the organization may need a particular skill set before you could realistically coach one of your team to develop it. In this case you would need to look at hiring someone outside of your team who already has the skill.

Step Six: Size up the learning environment
The final step before finalizing your coaching plan is to evaluate the learning environment that surrounds the individual who is the focus of your coaching efforts. You will want to evaluate the level of support that exists, assess resources you could potentially leverage, and identify the panel of judges (besides yourself) who will be evaluating the performance of the individual. This assessment will influence how much personal effort you will need to invest and your timeline. If you are able to leverage resources in the environment, you could speed up the coaching process because you would not be a bottleneck.

Step Seven: Create and execute your plan
Even if you are focusing on situational coaching you will want to have a plan that outlines your approach. You will want to set a goal or objective, define your coaching strategies and tactics, develop progress indicators to track improvements, and create a communication plan to manage expectations.

You will want to break down the target competency into teachable components that take into account the individual's baseline. These components are the building blocks that will allow you to establish early successes and build momentum. For example, if the goal was to improve a person's influence skills, an important building block to focus on first would be to evaluate and develop their skill in interpersonal assessment. Sizing up people accurately is an important influence precursor.

Elements of your plan could involve modeling or demonstrating behavior, providing feedback and support, challenging the individual to raise the performance bar, providing frameworks and models, teaching specific techniques, reinforcing practice and repetition, measuring, testing and evaluating, and providing them with an optimal learning environment.

By devoting the right amount of your time to fast track coaching, you will be able to quickly develop your high potentials and expand your leadership bandwidth.

ACT LIKE A THERMOSTAT

I find the concept of a thermostat a great metaphor for faster leadership. This device, found in just about every household, is a relatively simple mechanism that reads temperature and initiates action to maintain temperature within a desired range. Through constantly checking the temperature and triggering a heater or air conditioner to kick on for a specific time, the thermostat keeps your home's temperature where you want it by quickly making small adjustments rather than wide swings. It is the model of efficiency.

Faster leaders need to act like thermostats in their organizations by quickly doing three things: setting the range, developing a feedback system, and using action to either increase or decrease performance pressure.

The first step of setting a desired performance range is usually done by selecting goals and objectives you want the organization to achieve as part of your long-term plan. The challenge is to select stretch goals that are within the capability or potential of your organization. It is important to take into consideration the environment (i.e., business, competitors, and the economy) your organization is operating in because these outside forces can add stress. These variables combine to make up your desired performance range.

The second step is to develop an accurate feedback system that informs you about the real-time performance level and amount of stress the organization is currently experiencing. An objective feedback system is a critical counterbalance because your personal reactions to stress and tension can contaminate how you lead; your anxiety or uncertainty can drive your behavior. Sometimes when leaders are stressed, they pass that stress on to their organizations which only makes things worse. An objective feedback system can help you manage your behavior and prevent this reaction from affecting the organization.

I covered the importance of dashboards earlier in Chapter Nine and they are an important part of your feedback system. Your feedback system will need to incorporate metrics, observation, and feedback from other individuals. The most effective systems identify trends and spot leading indicators to help you act in time. The primary purpose of the feedback system is to trigger corrective action. The key is to put in place a system that has high accuracy and minimal time delay.

The third step is to develop and use a set of actions that either increase or decrease the performance pressure or demand in small increments. Rather than responding reactively, your actions should be planned ahead of time so they'll be ready for when you need them. **The faster leader is a deliberate leader.** For example, when an organization is experiencing high stress, the faster leader will *decrease* demand by organizing activities that allow people to blow off steam and relax a bit. Alternatively, if the team has become too complacent or the goals are not challenging enough, the leader will *increase* tension by raising the bar and holding people to a higher standard. It is important to be able to move the performance dial both ways (higher or lower) because over stressing the system causes performance to rapidly deteriorate, while not enough pressure leads to lack of urgency and distraction. It is important to constantly make small corrections and changes to avoid falling into a cycle of overcorrection or oscillation.

Additionally, be sure to take into consideration the delay between action and effect. Almost everything you do as a leader takes time to manifest itself in results. If you don't understand this and don't have enough patience to allow things to unfold, you will interrupt the cycle and jump into action because you are not seeing the results you expect. You fall prey to too much immediacy and urgency. You abandon things too quickly and end up going from one action to another and another. Quick decisions that look good on the surface can turn out to be bad ones when tracked over time. How can you avoid this? Set up systems that will help you to know when to act.

Managing your own reactions, understanding you may have to do what is counter-intuitive to you at times, having a feedback system in place that tracks the stress level of the organization, and having a repertoire of small adjustment behaviors you can rapidly deploy are all important factors in being an effective thermostat. By taking the example of the thermostat to heart, leaders can act fast to keep their teams on track and performing at a high level.

KEEP THE PERFORMANCE EDGE

Even high-performing teams can fall into ruts and develop bad habits. They can get lazy and careless. Top performers can get complacent and overly rely on their experience to solve problems rather than recognizing the novel and unique aspects of the challenges they face. Team performance can suffer when the challenges they face exceed their real or perceived capabilities. Top performers can hit the wall and fail.

Human performance is not linear. It goes through fits, starts, and detours. Rapid progress can be made in a short period of time, while consolidating the finer points of a skill can take years. Teams can be wildly productive and then hit patches of quicksand. Maintaining top performance can be fleeting and elusive.

Faster leaders realize an important aspect of their role is to keep their team and top performers on their toes. It takes real focus and discipline to do this because a downward performance slide is often gradual and subtle. If you are not watching for it, performance can get to the point where you have a crisis before you are even aware of it. You then have to launch into recovery mode to pull the team out of a nosedive. Remember, the right level of performance tension improves performance, whereas too much performance stress negatively impacts performance.

The faster leader challenges his team to stay at the top of their game by varying the practice regime, throwing unexpected situations at them, and constantly raising the performance bar. He continually challenges them to shave another minute off their team time. He demands that all team members keep their equipment in top working order by following a rigorous maintenance schedule. This kind of dedication and focus is critical to getting the best out of the team. Keep the following core principles in mind when managing the performance of your team.

Time and predictability erode performance. You will need to continually rejuvenate and challenge to get the best out of your team. Practice, a variety of experiences, and the right pacing keep things interesting and maintain the attention of the team.

Put people in stretch assignments and move them into different roles and functions to help keep things fresh. Boredom and distraction can easily set in if you don't take these steps. An occasional jolt or shift in direction can help break a team out of a performance rut.

Find the Sweet Spot. Think of the sweet spot as the optimal performance zone. Finding the sweet spot is difficult at times because teams and people make judgments that influence their performance. At times, they can set their sights too high and at other times too low. Regardless, people's beliefs about performance have a huge impact on how they actually perform. They become self-fulfilling prophesies. Leaders need to both recognize and challenge these beliefs. You need to identify achievable stretch goals to get the best out of your team.

To consistently find the sweet spot, leaders have to know what their team is capable of doing. It is important to test team members on a regular basis to get an accurate picture of their performance range because performance is not static. Even top performers have an upper limit and can get in over their heads and fail. Put your team through performance tests and drills on a regular basis and keep expectations in line with the sweet spot.

Beware the trap of experience. When time is at a premium, people have a strong tendency to rely on their experience to guide them. As long as the current situation is similar to what they have faced in the past, this strategy works. But with the rapid pace of change, it is much more likely your team will be facing novel situations. Applying historical approaches to a situation that is truly new often won't work. Here are a few consequences of the experience trap:

- Oversimplification
- Denial or distortion of events
- The confirmation bias (i.e., looking only for information that confirms what you believe to be true)
- Excluding entire classes of variables
- Missing the connections between events

To combat this trend, give your team new frameworks to handle new experiences. Supply them with perspectives that help them understand, assimilate, and apply new information rather than forcing it to fit into previous conceptions. Help them make sense of what they are, and will be, encountering. Consistent application of this practice helps build mental agility and learning intelligence.

Sampling. Faster leaders are often in a situation where they have broad organizational responsibilities and need to cover a lot of territory. I suggest leaders use the concept of sampling to efficiently get performance data on their teams. Sampling involves three steps.

1. Pick a confined area to explore. It should be an area that is important from a performance perspective but narrow in focus. You will need to vary the test area over time and don't give your team much advance warning. You are trying to get a true state assessment, not a well-rehearsed presentation.
2. Drill down into a lot of detail within the area of focus. The goals are to find out how well things are going, assess whether or not people are on top of things, find areas of misalignment or misunderstanding, and identify areas in need of additional focus.

3. Once you have gotten to sufficient depth and detail to answer the questions outlined above, withdraw your focus and attention and move on to the next sampling activity. The goal is not to stay at the detailed level for extended periods of time but to periodically drill deep to challenge, validate, and keep your team on its toes.

In this chapter, we've covered several important advanced pilot maneuvers that will help you improve your performance as a faster leader. Shaping behavior, fast track coaching, acting like a thermostat, and keeping the performance edge help you stay at the top of your game. In the next chapter, I'll wrap up with a few things for you to consider in your quest to continue building your faster leader skills.

ACCELERATION TOOL #13: PREPARE TO SHAPE BEHAVIOR

To effectively shape behavior, it is important to be prepared ahead of time. Having a consequence hierarchy and a framework for evaluating behaviors will enable you to quickly pick the right level of consequence to apply to a specific behavior and situation. Remember, shaping involves either trying to increase the frequency of a behavior or decrease the frequency of a behavior. I suggest a two step preparation process: develop a range of consequences and grade the target behavior.

Step One: Develop consequences

Start with three levels of consequence intensity and come up with as many consequences as you can in each category. A level one consequence is mild, a level two consequence is moderate, and a level three consequence is strong.

Consequences can be positive or negative. Consequences can be verbal or written feedback, tangible or intangible. You will need to match the intensity of the consequence with the magnitude of the target behavior and customize it to the individual.

Examples

Target Behavior: Individual met a routine deadline
Level two positive verbal consequence: You thank the individual in a 1:1 conversation.
Level one positive written consequence: Brief email "Good job"
Level one positive tangible consequence: Small amount gift card
Level two positive intangible consequence: Ask them to join you for coffee.

Step Two: Grade the behavior

After coming up with your consequences, you'll need to have a framework for assessing behaviors you want to modify or shape because you'll want to match the consequence with the behavior. Here are some things to consider when grading target behaviors:

- **Behaviors can be either negative or positive in their outcome**. When determining your consequence, think about the impact and results of the behavior. Larger impact behaviors need larger consequences.
- **The amount of effort and intensity** in producing the behavior can also be either positive or negative. Negative effort can encompass passive aggressive behavior to overt resistance. Positive effort can range from doing what is expected to exceeding expectation.
- **Difficulty** is another factor to be evaluated and can also be either positive or negative. For example, an individual might have the capability for a behavior but not demonstrate it. Other behaviors can represent a real stretch for an individual. They could be doing their absolute best.
- **Environmental factors** have an impact and can be either positive or negative. There are factors outside of the individual's control that are supportive and make the behavior easier to produce (i.e., adequate resources). There are other factors that make behaviors more challenging and difficult to accomplish (i.e., an antagonist team climate).
- **Your personal reaction** to the behavior can be either positive or negative. The behavior may produce a level of frustration or irritation in you. Alternatively, other behaviors can generate excitement and appreciation in you.

CHAPTER 14

Beyond the Horizon

Desire is the key to motivation, but it's the determination
and commitment to an unrelenting pursuit of
your goal—a commitment to excellence—that
will enable you to attain the success you seek.

MARIO ANDRETTI

YOU'VE BEEN STRAPPED IN AND pushed the pedal to the metal. Your
leadership is accelerating and you are helping your organization to
keep up the pace. What is beyond the next horizon that you can't
see?

Over the horizon (OTH) radar systems are designed to detect
oncoming objects at great distance. Their genesis began during
the Cold War and continues to this day. These systems are built to
give as much advance warning as possible about coming threats or
changes. Some systems can detect changes over 10,000 miles away.

I've written this book to function like a faster leader OTH
system. I've tried to capture important challenges that will show
up on the leadership radar and will have a significant impact on

your ability to lead. The fall out and consequences of these blips on the radar are only going to get stronger and stronger as time passes.

You'll be challenged to build high levels of team member engagement in a workforce that can be skeptical, cynical, and loyal only when it makes sense to them. You'll encounter resistance to your plans and strategies. At times this resistance will be overt, at other times it can be almost invisible. You'll need to constantly focus on optimizing everything the organization does as anything that slows you down can contribute to failure. You'll need to cultivate smart speed.

I'd like to wrap up with a summary of key points from the book that will help you further develop your **FASTER** leader skill set (**F**ocus, **A**lignment, **S**elf-awareness, **T**ime management, **E**ngagement, **R**esults) and get you ready to face the challenges ahead. I have refined a list of twenty-two summary strategies that will help you keep the pedal to the metal.

Strategy #1: Become obsessed with time—both yours and your team's. Time is precious and seconds matter. You can't lead if you don't have the time or are wasting time. Too many people get into a time deficit and are constantly scrambling just to keep their heads above water. Get better control of your time and reinforce a strong time sensitivity value within your team and organization by creating a strategic time allocation budget (STAB). Find ways to help your team avoid time wasting communication practices such as email. There are many new social communication tools that allow teams to communication and collaboration in real time. You will want to focus on minimizing reactive workflow, which is unnecessary work generated by others.

Strategy #2: Get ahead of things. Anticipate and look ahead. See the curve before you hit it. Being ahead of things allows you to manage situations rather than situations managing you. Anticipation allows you to get your team ready for changes that are coming. You can't lead if you are always reacting. Carve out time in your calendar to give yourself time to think and plan. This is territory you have to win for yourself—the pace of change doesn't allow you to call a time out.

Strategy #3: Focus on the critical path. In an accelerated world, the capacity for getting off track or distracted is quite high. That is why it is important for leaders to focus on the relatively few things that drive success and ignore or minimize the rest. Usually between three and six items, the critical path drives leadership attention and action.

Strategy #4: Focus both on results and how they are achieved. Results are critical but it is also important to focus on how those results are achieved. While certain results may look good on the surface, when you dig deeper, you can often see they were achieved inefficiently or with such collateral costs that the results were actually very poor. Become obsessed with continually making things better and more efficient.

Strategy #5: Reduce dependency on you by constantly building capability around you. Your capacity to lead is dependent on your team and organization. By growing them and cultivating talent, your impact is increased exponentially. Invest in key resources so they are ready when needed. Give your team the tools they need to succeed and perform at their best. Remember the paradox of the faster leader—you need to invest and be patient to develop an ecosystem that enables speed.

Strategy #6: Minimize resistance to your goals, plans, and initiatives. Resistance comes in many forms and is present in every organization. Too many leaders suffer setbacks or fail because they underestimate or fail to anticipate resistance. Resistance is a constant force leaders must learn to deal with and channel.

Strategy #7: Challenge and test constantly. Whether it is ideas, proposals, or people, you need to challenge all of these things on a regular basis. It is only when you challenge that you can get a clear sense of how strongly a person is committed to an idea, how clearly an idea has been thought through, or the performance someone is capable of. Since change is a constant, it is important to test things repeatedly over time.

Strategy #8: Build and maintain your credibility at all costs. Credibility is the foundation of faster leadership. You can manage without credibility, but you can't lead without it. Remember that it takes many small actions over time to build credibility and only one act to destroy it.

Strategy #9: Understand yourself and be self-critical. Your limits can become the organization's limits if you don't understand them and compensate for them. Flawed self-awareness is the number one leadership personality fault.

Strategy #10: Become a Super Learner. If there is one thing I know for certain, change requires leaders accelerate their capacity for learning. Leaders need to become super learners who cultivate the following characteristics:

- Have a capacity to build frameworks or mental models to quickly absorb large amounts of information and distill this information down into the most important issues and themes.
- Continually test and validate the assumptions at the heart of models.
- Attach very little ego to models and quickly discard those models when they no longer work.
- Are primarily concerned with the accuracy and power of models.
- Utilize rapid prototyping to enhance learning.
- Use action as a diagnostic.
- Have an appetite for data.
- Have a high level of comfort with ambiguity.

Strategy #11: Be hands on but get out of the way. The days of the pure manager are long gone. Leaders are expected to be more involved and be in command of critical details. Since many of the decisions leaders are involved with include levels of complexity and technicality, they have to be comfortable with a certain amount of detail to be able to evaluate the options and judgment of others appropriately. Leaders have to cultivate an appetite for detail to re-inforce this behavior in others. Leaders need to stay in touch with what is going on, and not rely on second and third-hand feedback exclusively. You need to roll up your sleeves and get involved.

Strategy #12: Cultivate your judgment. Your judgment is your GPS. It is what allows you to quickly see to the heart of things, prioritize accurately, and make decisions about a wide variety of issues.

Strategy #13: Embrace your leadership power. Leadership and power go hand-in-hand. Sometimes the process of influence is simply too slow given the demands of a situation. Know when to act and utilize the power and authority that are aspects of successful leadership. However, keep in mind the number of issues you should personally own or be responsible for is very small.

Strategy #14: Focus on efficiency in everything you do. Don't waste anything, repurpose whenever possible, and make sure your work processes actually make people's work easier, not harder. Accomplish the maximum with minimum effort. Focus on simplicity rather than complexity. Create feedback loops that will quickly allow you to know whether or not something is working. If it is not working, get rid of it quickly. Continually take things off the plate rather than constantly piling things on. Reduce the unnecessary complexity that continually creeps into work.

Strategy #15: Leverage your organization. Find ways to get the best out of your organization and people. Put people in the right roles and give them the autonomy and resources necessary to accomplish great work. Distribute ownership to keep people engaged.

Strategy #16: Set the vision and create momentum. Build organizational momentum by developing and communicating a compelling direction and vision. Create excitement, focus, and positive buzz around what you are trying to achieve by getting out and telling your story and vision. Make the rounds with your team and strive to keep your vision fresh and dynamic.

Strategy #17: Drive alignment. To be competitive, all parts of the organization need to pull together and in the same direction. This simple concept is at the heart of all successful organizations. When a team is out of alignment, members of the team go in different directions and pursue their own agendas. Coordinated action is non-existent. Tremendous inefficiencies result. The faster leader needs to set a clear direction and make sure the organization gets it and is aligned. Goals and objectives need to be linked and consistent across the organization.

Strategy #18: Build an accelerated work culture. Emphasize that the faster organization is the only way to compete globally. Reinforce quick and accurate decision-making, minimize organization hierarchy, build transparency, and ruthlessly deal with anything that slows the organization down.

Strategy #19: Build a great place to work. To attract and retain talent, you need to create a work environment where people are challenged and rewarded. You'll need to refine your great boss skills so your talent feels loyalty towards you and gives you their best. When people feel good about their work environment, they become effective ambassadors for the company.

Strategy #20: Communicate with impact to get your message gets through the first time. Information overload is a very big problem in organizations. People, by necessity, use filters to deal with too much information. A challenge for a leader is to communicate clearly so critical information gets through to people without distortion. Your communication needs to stick with people and not get lost in the background noise.

Strategy #21: Plan for scalability. Part of thinking and planning ahead is realizing that growth and competition test an organization's mettle. The faster leader develops strategies for scaling his organization to help manage growth in a disciplined way. The faster leader doesn't let the organization ramp capacity and hiring either too slowly or too quickly. He aims for the sweet spot. It is important to remember scaling can go up or down. In certain situations, the faster leader needs to be ready to scale back the organization to weather turbulence.

Strategy #22: Plan for succession. Faster leaders need to think about who will lead the organization after them. By ensuring there are multiple potential succession candidates in the pipeline, the faster leader helps to safeguard the organization's future. The succession plan doesn't have to be an elaborate formal exercise. The best succession plans are often informal and flexible, and keep expectations manageable, under control, and reasonable.

Keep these twenty-two strategies in front of you as you navigate the race course that is the terrain of the faster leader. Your engine's revving, the race is on, and you've become a Pedal to the Metal leader. Keep up the pace.

ACCELERATION TOOL #14: THE FASTER LEADER MANTRA

To keep yourself on track to becoming a faster leader, consider the following questions on a regular basis:

- How can I speed up my behavior and become more efficient at everything I do?
- How can I better handle the stresses associated with change and uncertainty?
- How do I manage my time more effectively so I have time to think and plan?
- How do I deal with all of the demands on my time?
- How do I know I am focusing on the right things rather than just what is urgent or immediate?
- How can I accomplish more with less?
- How can I best leverage my team and the resources I have?
- How can I quickly and accurately assess things so I know what is really going on in my organization?
- How can I quickly sort through all of the information I am bombarded with and find what is most critical?
- How can I manage the situation rather than having it manage me?
- What is the core value proposition of my organization? What is it that we provide that no one else can?
- What are the things that most impact the success of my business and team? What things, if absent, would cause me to fail?
- What are the most critical things I should be spending my time on? If I'm not spending the right amount of time on those things I have identified, what do I need to change?
- In every situation I find myself in, am I clear on what I am trying to achieve. Am I being purposeful or ambiguous?

- What is the best way to go about achieving my goals?
- Have I properly built alignment within my team and assigned the right resources and people to our goals?

Subject Index

❖ ❖ ❖

References

1. Dutra, Ana and Terry Bacon. "The CEO and Me." *Chief Learning Officer*, July, 2010, 27.
2. The Radicati Group, Inc., *Email Statistics Report, 2010-2014.* Palo Alto, CA 2014.
3. WWW.DOMO.com/blog/2014/04/data-never-sleeps-2-0/.
4. *State of the Workplace Report 2014.* Santa Monica, CA: Cornerstone OnDemand, 2014. www.csod.com.
5. *Airport Surface Operations Action Plan.* FAA. 1998.
6. "Employee Engagement Survey." *Gallup Management Journal,* (2009).
7. Ashford, Sue and Scott DeRue. "Five Steps to Addressing the Leadership Talent Shortage." *Harvard Business Review Blog Network* , June 2, 2010.
8. Davis, Jocelyn, Henry M. Frechette, and Edwin H.Boswell, *Strategic Speed: Mobilize People, Accelerate Execution.* Cambridge, MA: Harvard Business Review Press, 2010.
9. Friedman, Susan. *To Meet or Not to Meet- What are the Questions?* http://www.work911.com, 2012.
10. Smith, Rebecca. Attending Meetings Lowers IQ. *The Telegraph*, February 27, 2012.

11. Hadzima, Joe. How Much does an Employee Cost? *Boston Business Journal*, 2005.
12. Flaum, JP. *When it Comes to Business Leadership, Nice Guys Finish First.* Denver: Green Peak Partners, 2009.
13. Lakein, Alain. *How to Get Control of Your Time.* Signet, 1989.
14. Schwartz, Tony. No is the New Yes: Four Practices to Reprioritize Your Life. *Harvard Business Review Blog Network*, January 17, 2012.
15. Gary, Debbie. The Real Top Gun. *Air & Space Magazine*, July 2010.
16. Flight 1549: A Routine Takeoff Turns Ugly. *CBSNEWS.com*, February 8, 2009.
17. Ryan, John. Four Big Ways Leaders Exercise Good Judgment. *Forbes.com*, March 31, 2010.
18. Kopp, Carlo. The Modern Fighter Cockpit. *Australian Aviation and Defense Review*, March 1981.
19. Black Boxes Indicate Pilot Error in Air France Crash: Report. *Reuters.com*, May 23, 2011.
20. Long, Greg and Butler Newman. Speed to Market: Increasing Knowledge Velocity. *Chief Learning Officer*, October 2010, 40.
21. Colvin, Geoffrey. Why Dream Teams Fail. *Fortune Magazine*, June 8, 2006.

About the Author

❖ ❖ ❖

DR. ARLEN BURGER IS FOUNDER and CEO of Leadership Coaching, a Silicon Valley-based organizational and leadership development firm. Since 1990, he has built a stellar reputation for his work with CEOs, Board of Directors, senior management, and emerging leaders. An expert in leadership and organizational acceleration, he specializes in working with leaders who have to manage complex, fast-paced and demanding businesses. He has helped hundreds of individuals to successfully navigate through transition, challenge, and change.

Understanding that leaders have more demands on their time than they can typically address, he coaches leaders to maintain a rigorous focus on critical path variables that drive business success. By focusing on principles of accelerated leadership, he helps his clients to stay ahead of the curve and improve their impact. **His in-depth understanding of business and roll-up-your-sleeves approach to coaching consistently yields dramatic and sustainable results.**

Dr. Burger has been speaking on leadership topics throughout his career. He has given keynotes, seminars, trainings, and facilitated group development activities to a wide range of companies and associations. Currently, he is speaking on "Accelerate: Become a Faster Leader", "White Knuckle Leadership: Leading in challenging times", and "Become a Talent Magnet: Attract and retain the best".

He is featured in ***Leadership: Helping Others to Succeed;*** a highly successful book series from Insight Publishing. The book features interviews with best-selling authors and is currently available from Amazon.com in either paperback or electronic versions.

Dr. Burger's client list includes other companies ranging in size from start-ups to large Fortune 100 firms in the semi-conductor, venture capital, bio–medical, design tools, service, and e-business industries.

For more information check out his websites: www.fasterleader.com or www.leadershipcode.com

You can contact him directly at arlen@fasterleader.com

Check out the testimonials on his Linkedin® profile: www.linkedin/in/arlenburger

Follow him on Twitter®: www.twitter.com/DrArlen.

Made in the USA
San Bernardino, CA
09 June 2017